Urban Policy Problems

Urban Policy Problems

Federal Policy and Institutional Change

Edited by
Mark S. Rosentraub

Published in Cooperation with the Policy
Studies Organization

HT
123
.U7466
1986
West

PRAEGER SPECIAL STUDIES • PRAEGER SCIENTIFIC

New York • Westport, Connecticut • London

Library of Congress Cataloging-in-Publication Data

Urban policy problems.

Published in cooperation with the Policy Studies
Organization.

Bibliography: p.
Includes index.
1. Urban policy – United States – Addresses, essays,
lectures. 2. Federal-city relations – United States –
Addresses, essays, lectures. I. Rosentraub, Mark
S., 1950-   II. Policy Studies Organization.
HT123.U7466 1986   307.7'6'0973   86-596
ISBN 0-275-92120-4 (alk. paper)

Library of Congress Catalog Card Number: 86-596
ISBN: 0-275-92120-4

First published in 1986

Praeger Publishers, 521 Fifth Avenue, New York, NY 10175
A division of Greenwood Press, Inc.

Printed in the United States of America

The paper used in this book complies with the Permanent
Paper Standard issued by the National Information Standards
Organization (Z39.48-1984).

10 9 8 7 6 5 4 3 2 1

CONTENTS

INTRODUCTION

Most presidents since Franklin D. Roosevelt have tried, to varying extents, to reshape or direct America's future according to their own vision of a better tomorrow. Partisan politics aside, there does seem to be a common element to the administrations of several chief executives. President Roosevelt, in the 1930s, proposed a New Deal to rescue America from the Depression. His vision of a better tomorrow was based on a need to protect people from the vacillations of the market economy and to preserve democracy and capitalism in their national forms. To accomplish these goals, the Roosevelt administration sought a series of programs designed to produce an economic safety net for all Americans.

Three administrations later, John F. Kennedy proposed a reshaping of America domestically and internationally through his vision of a New Frontier. In his policy message to America, its allies, and adversaries, John F. Kennedy tried to remake America into the image of a youthful nation tempered by the history of two world wars and the Korean War, dealing with Europe and the future with a new vitality.

Lyndon Johnson changed the new frontier to the Great Society in a policy effort to realign permanently political power and economic opportunities in America. The Johnson administration not only tried to expand the economic security net for all Americans, but change the distribution of political power through the participation of millions of voters whose participation in local, state, and national elections had been inhibited by state and local governments. Johnson's goals, then, were to reshape opportunities, and through this reshaping, to improve the Democratic Party's control over political institutions at each level of government.

Democratic presidents have not been the only chief executives to attempt to reshape America in their image of a better tomorrow. Dwight Eisenhower, without the slogans of previous or future presidents, established the role of the federal government as an active participant in the enforcement of civil rights, and Richard Nixon established a

1

new system of relationships between the federal government and states and cities through his views of federalism and revenue-sharing programs. As important as these policy directions were, the most important directives by a Republican president were those issued by the administration of Ronald Reagan. In 1980, Ronald Reagan campaigned for the presidency, promising less government and less taxes. The road to prosperity and the creation of an economic security net for workers, he argued, did not lie in the largesse of federal programs, but in the dynamic strength of the free market in the U.S. economy. If unbridled, the Reagan argument went, the strength of the U.S. economy would make all Americans better off than they were under the Democratic leadership of Jimmy Carter.

Whether they were swayed by Ronald Reagan's arguments or disappointed with Jimmy Carter's leadership, the voters chose Reagan. In his 1981 budget message to Congress, President Reagan proposed a series of cutbacks which not only reflected his campaign rhetoric but, if followed, would have returned the role of the federal government to pre-Roosevelt levels. While Congress never endorsed the entire Reagan program, the changes initiated in 1981 fundamentally altered the course of America's domestic policies and future. By 1985, when Ronald Reagan presented his income-tax reform program, the capstone to his reshaping of America, the domestic policy landscape had been drastically transformed.

The changes finally made by the Reagan administration have not been, in relative terms, qualitatively different from the policy adjustments made by Presidents Roosevelt and Johnson. However, they have, it seems, produced more commentary and analysis. In part, this is a result of the previous reshaping of America by Reagan's predecessors. For example, one of John F. Kennedy's most important changes in the policy-development process was the inclusion of social scientists in the shaping of domestic policy. While Franklin Roosevelt had included social scientists in the New Deal, Kennedy brought the "best and the brightest" to Washington in larger numbers (Halberstam, 1969). These initiatives received additional impetus from the Johnson administration and, even through the Nixon years, social scientists were integrally part of the policy process.

The involvement of social scientists in the policy process was not only a function of the view policymakers had of the role for social scientists in the charting of America's future, but also a result of the changing technology of social-science analysis. The advent of data-processing equipment made large-scale analysis possible, and the perfection of numerous statistical procedures facilitated prediction and modeling. As national administrations called for more information and data analysis, America's academics were extremely eager to respond. With this response came not only more information about social programs and problems, but a cadre of university programs designed to produce administrative analysts capable of assessing the nation's problems and managing the programs designed to alleviate the harshness of urban and rural life.

In part, then, the preponderance of discussion and critique of the Reagan administration's plans and programs is related to the spillover effects of other presidents' views of America. Indeed, the changes made in America's course charted by Roosevelt, Kennedy, Johnson, and Nixon changed academic and social institutions. Perhaps the central issue to study when presidents recast America in their own image is the impact of these visions on the institutions which comprise the American dream.

POLICY CHANGES AND U.S. INSTITUTIONS

There is an old adage that begins, "When the [insert any giant or large institution] twitches, the [little people or smaller institution] quakes." We have each probably changed the giant in the story to any of the several large institutions or individuals and the same for the second part of the illustration. In terms of America's institutions, the giant is the domestic-policy apparatus of the federal government; and America's universities, businesses, and industries, to varying extents, become the units which change in response to the twitches in U.S. domestic policy. When the twitches are large in the sense of the policy changes of a Lyndon Johnson or Ronald Reagan, the changes in national institutions can be extremely large and fundamental.

The Great Society Programs

Several examples illustrate the effect of changing domestic policies on the operations, procedures, and priorities of institutions. For example, in the 1960s and 1970s, the federal government's domestic policies clearly emphasized the expansion of programs designed to help urban areas and the minorities that lived in these areas. In many instances, the federal government transferred resources to other levels of government to deliver programs; in other instances the federal government actually delivered programs and services itself in urban areas; and, in still other circumstances, the federal government gave money to private for-profit agencies to deliver services and programs in urban areas.

Many universities were among the institutions that were affected by the federal government's policies. They changed their policies and priorities in response to the government's leadership and financial support. Universities in various parts of the country began to develop open-admission programs to permit students from inner-city areas to attend college regardless of their high-school records. The logic behind these programs was that the inferior public schools available to minority students and racial policies inhibited the performance of otherwise gifted children. Whether or not these assertions were valid was seldom argued; open-admission programs, and the controversies they spawned, were instituted in the East, Midwest, and Far West by a number of public universities. Private schools also reevaluated their admission policies and began to offer opportunities to minority students to fulfill affirmative-action criteria and quotas.

Expanding opportunities for minority students were only one of the policy responses by universities to the federal government's domestic emphasis on urban areas and minorities. Several universities opened or expanded new campuses in nearby older or downtown areas. The University of Delaware, located in the small community of Newark, expanded its urban programs in that state's largest city, Wilmington. The University of Maryland, located in a Washington, D.C., suburb, enlarged its campus in Baltimore. In the Midwest, the University of Illinois continued the pattern of developing and expanding campuses in large, urban areas with the University of Illinois at Chicago Circle. In the Southwest, several new branches of the University of Texas were created at San Antonio, El Paso, and in the Dallas/Fort Worth area. Also, two institutes of urban studies were established--one for the University of Houston and one for the University of Texas at

Arlington. In the West, private schools such as the University of Southern California created a Center for Urban Affairs to coordinate a wide range of teaching and research programs focusing on urban issues.

Universities, of course, were not the only institutions affected by the federal government's domestic-policy emphasis. Because the federal government was also interested in supporting a wide range of service-delivery agents, numerous nonprofit organizations were formed in response to the availability of federal support. Existing nonprofit agencies expanded the scope of their services. In the private sector, corporate philanthropy also followed the lead of the federal government and a variety of urban-related programs were supported. For example, the much-publicized experiments in community control received a considerable amount of support from the Ford Foundation (Berube and Gittell, 1968) and the Ford and Mellon foundations were particularly active in providing educational support for universities developing programs specifically designed to address the urban agenda that had emerged.

The New Federalism of Ronald Reagan

As far-reaching as the changes were as a result of the Great Society programs of the Johnson administration, the domestic policy changes drafted under Ronald Reagan and enacted by Congress in 1981 and 1982 were, if anything, larger. The Reagan plan for a better tomorrow involved the relaxing of restraints on business in an effort to stimulate productivity and create new jobs and wealth. To accomplish this goal, the Reagan strategy involved two separate tasks: (1) reduce government spending, and (2) reduce the taxes paid by Americans for programs of questionable value and productivity.

As introduced in 1981, the Reagan plan for spending by the federal government would have made numerous changes in expenditures from 1981 to 1986; Table I.1 details these changes. The programs which would have been reduced the most were employment and training, education, and social services. Several programs would have received increased funding support, including social insurance and health (Medicare and Medicaid). However, since costs could have been expected to increase by 30 percent over the time period of 1981 to 1986, even these increases would have been small.

TABLE I.1

Proposed Changes in Federal Spending by Policy Areas,
Fiscal Years 1981 and 1986

Policy Area	FY1981 Expenditure (billions of $)	FY1986 Expenditure (billions of $)	Percentage of Change
Income assistance	35.9	34.4	−4.2
Social insurance	182.2	261.0	43.2
Health	66.0	102.4	55.2
Education	15.1	8.8	−41.7
Social services	6.5	5.0	−23.1
Employment and training	9.8	3.6	−63.3
Housing and community development	12.7	12.4	−2.4
Transportation	23.3	19.6	−15.9
Veterans' benefits	23.0	27.9	21.3

Source: Palmer and Sawhill, 1982.

The second part of the Reagan plan involved a series of changes in the taxes paid by businesses and individuals. Passed as part of the Economic Recovery Tax Act of 1981, the changes created a tremendous movement of capital from the public to the private sector. Reviewing the changes made, Okner and Bawden (1983) estimated that in tax year 1984, the federal government would have received $95 billion more if the tax rules of 1980 were still in effect. For tax years 1982, 1983, 1984, and 1985, then, it is possible that the Reagan plan could have accounted for the transfer of more than $350 billion from the coffers of the federal government to the private sector.

It may be possible to debate whether the changes made by Ronald Reagan were as large, larger, or smaller than the initiatives of Lyndon Johnson. Regardless of the relative magnitudes, each set of changes had the ability not only to change America's course and image, but to affect the operation, policies, and procedures of America's institutions drastically.

ASSESSING THE IMPACT OF
FEDERAL DOMESTIC POLICY

The emphasis of the federal government on urban areas and opportunities for minorities by the Johnson administration changed life in America for individuals and institutions. Much of the analysis on the effects of Great Society programs has focused on the changes on individuals and the distribution of wealth and services. For example, there have been studies on income redistribution, the level of services, opportunities for economic advancement, political power, and the general quality of life of all Americans. There have been fewer considerations of the effect of the Great Society programs on institutions.

The impact of shifts in domestic policies on U.S. institutions is the concern of this volume. The point of embarcation for this analysis is the policies of the Reagan administration. For selected institutions, the various contributions to this volume assess the implications and meaning of Reagan policies. In some instances, the concern of an author is with the image created for a particular institution in terms of the administration's objectives of achieving certain policy outcomes. In other instances, the focus is not on the effects of the changes made by the Reagan administration, but on how an institution may need to change in response to the new service demands or definitions. To aid understanding, it may be best to specify, in general or theoretical terms, how institutions may be affected by the domestic policy decisions of the Reagan administration. In this manner, the initial examples of reaction and change to the domestic policy initiatives discussed earlier can be recast and grouped into a meaningful typology.

Domestic Policy and Policy Images

Presidents have a great power to change institutions by changing the public's perception of these institutions or groups. Presidents, or any national leader, can accomplish this transformation through the images conveyed to the populace. The ability of messages generated by leaders to interpret, change, or enhance images in the public's mind has been of substantial interest to political scientists and sociologists. Much of this interest, of course, was tied to the propaganda efforts of the Nazi regime and its portrayal of Jews. In a similar vein, other social scientists have enhanced the ideas suggested by McLuhan (1964) and have studied the images that exist in the public's mind as a result of the ways in which public officials and the media describe various institutions (Bagdikian, 1971; Rosentraub and Burke, 1979). These various studies and commentaries clearly indicate that the popular perception of institutions can be shaped by images portrayed by the media and opinion leaders. In turn, the actions, policies, and decisions of people at all levels of society are then affected by the images of institutions which may be related to the political agenda of a leader or the media.

Yet, even with this rather negative assessment of imagery and policy, the symbolic use of images to gather support for policies and programs is a central task for any administration. The notion that issues and ideas may be manipulated for political ends is generally viewed in an unfavorable light. Yet, the manipulation of ideas for policy seems to be a constant. Edelman's (1964) classic discussion of The Symbolic Uses of Politics simply articulated what most leaders have implicitly or explicitly understood. When parties or persons out of favor rely on images for policies, the pejorative term propaganda is applied. When groups or individuals in favor use the same manipulation of images, the descriptive term applied may be the "facts" or "the truth."

Without imputing motives or suggesting that the images conveyed by the Reagan administration are the same as the tactics used by other presidents or leaders of governments who have been or are adversaries, Ronald Reagan is, indeed, a master of imagery and the symbolic use of politics. Three issues can serve as excellent examples of his use of imagery. First, in terms of reflecting his ideas of the problems with the economy and the beliefs of many Americans, the president has projected, if not an antiunion stance, at least one that indicates that the power of unions is partly responsible for the economic problems of the country. The strike of the air traffic controllers gave the president the opportunity to illustrate that he would "stand up" to the dictates of unions. In this way, the president not only accurately read a strain in his supporters' politics--an antiunion tendency--but tied his position to the idea that big unions were actually hurting workers and those people interested in work. His direct appeal to the air traffic controllers before the ultimatum involving dismissals appealed to his many supporters. This support was so strong that when the president fired the air traffic controllers, labor unions tacitly went along and did not call for any sympathy strikes. The president had beaten the unions in imagery and by his actions and success was able to assume a nonunion position that, in 1984, caused him no problems at the polls. Reagan simply went beyond the union leaders to the individual worker; the average American proved too afraid of economic problems to challenge the president's views.

A second example of the symbolic use of facts or politics for appropriate images involves the spending policies of certain state and local governments. In the 1970s, before Reagan assumed the presidency, the fiscal plight of many Eastern and Northern cities had captured the nation's attention. In his campaign, and in the first years of his presidency, Reagan used these cities as examples of the excessive reliance on social programs for economic security and the economic insecurity and high taxes that such policies produce. Less government spending, not more, was needed to address the problems of these cities. In 1985, while campaigning for his tax-reform plan, Reagan argued that citizens of states with low taxes should not subsidize states with higher taxes. He proposed that state and local taxes should no longer be allowed as deductions from federal taxes.

While it is possible that Reagan was correct and that fewer social programs and less taxes would help these communities' economies, it is also true that the cities that were encountering fiscal problems were the same cities which had historically provided a wide range of social services to immigrants. In many instances, these immigrants had received the benefits of these programs and with new skills had moved to jobs outside of the taxing jurisdiction of the provider cities. With more and more beneficiaries leaving the taxing jurisdictions of older cities, and a new wave of lower-class immigrants still arriving in the cities, a shortfall did exist. Yet, the question facing these cities seemed to be fiscal insolvency from a continuation of programs or a social bankruptcy if programs were curtailed. This was a substantially different image from the one projected by the national administration of these cities and a very different image in media portraits of New York City, Cleveland, Newark, and the other cities with fiscal crises in the 1970s and 1980s.

The argument above is not meant to suggest that there was no mismanagement of municipal finances that could have contributed to the fiscal problems of the city. Indeed, from the studies of New York City's crisis, there was evidence of mismanagement. Yet, mismanagement is not limited to urban management, nor was it the only cause of the problems of cities. The fiscal-boundary problem briefly discussed above, which involved beneficiaries of municipal expenditures leaving the taxing jurisdictions of cities before making contributions to the local tax base, was also a contributing factor, as were several other factors. Yet, what is critical here is that the image provided by the national administration was one of mismanaged cities indulging in programs which would not help the lower class, would not produce an economic safety net, and would cost taxpayers their hard-earned money.

A third example of the use of images to foster policy objectives by the Reagan administration was its continuous reference to a federal government of Democratic presidents and Congresses that had stretched its tentacles into every facet of American life. The Democrats, it was argued, had forgotten the time-honored traditions of local control and decision making and were attempting to direct life from Washington, D.C. Indeed, the Reagan administration provided a portrait of federal control that suggested the federal government operated each of the many programs it financed from huge bureaucracies hiding behind a facade in Washington. The problems of big government, the Reagan argument went, could only be solved if Washington returned to the states and local leaders the responsibility for programs delivered at the local level. Yet, while the Reagan administration wanted to transfer this political power, the reduction in federal support for programs important to cities would actually mean a decline in local power.

The issue of images, symbolic use of politics, and institutional change are the subjects of three different chapters in this volume. The president's acumen aside, the basic question in this imagery is the extent to which the factors and institutions identified by the president as in need of change are indeed correctly described. If there are errors in the depiction, it is not only possible that the policies and programs identified by the president may not reach his goals, but it is also possible that his goals may have already been achieved. If that was the case, then the entire policy program might need to be adjusted.

The first image examined is that of unions and municipal fiscal strength. In "Militancy, Union Penetration, and Fiscal Stress: Are They Really Connected?" Robert Rodgers and Jeffrey Straussman examine one of the central ideas in the discussion of municipal fiscal solvency. A popular image in the considerations of municipal finance is that public-employee unions have contributed to the collapse of major urban areas. As Rodgers and Straussman note in their introduction, "Some mayors seem not only willing to play hardball with municipal unions, they practically relish the opportunity." Mayor Edward Koch of New York City is one example. Given the perceived political benefits in the fight and the extremely limited potential losses, why wouldn't a mayor want to "play hardball" with municipal unions? President Reagan played his version of hardball and not only did he win the battle, but in his reelection bid, organized labor failed to mount any concerted effort against him. Fighting unions under a guise of reducing costs, eliminating unnecessary programs, and saving taxpayers may now be the best game in town in terms of reelection politics.

Yet, the data presented by Rodgers and Straussman suggest that public-employee unions may well have emerged as a convenient scapegoat for tax-conscious politicians. The authors do not mean to suggest that public-employee union demands have not increased municipal costs; rather, they argue that fiscal stress is caused by numerous factors and the existence of public-employee union demands does not, by itself, explain a large portion of the municipal fiscal problems.

In terms of local policy and urban issues, no topic has been of more pronounced importance than the fiscal crisis of the city. Since the administration of Gerald Ford, each president has had to address the issue. The importance of this policy issue is underscored by the inclusion of a second chapter on fiscal stress and images by David R. Morgan and Robert E. England. When large problems similar to the fiscal crisis of cities emerge, the most common questions posed are "Who is to blame?" and "What caused the problem?" In part, the desire for these answers is tied to America's faith in pragmatism and the ability to solve any problem once the causes are identified. The issue of municipal stress is, of course, particularly critical because of the federal, state, and local policies developed based on the perceptions of the problem and its causes.

Morgan and England identify not only some of the important factors, but also the policies and programs that would need to be considered if the "facts" of the crisis are considered instead of the popular images. It is possible that cities, like other entities, have life cycles and a similar propensity, over time, to attract a large lower class which is more dependent on publicly provided services. If this thesis was valid, then even the bustling cities of the Sun Belt would encounter fiscal stress as they aged. Professors Morgan and England examine this issue and offer important information in terms of the image of the cities portrayed by the Reagan administration and the press.

The third and last example of imagery and policy is James Musselwhite and Lester Salamon's assessment of the impact of the Reagan administration's policies on non-profit organizations. One of the stated goals of the administration's New Federalism is to return control of programs and policies to the state and local level. Yet, it may well be that control over policies and programs was already at the state and local level. Musselwhite and Salamon argue that the unique U.S. system of provision and production had already transferred extensive control of programs to the state and local levels. Indeed, if their data and conclusions are correct, the Reagan administration's policies might eventually destroy or weaken the ability of state and local leaders to shape domestic policy and service provision. In this sense, since the desired goal of the Reagan administration had already been met, the policies and programs initiated to reach the goal may actually change the system which, in operation, was accomplishing what the New Federalism wanted to establish.

Domestic Policy and Institutional Reactions

The second issue addressed by this volume is the responses by several different institutions to the domestic policy changes of the Reagan administration. There are, of course, numerous institutions which could be selected for study; indeed, it would be possible to produce a separate volume on the effects of the administration's policies on many institutions. What is attempted here is a more modest examination of the effects and implications of the new policies on only four areas. The areas were selected because of the particular interests of the authors and do not attempt to project a representative view of change. However, these institutions are important and their changes and reactions will have critical implications. In a sense, this section of the book is not concerned with whether or not the images addressed by the Reagan administration's federalism are valid, but what different institutions will encounter given the current U.S. policy orientations.

No area is more thoroughly discussed and debated than health care. The costs for health care have, during the first half of this decade, risen faster than the costs for any other consumer good or government program (Rosentraub, Musselwhite, and Salamon, 1985). Medicaid and Medicare have propelled the administration's interest in cost-containment strategies and the management of the health-care industry. The role of these two programs in the delivery of services to the poor and the elderly clearly established the center-stage importance attributed to health care. The most recent programs introduced by the Reagan administration to control its own investments in health care have been the limitations in the deductability of health expenses from taxpayers' income, the desire to tax employer-paid health-insurance premiums, and a payment system for Medicare and Medicaid recipients based on diagnostically related groupings (DRGs). This last reform has, of course, attracted the most attention because of the size of the federal government's payments. Basically, the DRG program specifies, in advance, how much the federal government will reimburse service providers for certain procedures and treatments. In a curious fashion, the DRG program represents a price list for medical treatments with excess costs being the responsibility of the parties involved. This usually means that the patient has to pay the additional charges. However, since many of the patients cannot afford to pay any extra charges, the DRG plan can mean that service providers will either have to lower their costs or transfer patients before a bill surpasses what will be received from the federal government.

With such intense pressure to control costs, the health-delivery industry is acutely interested in any programs and policies that could reduce costs and help these institutions respond to the domestic-policy changes of the federal government. The federal government's policies toward health care seem to be designed to make consumers and suppliers more conscious of the cost of medical services. Myrna Pickard considers one possible response to the new federal policies in her chapter, "Changes in White: Health-Delivery Options in a Time of High Cost." Basically, Dr. Pickard argues that it is time to consider changing the labor costs associated with the production of medical services. This can be accomplished, she argues and demonstrates, through a more effective and extensive use of nurse practitioners and schools of nursing in the delivery of medical care. These changes can be a very positive response to the policies being implemented with regard to the financing of health care in the United States.

Federal domestic policy was critical to the advancement of affirmative action programs and the expansion of employment opportunities for the women. During the last two decades, the federal government was the prime mover behind a series of laws and executive orders designed to prohibit discrimination against women. During his campaign in 1980, Ronald Reagan made it clear that he was not in favor of a strong federal role in the enforcement of affirmative-action programs and plans. His sentiments became even more apparent with a series of budget reductions and the modification of the federal government's emphasis on the enforcement of affirmative-action goals. A central question for women and the public-employment sector which was so affected by the affirmative-action policies of the federal government before the Reagan administration is: "What will be the effect of the new domestic policies?" This question is the focus of Patricia Huckle's "Changers and the Changed: Affirmative Action and Local Governments." Dr. Huckle first reviews the policies of previous administrations and the changes made by the Reagan administration. Her findings may be a bit surprising as she finds "solace for both sides" as the federal courts may be able to preserve some of the policy initiatives of past administrations. Regardless of this outcome, Dr. Huckle's chapter raises the more profound question of who should shoulder the responsibility for enforcing the civil-rights legislation painfully achieved in the past. Her findings and conclusions raise important policy questions for public officials as the course of the federal government, in this policy area, seems to be inexorably changed.

Of all the policy areas the Reagan administration wanted to change, economic policy and development would have ranked at or near the top of their list. In the president's view, America had been led by a series of Democratic administrations and congresses down a path that was destined to lead to the creation of an unproductive state. The Republican presidents, in recent years, had been hardly more effective in moving America away from its drift toward a welfare state. Presidents Eisenhower, Nixon, and Ford may have stemmed the flow, but by 1980, America, in the view of Ronald Reagan and his staff, had moved dangerously close to the point of being dominated by government. To reverse that trend and to place America on the "right track" toward prosperity and development, a new plan was needed.

The appropriate track for economic development and growth that benefits all economic classes and ethnic/racial groups in America has been a central issue for virtually all administrations. Despite claims of caring more for the "underclasses" than the Republicans did, the record of Democratic administrations still left a great deal undone. Ronald Reagan could ask all economic and racial groups if they were better off under Jimmy Carter in 1980 than they were in 1976 and most would say they were not. Since most people were not better off in 1980 than they were in 1976, why not try the policies and programs of Ronald Reagan? There is no way to determine how many people followed this logic in supporting the first term of Ronald Reagan's presidency.

Balancing economic growth and development has been a difficult issue for the United States as it has for basically every other nation. In some cases, there is no interest in balancing development and discrepancies or imbalances should be expected. In some instances, societies do try to balance or, at least, distribute opportunities. These different approaches are not of direct concern here. Rather, Lyke Thompson focuses on the question of economic development and raises the interesting possibility that the entire theoretical orientation of both Democratic and Republican administrations may not accurately portray how growth occurs and what affects its distribution. In this sense, his chapter, "Economic Differentiation, Growth Centers, and the Failure of National Economic Policy," is a critical assessment of the failure of domestic policies to affect economic development. In his assessment, neither the policies or programs of the Republicans or Democrats can affect the distribution of growth. However, he does not limit his observations to what has failed; a new perspective for domestic policy is suggested to change the large institution of economic development which might permit a more balanced distribution of growth.

The fourth policy area reviewed concerns the Reagan administration's emphasis on deregulation and telecommunications. Deregulation, of course, was a popular strategy for the Carter administration in its efforts to change the way in which the airlines of this country operate. Deregulation also fits the Reagan administration's economic philosophy and the mood of the popular culture at this time. Deregulation, then, will be a new issue for all levels of local government and, in particular, major cities. The importance of deregulation for major cities is related to the concentration in major cities of the activities and industries which are affected by deregulation.

The need for cities to consider the implications of their new responsibilities under deregulation are discussed by Mitchell Moss in his assessment of "Urban Policy and Telecommunications Systems." To manage development and their own futures effectively, cities, in Moss's opinion, must not be "enamored of new technologies . . . [but understand] the changing technological infrastructure and the broad-based way in which . . . [these changes] will influence almost all aspects of urban government services and economic development."

Policy Changes and the Oracles

The images of institutions and institutions themselves are not the only factors or forces that are altered by domestic-policy initiatives. The institutions sometimes regarded as the oracles of change, the academic disciplines which are supposed to raise questions about the organization of a society and the distribution of its resources, are also affected by domestic-policy changes. The involvement of social scientists in the development of policy by Presidents Roosevelt, Kennedy, Johnson, Nixon, Ford, Carter, and Reagan has drastically changed both the universities from which these academics came and their disciplines. Universities have been changed in a number of ways, some of which have already been discussed. For example, in the 1960s and 1970s, numerous universities in all parts of the country changed their orientations to include a variety of urban-oriented teaching, research, and service centers. These same programs which were extremely popular slightly more than a decade ago are now being curtailed, reduced, and, in some instances, eliminated. With the national administration and students themselves more interested in private economic development, university programs designed to study the city and the distribution of services and resources are now simply not in vogue (Rosentraub and Warren, 1986).

It is clear, then, that universities, as institutions, are changed by domestic-policy orientations. The question which the last section of this volume focuses upon is not whether universities change, but what are the effects of domestic-policy changes on academic disciplines? Three academic disciplines were selected for analysis in this last section because of their clear relevance to the development of domestic policies. Sociology and sociologists have been involved with the development of domestic policy since the administration of Franklin Roosevelt. Substantial inputs into the development of the New Deal were made by faculty from the University of Chicago. The importance of sociologists to the development of domestic policy has continued through the participation of individuals such as James Coleman, Irving Horowitz, and numerous other scholars. The appropriate role for sociologists in the development of domestic policy and the challenges it faces with the new emphases of the Reagan administration are considered by Scott Cummings in "Urban Policy Research and the Changing Focus of the State: Sociology's Ambiguous Legacy and Uncertain Future." Cummings argues that the very creation of new knowledge is a function of the spending policies of the state. When the state changes its emphases, the quality and kind of information produced on different subjects will also change. As he notes: "In the present political climate, a policy market exists only for ideas endorsing Reaganomics and programs promoting private profit accumulation." If this assertion is valid, then a major conflict may exist for disciplines that identify with notions of equity in the distribution of resources, power, and opportunities, especially if reaching these objectives requires some form of collective action. This is part of the discussion included in the Cummings's chapter as he ponders sociology's ability to contribute to the development of information, ideas, and theories to solve the urban problems that still plague metropolitan areas and the ethnic/racial and economic minority groups that still call America's cities home.

As important as sociologists have been in the development of domestic policy, economists have probably surpassed the importance of the representatives of any aca-

demic discipline.   John Kenneth Galbraith was among the
first economists involved in national-policy processes in
the administration of Franklin Roosevelt.   Since that time,
and continuing through the administration of Ronald Reagan,
economists have assumed a prominent, if not leading, role
in the development of domestic policy.   As economics has
grown in importance in the development of domestic policy,
the critical nature of economic theory as it is applied to
urban policy becomes evident.   As argued by Jeffrey Chapman, Gary Reid, and Donald Winkler, the ideas which formulate economic theory, as applied to domestic policies,
are at an important junction.   Many noneconomists and
policymakers, baffled by the much-publicized inaccuracies
of macroeconomic predictions, may be disregarding the
recommendations and analysis of applied microtheorists.
The applied work of microeconomic theorists has, on occa-
sion, even fallen into more disrepute because of the tendency among some researchers to subsume questions of income distribution and political implementation in discussions dominated by the concept of efficiency.

The challenge, then, for economics, may be to unify
its theoretical framework with the policy requirements for
discussions of efficiency that include, on an equal footing,
the issues of the distribution of resources and opportunities
and the politics of implementation.   A "realistic" approach
to the study of economic policy by microtheorists will then
have the strength to confront even the most dedicated skep-
tics who are concerned with the inaccuracy of some macroeconomic projections.

Despite the importance of economists to the policy
process, the entire process of public policy is a major
orientation of students of political science and public administration.   Within the large number of studies of public
policy which students of these disciplines have produced,
two issues have emerged as being most critical, equity and
efficiency.   Indeed, as Robert Warren notes, these issues
have often been presented as ideas in opposition to each
other.   This is not to suggest that equity implies an inability to be efficient or that efficiency means inequity.
Yet, the current political climate clearly implies that efficiency must be the goal of politics, even if inequities exist
or are produced.   Warren takes issue with this point and
declares "efficiency in the abstract has no meaning."   Indeed, what political science and public administration have
failed to do is to specify carefully the ways in which poli-

cies can be inefficient in their generation of inequitable costs. To accomplish this challenge, Warren argues, a new paradigm to guide the analysis is required. This new paradigm is developed in "Equity and Efficiency in Urban-Service Delivery: A Consumption and Participation Costs Approach."

A CONCLUDING NOTE

Philosophers offer conflicting advice regarding change. On one hand, we are told, the more things change the more they are the same. On the other hand, we are also told that there is nothing as constant as change. The administration of Ronald Reagan will be re- membered for many things, not the least of which was a qualitative alteration in the flow of federal policy. In charting this new course in several areas, the chapters in this volume clearly indicate that the changes in federal policy have left things different. This is not a case where things are the same after changes take place. In- deed, if this collection has accomplished anything, it has identified what changes have resulted from the policies of the Reagan administration and what issues students of pub- lic policy must respond to in light of these changes. Things in the 1980s are not the same as they were in the 1960s and 1970s and the legacy of the 1980s will mean more differences for local governments in the future. No, things are not the same, nor are they likely ever to be the same again.

REFERENCES

Bagdikian, Ben H. 1971. The Information Machines. New York: Harper and Row.

Berube, Maurice, and Marilyn Gittell. 1968. Confrontation at Ocean-Hill Brownsville. New York: Praeger Pub- lishers.

Edelman, Murray. 1964. The Symbolic Use of Politics. New York: Harper and Row.

Halberstam, David. 1969. The Best and the Brightest. New York: Random House.

McLuhan, Marshall. 1964.   Understanding Media: The Extensions of Man.   New York: McGraw-Hill.

Okner, Benjamin, and D. Lee Bawden. 1983. "Recent Changes in Federal Income Redistribution Policies." National Tax Journal 36(3): 347-60.

Palmer, John L., and Isabel V. Sawhill. 1982. The Reagan Experiment. Washington, D.C.: Urban Institute.

Rosentraub, Mark S., and Barbara A. Burke. 1979. "Mass Communication and Decision-Making: A Case Study of the Geography of Newspaper Information and Local Government." Journal of Environmental Systems 8(3): 267-91.

Rosentraub, Mark S., James C. Musselwhite, Jr., and Lester M. Salamon. 1985. Government Spending and the Nonprofit Sector in Dallas. Washington, D.C.: Urban Institute.

Rosentraub, Mark S., and Robert Warren. 1986. "Urban Universities and the Distribution of Growth in Developed Nations." Policy Studies Review. Forthcoming.

Part I

Domestic Policy and Policy Images

1

Militancy, Union Penetration, and Fiscal Stress: Are they Really Connected?

Robert C. Rodgers and
Jeffrey D. Straussman

INTRODUCTION

If the "days of wine and roses" are over (to recall a comment made a few years ago by the former governor of New York, Hugh Carey), we might expect public employees to be among the first groups with empty glasses and flower-less vases. The reason is simple. If public managers really want to engage in cutback management, in response to demands for tax relief or declining federal funds, they must trim the largest set of costs--wage and nonwage compensation. This means battling with public employees and their respective bargaining units. Some mayors seem not only willing to "play hardball" with municipal unions, they practically relish the opportunity. The next few years promise to give many other public officials a chance or two to play the game.

It was not very long ago that specialists in public sector labor relations spoke about the "catch-up" phase of public unionism. Indeed, the 1960s and the first half of the 1970s were a period when public unions seemed to nar-row the gap between their private-sector counterparts on three basic dimensions--militancy as expressed by strikes, the legal environment as evidenced by state and local gov-ernment collective-bargaining legislation, and perhaps most important, wage and nonwage compensation. There is a considerable body of empirical research on this period (Lewin, Feuille, Kochan, 1981). In general, the impact of public unions on a range of questions (from compensation to management prerogatives) suggests that public unions have not dramatically altered the political and economic contours of state and local government.

But all this is academic. A new era--the one alluded to by Governor Carey--is upon us. Since 1975, many state and local governments have experienced fiscal austerity. The causes are many. For some local governments such as Detroit, Cleveland, and New York, fiscal austerity is a response to both an acute financial crisis and a more general chronic economic decline. For other governments, austerity was precipitated by taxpayer revolts such as California's Proposition 13 and Massachusetts' Proposition $2\frac{1}{2}$. And for hundreds, probably thousands of other local governments, austerity and its accompanying cutback management will be initiated by the intergovernmental fiscal fallout of the Reagan administration's cutback policies.

The expectation that public unions have contributed to urban fiscal stress seems straightforward. Consider the following logic. The labor share of local-government budgets is approximately 75 percent. The most important issue for organized public employees has, in general, been wage and nonwage compensation. Consequently, to the extent that unions can exert wage pressure on city budgets, stress should increase. Naturally, stress would be ameliorated if, as in the private sector, increased labor costs are "passed on" to consumers. But the analogy is not very useful because in the local public sector, the consumers are taxpayers and their employees, elected officials, are wary about raising taxes.

Where does this leave public-sector unions? Recent signals say, not in a very good position. Indeed, public employees have complained that "bad press" has adversely affected their negotiating position. Aside from image, public unions will likely be asked to take part in local government efforts to maintain (or restore) financial solvency. This has meant, and will continue to mean, acquiescence on labor's traditional compensation and noncompensation demands.

An illustration of this comes from the financially besieged city of Detroit. As part of a comprehensive state and local plan to return Detroit to financial solvency, municipal workers had to agree to a two-year wage freeze. The unions balked. Mayor Coleman Young threatened to obtain the equivalent savings through layoffs if the unions did not accept the wage freeze. And Mayor Young has always been portrayed as pro-union!

Does the Detroit example highlight the future of public-sector labor relations? Will local governments under fiscal siege try to extract large concessions from their public employees? And what will be the response of public unions? Will they "take it on the chin" and keep a low political profile because public sentiment is antiunion? Or, on the contrary, will public unions be more militant, refusing to be scapegoats?

There are no public-sector labor relations crystal balls to answer these questions. Yet, the future of public-sector labor relations, particularly the association of unionism with fiscal stress, should be influenced by what has happened in the recent past. However, if fiscal stress has become routine, we simply do not know if public unions have responded differently in fiscally stressed jurisdictions compared with healthy ones. It is also possible that some of our impressions about public unionism and fiscal stress are misinformed. Maybe public unions are not quite the villains of the financial drama critics make them out to be. We ask three questions by taking a look at the not-so-distant past (1975 to 1979) so that we may have a sounder empirical basis for forecasting the future of public-sector labor relations in an environment of fiscal austerity.

THE IMPACT OF UNIONS ON WAGES

There are a plethora of studies that try to determine the impact of public unions on public employee wages. While these studies have produced mixed results, it is safe to conclude that, on balance, unions have exerted mild upward pressure on municipal wages. More recent work suggests that traditional wage studies have underestimated the impact of unionism. That is, nonwage compensation has been an important dimension of significant cost outlays that municipalities incurred (Dickson and Peterson, 1981).

Studies that consider the cause-and-effect relationship between public-employee union activities and fiscal stress have reported consistent relationships. Clark (1970), in an analysis of 51 cities, found a positive association between the existence of a union contract and fiscal strain. Benecki (1978) found modest support for the hypothesis that collective bargaining is associated with higher expenditure levels. Two studies point to increased pressure on the budget process which is caused by collective bargaining.

Kearney (1980) studied collective bargaining in 23 Iowa cities and found that it "complicated" the budget process. Derber and Wagner (1979), in their study of 27 Illinois local governments, found that jurisdictions with "tight fiscal conditions" were more likely to consider their ability to pay as a salient consideration in the bargaining process. Case studies also hint at the association of public unionism and fiscal strain. Irene Rubin's study (1982) of a Midwestern city, Running in the Red, notes that excessive wage concessions to municipal unions contributed to the city's fiscal woes. And, of course, we cannot forget the 1975 financial crisis of New York. Virtually every account of that period places some blame on unions in contributing to the city's fiscal problems (see Morris, 1980).

There is a fundamental reason to expect public unions to exacerbate fiscal strain. Specifically, public employees enjoy a monopoly situation for many local-government services. The monopoly arrangement allows unions, at least in principle, to use the threat of the withholding of services as a way to extract wage and nonwage concessions. This feature of local-government services makes public-sector collective bargaining substantially different from private-sector negotiations (Wellington and Winter, 1971).

Observers of public unions who do not fully accept the idea that public unions have an inherent advantage in their monopoly position concede that at least "essential" employees--typically police and fire fighters--require separate treatment (Burton and Krider, 1975:135-77). In this connection, Juris and Feuille (1973:43) noted that fire fighters in Dayton, Ohio, and police and fire fighters in Cleveland, were the last to be laid off in budget crunches even though their salaries were higher than other municipal employees. Mayor Henry Maier (1972:61) of Milwaukee has summarized the position of the city faced with monopoly pressure: "The greatest overriding problems for the municipal leader is the fact that in labor relations he is dealing with critical monopolies in some areas and that no weapon has been developed to firmly strengthen his legal hand in dealing with these situations on behalf of the public."

Once fiscal stress is acknowledged as a fact of municipal life, we would expect public unions to develop a defensive posture. Unions, on the political retreat, should be more submissive in the face of the financial woes of cities and the accompanying "taxpayer revolts." Although empirical studies are nonexistent, there are a few hints that the submissive hypothesis has some credence. The "get tough" approach of some big-city mayors, complaints about negative media image, and even the defensiveness of union-sponsored television commercials, all portray a reaction that is tempered by the new fiscal realities. Some cities have even negotiated productivity improvements as part of a labor package, or asked for union givebacks of benefits which were won in earlier collective-bargaining agreements.

Two distinct situations are suggested by the above. While previous studies suggest that there is a correlation between public unionism and fiscal stress, research has been restricted to the link between unionism and fiscal stress. This study considers the possibility that public unions may be affected by, and thereby responding to, fiscal scarcity in ways fundamentally different from the less-stringent earlier periods. Are unions, fearing further declines in their political power and anticipating still further taxpayer backlashes, more accommodating to the realities of an austere fiscal climate? For example, are unions less likely to initiate strikes after evidence of fiscal stress?

As a means of addressing these research questions, two recent periods have been selected for examination. The first is 1975 through 1977. This base period was selected because it reflects a period when fiscal stress surfaced as a noticeable phenomenon in many cities. The selection of the followup period, 1977 through 1979, allows us to explore the second question: Is public union activity related to the fiscal conditions of an earlier time period?

URBAN STRESS AND FISCAL STRAIN

Urban stress is an elusive concept. While there are several "trouble lists" that attempt to portray the relative position of cities, the indicators used to rank cities actually tap different dimensions of city health. For example, the Brookings Hardship Index taps "social-need" conditions, the Congressional Budget Office study considers economic-need conditions, and the Treasury Department's index addresses fiscal-need conditions. These various indices of city stress have been subjected to comparison and criticism (see Burchell et al., 1980:159-229). Weaknesses of the indices include the following:

_The indices generally focus on only one dominant feature of stress (economic, social) but are used to make inferences about other aspects of stress (such as fiscal).

_There is no well-defined causal link among different dimensions of stress.

_Comparisons across municipalities are precarious because of differential functional responsibilities.

_Comparisons are sometimes complicated because of underlying and overlying jurisdictions.

_Cross-sectional comparisons are unable to detect anomalous values on specific stress data at one point in time.

City stress is clearly multidimensional. Public unions may influence changes in various dimensions of stress. For example, one might argue that public unions drive up the cost of municipal services, which requires increases in local taxes. These tax increases, in turn, influence plant-location decisions, which affect the economic base of the municipality. The causal chain of events is mere speculation, but it is, in principle, susceptible to examination.

Our objective is more modest. We argue then that if public unions influence urban stress, this influence should be reflected in the fiscal condition of the city. Our reasoning is straightforward. When unions organize to bargain collectively, and when they strike, their ultimate objective is to obtain wage and nonwage compensation concessions for their respective memberships. To the extent that these activities are effective, cities are likely to bear increased fiscal burdens. Of course, unions organize, bargain, and strike over issues that are "noneconomic." But on the average, and over time, most of the issues of interest to a membership have long-range cost implications.

MEASURING STRESS

For the purposes of our analysis we have selected four measures of fiscal strain. (Our measures, variable descriptions, and data sources are listed in Appendix A.) One measure captures the change in the tax burden on city residents. The second captures the change in fiscal dependency--the reliance on intergovernmental aid. The third depicts the change in the total debt retired, and the fourth is derived from downward adjustments in the Moody's bond ratings as an indicator of the cities most severely wrought with fiscal stress.

Tax Burden

The concept of tax burden is well acknowledged in analyses of fiscal conditions of local governments. John Peterson (1980:231-48) used a similar measure--city revenue effort--(own source revenue/personal income) and found a strong relationship between this measure and Moody's ratings for general-obligation bonds. The Congressional Budget Office (see Burchell, 1980:188) has created an urban-need index that includes indicators of fiscal need. One indicator is taxes as a percentage of personal income. Similarly, the U.S. Treasury Department (see Burchell, p. 188) has created a fiscal-strain index for the 48 largest cities. Included in this index is an "own source revenue burden change." Similar to the index used by the Treasury Department, our tax burden index (CRE) is the change in own source revenues divided by total per capita personal income (see Appendix A).

Fiscal Dependency

This measure captures the cities' dependency on intergovernmental aid. The overall pattern has been a growing reliance on revenues other than "own source" during the decade of the 1970s. Even cities not usually associated with stress have become dependent on intergovernmental aid. For example, Catherine Lovell (1981:194) has pointed out that even growing cities such as Phoenix and Houston have come to rely on intergovernmental revenues.

Why is the proportion of revenues that are derived from intergovernmental aid a useful fiscal indicator? We can think of this indicator as a "warning signal." When a city begins to rely on intergovernmental aid, it provides services that often have political constituencies. When the aid ends, or is withdrawn, the city must either terminate the programs or pick up the cost, thereby increasing the tax burden on local residents. If political support has been generated, this puts public officials in a difficult position. Terminating the programs in question is undesirable; so is raising taxes.

This second fiscal strain measure (CGV) is relatively straightforward. It is measured as the ratio of the change in total intergovernmental revenues from all sources, divided by the change in total expenditures.

Change in Debt Status

Change in debt status can be affected by a variety
of short-term and long-term considerations. Case studies
of the New York City financial situation of 1975 have all
pointed to the growth of short-term debt as one indicator
of crisis. Debt measures as proxies for fiscal stress have
been used by Nivola (1982), Clark (1970), and Aronson and
King (1978). Following the latter, we selected for consideration a dimension of a city's debt that is most likely to
be affected by short-term (that is, two-year) factors. Furthermore, we treat debt in terms of a burden on local revenues. The change in debt status (LDR) is measured by
the change in long-term debt retired, plus the interest
paid on the general debt, divided by the change in own
source revenue.

Distressed Cities

The fourth variable (DIS) used to depict fiscal stress
identifies those cities having a "severe" form of stress.
That is, we tried to identify the most distressed cities in
our population by selecting the cities that had a down-
grading in their Moody's bond rating for general-obligation
bonds between 1975 and 1980 (see Appendix A for rating
criteria).

THE CITIES SELECTED FOR ANALYSIS

There is little consensus as to what is an appropriate population or sample of cities to study. Lists of
troubled cities referred to above generally include only the
largest cities in the United States. While this approach
has the virtue of including the most obvious cases (New
York, Cleveland, Detroit), it ignores smaller cities that do
not receive national attention.
An alternative approach has been adopted by Terry
Clark (1970). Clark used a 51-city sample in analyzing
fiscal stress. Nivola has pointed out that this sample includes some of the largest cities that are really suburbs.
Nivola's point is that cross-sectional comparisons can distort the meaning of fiscal stress when gross disparities are
found among the cities because they are qualitatively different (1982:380).

We have elected to include both large and small cities that have previously been used in analyses of fiscal stress by the Advisory Commission on Intergovernmental Relations (1980). These 127 cities, listed in Appendix B, include all cities located within the 85 largest Standard Metropolitan Statistical Areas (SMSAs) and, in addition, a selection of 25 smaller cities. This group of cities is geographically representative of population concentrations in the country; it also includes cities that are growing and declining in population.

MEASURING PUBLIC-EMPLOYEE UNION ACTIVITY

In this analysis we have focused on two dimensions of public unions: militancy and union penetration. Militancy is straightforward. It refers to the incidence of strikes by organized public employees. Strike activity is often thought of as an indicator of union power. Moreover, despite the fact that strikes by public employees (with a few exceptions) are prohibited by law, the incidence of strikes by public employees has increased since the mid-1960s.

Should strikes affect the fiscal condition of local governments? While this subject has not been addressed directly, there is a plausible logic that would answer the question in the affirmative. The logic is as follows. Following the Wellington-Winter (1971) argument, if public employees have monopoly power, then local governments are unable to find alternatives if services are withheld through strikes--at least in the short run. Local government officials are thus forced into a position of making concessions. The cost of local government thereby increases. This, over time, creates fiscal deterioration.

In our analysis we have focused on four different dimensions of public-union strike activity, for each of the two time periods, respectively:

LST The proportion of work time lost as a result of all work stoppages (by six or more employees) lasting one day or longer;

USP Union support for the strike, or the proportion of all work stoppages that were sanctioned by a recognized bargaining agent;

ECO The proportion of work stoppages that occurred primarily over "economic" issues (essentially wage and nonwage compensation disputes);

ARB The proportion of strikes that were settled by interest arbitration. This dimension of strikes—the method of dispute settlement—is important because: (a) Unions tend to favor arbitration as a way to resolve disputes, and (b) There is some evidence that arbitration may produce outcomes advantageous to public unions (Olson, 1980).

Union penetration will also be considered. Conventional wisdom suggests the greater the "presence" of unions, the more likely that the fiscal condition of a jurisdiction will be in stress. These dimensions of union penetration will be considered.

ESS The extent to which essential employees (fire fighters and/or police) are organized to bargain collectively. With the introduction of ESS, the monopoly argument is taken into consideration, the view that government services, especially police and fire, are not substitutable in the private market. As a consequence, public employees who provide essential services are in an advantaged position if they are organized;

ORG The relative percentage change in proportional bargaining unit membership during the two time periods, respectively;

UNT The percentage change in the number of bargaining units having recognition to bargain collectively for the two time periods, respectively.

ANALYSIS

Our analysis is in three parts. First, we look at the simple correlations between public unionism and fiscal strain in each of the two time periods—1975–77, and 1977–79. Table 1.1 lists the hypothesized relationships between the public unionism measures and our bivariate results for 1975–77.

The inconsistency between the expected and actual signs, and the absence of significant relationships prove to be disappointing to those who hold strongly to the view that public unionism is associated with fiscal stress. Notice

TABLE 1.1

Predicted and Cross-section Correlations between Public Unionism and Fiscal Strain, 1975-77

Independent Variables	Predicted Relationship	$CRE_{t_2-t_1}$	$CGV_{t_2-t_1}$	$LDR_{t_2-t_1}$	DIS
Lost time in strikes (LST)	+	.00	.05	-.02	.05
Strikes over economic issues (ECO)	+	-.24[a]	.10	-.05	.03
Union support for the strike (SUP)	+	.03	.11	-.29[b]	.04
Strikes settled by arbitration (ARB)	+	-.16	.09	-.03	.10
Essential employee index (ESS)	+	.06	.11	.19[a]	.23[a]
Change in union membership (ORG)	+	.03	-.10	-.10	-.18[a]
Change in number of units (UNT)	+	.08	-.06	.00	-.02

[a]Signifies the relationship is significant at the .05 level or better.

[b]Signifies the relationship is significant at the .01 level or better.

Note: N = 127.

Source: See Appendix A at the end of this chapter.

in the earlier time period (1975 to 1977) only five relationships are significant, and three are in the opposite
direction from that expected. The later time-period results
(1977 to 1979) are only somewhat more suggestive.

The relationship between essential employees and
the distressed cities variable comes closest to confirming
the conventional wisdom. Notice that the relationship is
both positive and significant for both time periods. This
suggests that there may indeed be an association between
the extent of unionization among essential employees and
city fiscal stress, thereby giving some credence to the essential argument mentioned earlier.

A host of methodological artifacts and data limitations may explain the absence of significant relationships
in Tables 1.1 and 1.2. Consider one possible explanation.
Perhaps the reason why we have not found significant relationships in our two cross-sectional analyses is that the
influence of unionism on fiscal stress does not take effect
until a later time period. We could ask: Did strikes and
union penetration in the mid-1970s lead to deteriorating
fiscal conditions in the late 1970s? This question suggests
a time-ordered test. The results are reported in Table 1.3.

The results in Table 1.3 similarly fail to confirm
the conventional wisdom. All of the significant relationships except one have negative signs, contrary to our
hypotheses. We can offer one, albeit post hoc, explanation. It is possible that there is a relationship between
unionism and stress, but not for the time periods under
consideration. Perhaps the relationship held for the pre-
1975 period. Clark's (1970) finding that unions are associated with stress is based on data from the first half of
the 1970s. Similarly, analyses of the New York City financial crisis of 1975 generally portray public unions as making a significant contribution to the crisis. Here also the
time period is the late 1960s to the early 1970s. It is
conceivable that public unions began to moderate their activities by the mid-1970s.

If public unionism is not associated with stress,
perhaps stress influences union activities. That is, even
if unions may not have contributed to fiscal stress, it is
still conceivable that public unions respond to increasingly
austere fiscal environments. One might argue, for example,
that a period of stress is followed by a moderation of militant activities. Unions fearing a citizens' backlash and
knowing that the city is in the midst of fiscal troubles may
wish to adopt a low profile.

TABLE 1.2

Predicted Cross-section Correlations between Public Unionism and Fiscal Strain (1977–79)

Independent Variables	Predicted Relationship	$CRE_{t_3 - t_2}$	$CGV_{t_3 - t_2}$	$LDR_{t_3 - t_2}$	DIS
Lost time in strikes (LST)	+	-.12	-.10	-.03	.25[a]
Strikes over economic issues (ECO)	+	-.05	-.13	-.12	.05
Union support for the strike (USP)	+	-.22[a]	-.05	-.03	.00
Strikes settled by arbitration (ARB)	+	.22[a]	.01	.02	-.02
Essential employee index (ESS)	+	-.22[a]	-.03	.03	.23[a]
Change in union membership (ORG)	+	-.12	.03	.06	.02
Change in number of units (UNT)	+	-.08	.09	.01	-.09

[a]Signifies the relationship is significant at the .05 level or better.

Note: N = 127.

Source: See Appendix A at the end of this chapter.

TABLE 1.3

Predicted and Time-ordered Correlations between
Public Unionism (1975-77) and Fiscal Stress (1977-79)

Independent Variables	Predicted Relationship	CRE t_3-t_2	CGV t_3-t_2	LDR t_3-t_2
Lost time in strikes (LST)	+	$-.26^a$	.06	-.00
Strikes over economic issues (ECO)	+	.05	.05	.04
Union support for the strike (USP)	+	.05	$.32^b$	-.01
Strikes settled by arbitration (ARB)	+	-.08	.04	.03
Change in union membership units (ORG)	+	.07	-.18	.03
Change in number of units (UNT)	+	-.05	-.05	-.03

[a]Signifies the relationship is significant at the .05 level or better.
[b]Signifies the relationship is significant at the .01 level or better.
Note: N = 127.
Source: See Appendix A at the end of this chapter.

Similarly, organizing activities may slow as public employees become more concerned about job security. Job security may take precedence over traditional union activities. We explored this theme by examining the relationship between fiscal stress in 1975 to 1977, and union activity between 1977 and 1979. We expected both militancy and union penetration to be moderated by the fiscal strain of the 1975 to 1977 period. As Table 1.4 illustrates, our expectations were, again, not fulfilled.

Notice the result of lost time in strikes. While we hypothesized an inverse relationship between fiscal stress and militancy, we actually found a positive and significant relationship with our change in tax-burden measure. Similarly, while we expected a negative relationship between

TABLE 1.4

Predicted and Time-ordered Correlations between Fiscal Stress (1975–77)
and Public Unionism (1977–79)

Independent Variables	Predicted Relationship	LST Lost Time in Strikes	ECO Strikes over Economic Issues	USP Union Support	ARB Strikes Settled by Arbitration	ORG Δ in Union Membership	UNT Δ in Number of Units
$CRE_{t_2}-t_1$	--	$.20^a$	.12	-.06	.00	.08	-.03
$CGV_{t_2}-t_1$	--	.09	$.19^a$	-.03	.08	.02	.15
$LDR_{t_2}-t_1$	--	.10	-.00	-.09	-.00	.06	.08

[a] Signifies the relationship is significant at the .05 level or better.

Source: See Appendix A at the end of this chapter.

strikes for economic reasons and fiscal stress, our actual result is positive and significant with our measure of fiscal dependency. Contrary to conventional wisdom, militancy by public unions did not seem to be affected by fiscal stress.

The correlations in Table 1.4 cannot be used as a test of causality. They only reflect the existence of a relationship. Even when using accepted tests such as cross-lagged correlational tests, we find no evidence of causal impact of fiscal stress and union activity. There are three post-hoc explanations for these results. First, we considered objections to the inclusion of the smaller cities in the analysis as a possible explanation for why so many of the predicted relationships were not confirmed. Therefore, we repeated the analysis for the 85 cities in the largest SMSAs. The results were consistent with those reported in Tables 1.2 through 1.4. We also considered the possibility that cities not faced with stress may simply respond differently to the demands of unions, and vice versa, than the cities that are essentially in a "stress" condition. This would suggest that relationships in the "no stress" cities are being canceled by relationships found for the stress cities. This possibility was examined by selecting for analysis only those cities that had been determined by the Department of Housing and Urban Development to meet the standards of minimum fiscal stress. Results once again were generally consistent with the results found in Tables 1.2 through 1.4.

Second, public unions may not have dramatically altered their basic activities after the onset of fiscal stress. Indeed, after a decade of "catch-up," public employees may have lost some economic ground during the mid-1970s and were therefore unwilling to curb their activities in the face of retrenchment. It is also possible that public unions simply would not accept the reality that many cities were beginning to face austere fiscal conditions. Indeed, the Derber and Wagner (1979:23) study found: "About half the union negotiators accepted management's claims of budget constraints and accommodated their bargaining to the situation. The other half disbelieved management or asserted that, regardless, it was up to management to get the necessary funds for acceptable pay increases." This study, limited to an examination of 27 public units in Illinois, is, as with our study, only suggestive. Nevertheless, it is possible that many public unions do not pay much attention to the fiscal condition when deciding on strike actions. And even if they are concerned with fiscal retrenchment, it is also possible that a large number of unions are willing to take actions to maintain the economic position of their members even at the risk of personnel layoffs.

The third interpretation is based on a conceivable management response to unions in the aftermath of fiscal deterioration. Perhaps public officials are more willing to "take a strike" for two basic reasons. Public officials may feel that citizens do not want them to succumb to union pressure. Rather, public officials may perceive support for a "get tough" position even if this causes inconveniences due to striking public employees. Mayor Edward Koch of New York certainly experienced this reaction during the transit strike of 1980. Cities may also save money during a public-employee strike, notwithstanding the necessity of incurring additional costs when services are continued. While public officials will certainly not acknowledge that they welcome strikes by public employees, strikes may not be as onerous as they once were. Indeed, Philadelphia's cash-flow problems were eased a few years ago when teachers went out on strike. Again, all this is only speculation, but it is a plausible explanation for our nonintuitive results.

CONCLUSIONS

Can we dismiss the notion that public unions have contributed to fiscal deterioration? Not yet. An obvious caveat is the fact that our analysis merely considered the association of unions and stress; we made no causal claims. Furthermore, the concept and measurement of fiscal stress remains problematical. In particular, analysis of a sample of local governments is hampered by the quagmire of intricate relationships among jurisdictions. Fiscal stress for any local government is affected by the number of types of overlying and underlying governments. Stress may also be affected by the functional responsibilities assigned to local governments. Consequently, measures of fiscal stress for single jurisdictions that are examined in a cross-sectional context are invariably suspect, and causal inferences are precluded from a consideration of bivariate correlations. Our data and analysis, as with previous studies, have not escaped these criticisms.

It is also possible, indeed probable, that there are a host of factors other than public unions that account for variations in fiscal stress. One common explanation for fiscal stress, for instance, is the claim that economic decline produces stress. It is certainly plausible that there are important interactive effects between economic phenomena such as unemployment and public unionism that, together, may be more effective in explaining fiscal stress. Indeed, it would seem appropriate for future research to include public unionism as one group of explanatory variables in models of fiscal stress.

However, even if public unions have been unfairly blamed for the fiscal infirmities of many cities, they will not be able to ignore the fiscal realities of the late 1980s. Cities that have suffered from revenue shortfalls caused, in part, by taxpayer revolts and President Reagan's New Federalism have been searching for ways to trim their budgets. Options such as contracting for services or privatization clearly threaten the traditional interests of labor in the public sector. Charges of "union busting" will unlikely stop city administrators from considering personnel options that could cut labor costs. This means that solutions to fiscal deterioration will require adjustments from public unions that reflect the realities of the second half of the 1980s—adjustments that may indeed be painful to public employees who reaped gains from the catch-up period of a bygone era.

Variable Descriptions, Means and Sources

Dependent Variables	Mean Values t_2-t_1	t_3-t_2	Variable Description	Source
$CRE_{t_2-t_1}$	.043		1000 x the ratio of change in own-source revenues from 1975 to 1977, divided by total per-capita personal income, 1975	City Finances 1975, 1977
$CRE_{t_3-t_2}$		.014	1000 x the ratio of change in own-source revenue from 1977 to 1979, divided by total per-capita personal income, 1977	City Finances 1977, 1979
$CGV_{t_2-t_1}$	.461		the ratio of change in total intergovernmental revenues, divided by the change in total expenditures, 1975-77	City Finances 1975, 1977
$CGV_{t_3-t_2}$		-1.117	the ratio of change in total intergovernmental revenues, divided by the change in total expenditures, 1977-79	City Finances 1977, 1979
$LDR_{t_2-t_1}$	10.952		the ratio of change in long-term debt retired and interest on the general debt outstanding, 1975-77, divided by the change in own-source revenues, 1975-77	City Finances 1975, 1977
$LDR_{t_3-t_2}$		.673	the ratio of change in long-term debt retired and interest on the general debt outstanding, 1977-79, divided by the change in own-source revenues, 1977-79	
DIS	.142	.142	a dummy variable (1=yes, 0=no) constructed to represent cities in the worst financial condition 1975-79, as reflected by Ba or Baa lowering of their bond rating	Moody's bond-rating service

(continued)

Dependent Variables	Mean Values t_2-t_1	t_3-t_2	Variable Description	Source
LST	.246	.294	the percentage of total work time lost from stoppages of one day or longer, by six or more employees	BLS Work Stoppage Data (1974–80)
USP	.931	.910	proportion of strikes that were officially supported by bargaining agent having recognition to bargain collectively	Same
ECO	.302	.389	proportion of all strikes that were primarily over economic issues	Same
ARB	.086	.017	proportion of all strikes that were settled by interest arbitration	Same
ESS	1.69	1.69	an index reflecting the organization of fire fighters and/or police to bargain collectively, where ESS=0 when neither the police nor the fire fighters have recognition; ESS=1 when either the police or fire fighters have recognition; and ESS=2 when both have recognition	Annual Government Employment Survey (1977)
ORG	−8.62	37.96	percentage of change in the proportion of members of bargaining units in 1977, minus the proportion of the workforce organized in 1975; also for 1977–79	Bargaining Unit Data File (1975, 1977, 1979) Census
UNT	−8.13	21.84	percentage of change in the number of bargaining units in 1977, less the number of units in 1975; also for 1977–79	

Note: t_1 denotes 1975; t_2 denotes 1977; and t_3 denotes 1979.

APPENDIX B

Listing of Cities Included in Analysis

East	Midwest	South	West
Bridgeport	Chicago	Birmingham	Phoenix
Hartford	Cicero	Mobile	Tucson
New Britain	Peoria	Jacksonville	Anaheim
Washington, D.C.	East St. Louis	Miami	Garden Grove
Portland	Fort Wayne	Tampa	Santa Ana
Baltimore	Gary	St. Petersburg	Fresno
Boston	Hammond	Atlanta	Los Angeles
Springfield	Indianapolis	Columbus	Long Beach
Chicopee	Des Moines	Savannah	Pasadena
Worcester	Sioux City	Louisville	Sacramento
Manchester	Wichita	Baton Rouge	San Bernardino
Jersey City	Detroit	New Orleans	Riverside
Newark	Flint	Shreveport	Ontario
East Orange	Grand Rapids	Jackson	San Diego
Paterson	Lansing	Charlotte	San Francisco
Clifton	Saginaw	Oklahoma City	Oakland
Passaic	Duluth	Tulsa	Berkeley
Camden	Minneapolis	Knoxville	Richmond
Albany	St. Paul	Memphis	San Jose
Schenectady	Kansas City	Nashville	Denver
Troy	St. Joseph	Austin	Honolulu
Binghamton	St. Louis	Corpus Christi	Albuquerque
Buffalo	Omaha	Dallas	Portland
New York	Akron	El Paso	Salt Lake City
Rochester	Canton	Ft. Worth	Seattle
Syracuse	Cincinnati	Houston	Spokane
Utica	Cleveland	San Antonio	Tacoma
Altoona	Lakewood	Norfolk	
Philadelphia	Columbus	Portsmouth	
Pittsburgh	Dayton	Richmond	
Providence	Springfield	Huntington	
Warwick	Toledo		
Pawtucket	Youngstown		
	Warren		
	Madison		
	Milwaukee		

REFERENCES

Advisory Commission on Intergovernmental Relations. 1980. Central City--Suburban Fiscal Disparity and City Distress, 1977. Washington, D.C.: ACIR.

Aronson, J. R., and A. King. 1978. "Is There a Fiscal Crisis Outside of New York?" National Tax Journal 31: 153-63.

Benecki, S. 1978. "Municipal Expenditure Levels and Collective Bargaining." Industrial Relations 17: 216-30.

Burchell, R., et al. 1980. "Measuring Urban Distress: A Summary of the Major Urban Hardship Indices and Resource Allocation Systems." In Cities Under Stress, edited by R. Burchell and D. Listokin. New Brunswick, N.J.: Center for Urban Policy Research.

Burton, J., and C. Krider. 1975. "The Incidence of Strikes in Public Employment." In Labor in the Public and Nonprofit Sectors, edited by D. Hamermesh. Princeton, N.J.: Princeton University Press.

Clark, T., et al. 1970. "How Many New Yorks?" Mimeographed. Department of Sociology, University of Chicago.

Derber, J., and M. Wagner. 1979. "Public Sector Bargaining and Budget Making Under Fiscal Adversity." Industrial and Labor Relations Review 33: 18-23.

Dickson, E., and G. Peterson. 1981. Public Employee Compensation: A Twelve City Comparison, 2d ed. Washington, D.C.: Urban Institute Press.

Juris, H., and P. Feuille. 1973. Police Unionism. Lexington, Mass.: D. C. Heath.

Kearney, R. 1980. "Municipal Budgeting and Collective Bargaining: The Case of Iowa." Public Personnel Management 9: 108-14.

Lewin, D., P. Feuille, and T. Kochan. 1981. Public Sector Labor Relations: Analysis and Readings, 2d ed. Glen Ridge, N.J.: Horton.

Lovell, C. 1981. "Evolving Local Government Dependency." Public Administration Review 41: 189–202.

Maier, H., and S. Zagoria, eds. 1972. "Collective Bargaining and the Municipal Employer." In Public Workers and Public Unions. Englewood Cliffs, N.J.: Prentice-Hall.

Morris, C. 1980. The Cost of Good Intentions. New York: W.W. Norton.

Nivola, P. 1982. "Apocalypse Now? Whither the Urban Fiscal Crisis." Polity 14: 371–94.

Olson, C. 1980. "The Impact of Arbitration on the Wages of Firefighters." Industrial Relations 19: 325–39.

Peterson, J. 1980. "Big City Borrowing Costs and Credit Quality." In Cities Under Stress, edited by R. Burchell and D. Listokin. New Brunswick, N.J.: Center for Urban Policy Research.

Rubin, I. 1982. Running in the Red. Albany, N.Y. Suny Press.

Wellington, H., and R. Winter. 1971. The Unions and the Cities. Washington, D.C.: Brookings Institute.

2

Fiscal Stress and American Cities

David R. Morgan and Robert E. England

The so-called "taxpayers' revolt," coupled with recent reductions in federal aid to cities, has sparked renewed concern for the fiscal plight of U.S. cities. The
concern is real and immediate. "Since 1977 more than half
the states have passed tax and spending limitations (Palmer
and Sawhill, 1982:3)." Proposition 13 in California and
Proposition $2\frac{1}{2}$ in Massachusetts are but two examples of
citizens' demand for fiscal retrenchment. Fiscal austerity
on the part of local governments has been aggravated further by the current administration's Program for Economic
Recovery which, in part, proposes a state takeover of previously funded federal programs (see Donnelly, 1982). In
1980, for example, "federal aid constituted almost 25 percent of state and local expenditures. If all the administration's proposals were to come to fruition by 1991, . . .
the federal share in state and local budgets would be reduced to 3 to 4 percent (Peterson, 1982:159)." In FY 1982
alone, discretionary grants to state and local governments
were cut 15 percent below the funding levels they would
have reached under prior policies (Palmer and Sawhill,
1982:14).

As Pelissero (1983:1) so aptly reminds us: "American
cities continue to experience problems that are beyond their
own means to resolve." And there is considerable doubt
about the willingness and/or ability of state governments
to respond to the needs of their legal offspring (Herbers,
1981). The "urban crisis" is not over; it merely has been
redefined and relabeled as fiscal retrenchment and fiscal

stress. In order to make urban America a more viable
partner in the federal system: (1) a better understanding
of the factors associated with fiscal decline is required,
and (2) public policies that clearly delineate the responsibilities of federal, state, and local governments to combat
decline must be forthcoming.

This chapter primarily focuses on point one above.
After briefly considering previous research bearing on the
subject of urban fiscal stringency, a causal model of those
forces affecting urban fiscal stress is introduced and tested.
In the discussion and implications section, attention turns
to point two—public policy options for combatting urban
fiscal decline.

COMPARING MODELS OF FISCAL STRESS

Although federal cutbacks may be an immediate
cause for worry, most careful observers have recognized
for some time that many forces have been operating to
push some cities to the brink of bankruptcy. Although no
overall agreement has been reached regarding the causes
of fiscal decline, two general approaches or models can be
identified (Nivola, 1982). The first model places primary
emphasis on the long-term economic and social decline suffered by many large, old cities, particularly in the North.
The second approach contends that more immediate political
causes are to blame, for example, uncontrolled city spending
resulting from unionization and padded payrolls. The central research issue now is to offer further and perhaps
more elaborate tests of these competing explanations.[1] Before offering an integrated model of fiscal decline, a brief
overview of previous efforts to explain fiscal stress is in
order.

The socioeconomic decline model of fiscal stress is
based largely upon the assumption that the loss of people
and jobs eventually culminates in fiscal strain (see Chinitz,
1979; Garn et al., 1977). Those places most vulerable are
older Northern and Eastern manufacturing cities that lost
human and capital resources as a result of the nation's
gradual shift to a postindustrial and service economy. As
their economic vitality diminished, a decline in the tax
base ensued. The exodus of the middle and upper classes,
coupled with the influx of rural and disadvantaged minority groups, imposed a significant fiscal burden on many

large cities. This increasingly dependent population--the unskilled, the hard-to-employ, the poor, and the elderly-- required an enlarged package of urban services, including more welfare, job training, education, and health benefits. In short, many of these large, old cities found themselves in dire financial straits, confronted with rising needs in the face of declining resources. Muller (1975), for example, accepts the basic premise that the large city's fiscal diffi- culties can be traced to loss of people and jobs that in turn affects the jurisdiction's capacity to pay for local services. In addition, Stanley's (1976:5) analysis recog- nizes that large cities may find themselves in financial trouble when (1) the population and economic base declines, (2) service costs rise, (3) revenues lag, and (4) fiscal management is indifferent or expedient.

The socioeconomic explanation of fiscal stress is also well illustrated by the work of Howell and Stamm (1979). To measure fiscal stress, they begin with more than 100 "financial data items" (for example, ratio of local taxes to personal income, per-capita total debt) for 66 medium-to- large cities (mean population about 250,000). Using a two- stage factor analysis and their own judgment, this list is reduced to 13 variables representing three basic categories-- revenue, debt, and expenditures. Grouping these 66 cities into 16 clusters based on a set of economic and social conditions, the authors conclude that older industrial cities are the most likely to be in financial trouble.

The second model of fiscal stress is best represented by the research of Clark (1976) and Nivola (1982). As Nivola indicates, the second view of city financial decay is directed less at broad patterns of urban economic devel- opment and more at the internal political dynamics of local government. According to this persective, it is the distri- bution of power inside the community and how the city manages its resources that decides its fiscal fate. This view often singles out government mismanagement, especially in response to growing employee pressures, as the most proximate cause of fiscal debilitation. Part of the employee- cost burden may result from payroll expansion to meet the demands of increasingly politicized minority groups with special needs that might be addressed with more or en- larged municipal programs. Katznelson (1981:180), for ex- ample, argues that the rapid increase in city spending in the late 1960s and early 1970s was a desperate attempt to appease angry claimants and to restore social peace.

Others (see Stanley, 1976) point the finger of blame directly at organized employee groups. Piven (1976), without mentioning unions, contends that indeed organized provider groups rather than the poor reaped the lion's share of the new money flowing to cities during the 1960s. Nivola's analysis, although limited to partial correlations, confirms that employee cost-related variables are better predictors of fiscal stress than a measure of city hardship.

Clark (1976), using the 51 cities from the National Opinion Research Corporation's Permanent Community Sample, develops 29 financial-policy indicators to construct measures of municipal fiscal strain. Factor analysis is used to reduce these to four dimensions--debt (long-term and short-term), expenditures, and tax effort. The clearest fiscal stress indicator for each dimension is then selected to represent that factor (for example, sum of per-capita expenditures for nine common functions to represent "expenditures"). In general, Clark concludes that population, age, size, and growth rate are of little direct import. On the other hand, lower taxable property values, greater service extensiveness, and more poor residents do lead to problems. The percentage of Irish in the city and certain leadership indicators are also useful predictors of stress. Despite finding that socioeconomic resources are not good predictors of fiscal strain, Clark and Ferguson (1983:171) show that organization and political activities of municipal employees have little impact on city financial distress. It seems that where employee groups are strong, the city pays them well but hires fewer workers, so the overall effect is minimal.

Recently, Stonecash and McAfee (1981) have offered a model of fiscal stress that combines elements of both approaches. These authors posit a causal sequence in which cities undergoing economic decline tend to experience a growing dependent population. This leads to increases in the demand for services that, in turn, generate more spending. The eventual outcome--fiscal trouble. Stonecash and McAfee emphasize that cities respond in different ways to a deterioration in their local economy so that the relationship between socioeconomic conditions and fiscal response is quite variable. Although the authors contend the developmental model of urban fiscal stress is probably valid, they offer no multivariate test of its adequacy.

The analysis that follows attempts to integrate into a single model aspects of both the socioeconomic and political approaches outlined above. That is, we accept the view advanced by Stonecash and McAfee that the socioeconomic decline model must be supplemented by an attempt to take account of internal political forces within each city that may help determine that city's response to changes in its socioeconomic environment. The 54 U.S. cities of 250,000 or more population are included for analysis.[2]

DATA AND METHODS

Following the approach employed by Clark (1976), three basic components of urban fiscal decline were identified. Each of the three basic measures was divided by per-capita income to take ability to pay into account. These three stress variables were then standardized (z-scored) and summed. The use of one measure makes comparisons easier, and an argument can be made that a single indicator of stress more realistically portrays a city's overall financial condition than would several separate but more limited indicators. The fiscal stress (FS) variable is thus a composite score of the following items z-scored and summed (taken from standard Census Bureau sources): (1) long-term debt per capita/per capita income, (2) per-capita expenditures for nine common functions/per-capita income, (3) own source revenue per capita/per-capita income.[3] Short-term debt is not included, since a number of the 54 cities had none, and where it does exist, some question exists as to whether it represents a genuine obligation of the municipality (see Clark and Ferguson, 1983:64).

Since stress is a long-term, dynamic process, our primary concern will be to examine those forces that contribute to financial deterioration over time, in this case between 1960 and 1979. This change measure is constructed by regressing 1979 FS scores on 1960 FS scores.[4] The residual from this equation becomes the change measure, reflecting the degree to which each city's FS score for 1979 can be predicted by its 1960 score. The advantage of this residualized change measure (with a mean of zero and a standard deviation of one) is that it is not affected by a city's fiscal stress position in 1960.

The 54 cities with their fiscal stress scores for 1960, 1979, and a change measure are shown in Table 2.1 (positive scores indicate greater stress). The change measure, expressed in standard-deviation units, reflects the extent to which the city became more or less stressed in 1979,

TABLE 2.1

Fiscal Stress Scores for 1979, 1960, and Change
between 1960 and 1979 for 54 U.S. Cities
of 250,000 Population and over

City	1979 Z–Score[a]	1960 Z–Score[b]	1960–79 Std. Dev. Change[c]
Boston	12.406	5.194	7.21
New York City	10.723	5.899	4.82
Newark	9.226	4.078	5.15
Philadelphia	7.567	2.414	5.15
Atlanta	7.404	−0.828	8.23
Baltimore	6.648	3.519	3.13
Detroit	6.586	0.913	5.66
Birmingham	6.028	−0.663	6.69
Cleveland	5.829	0.807	5.02
San Francisco	5.065	0.874	4.19
Rochester	4.598	0.213	4.39
Denver	4.443	−0.469	4.91
Nashville	4.384	6.678	−2.30
St. Louis	4.216	0.557	3.66
Tampa	3.974	0.239	3.74
Cincinnati	3.912	1.415	2.50
Austin	3.833	0.464	3.37
Jersey City	3.737	2.947	0.79
Buffalo	3.733	0.766	2.97
New Orleans	3.578	−0.039	3.62
Norfolk	3.527	0.983	2.54
St. Paul	3.524	−0.403	3.93
Louisville	3.301	0.708	2.59
Miami	3.045	3.080	−0.04
Kansas City	3.026	−1.002	4.03
Memphis	2.801	2.950	−0.15
Columbus	2.782	−1.448	4.23
Tucson	2.428	−3.032	5.46
Jacksonville	2.388	5.767	−3.38
Seattle	2.272	−1.384	3.66

(continued)

Table 2.1, continued

City	1979 Z-Score[a]	1960 Z-Score[b]	1960–79 Std. Dev. Change[c]
Oklahoma City	1.826	−2.309	4.14
Long Beach	1.726	−0.531	2.26
San Antonio	1.721	−1.642	3.36
Oakland	1.534	−1.591	3.13
Sacramento	1.495	−1.861	3.36
Minneapolis	1.451	−1.894	3.35
Los Angeles	1.055	−1.448	2.50
Portland	1.038	−1.129	2.17
Dallas	1.015	−1.487	2.50
Pittsburgh	0.999	−0.896	1.90
Milwaukee	0.983	−0.012	1.00
Akron	0.980	−2.331	3.31
Wichita	0.859	−1.529	2.39
Phoenix	0.810	−2.398	3.21
Chicago	0.747	−1.311	2.06
Tulsa	0.370	−2.118	2.49
Toledo	0.323	−1.765	2.09
Indianapolis	−0.115	−1.849	1.74
Omaha	−0.294	−3.305	3.01
Houston	−0.386	−1.667	1.28
Fort Worth	−0.538	−1.336	0.80
El Paso	−0.819	−1.750	0.93
San Diego	−1.347	−2.642	1.30
San Jose	−1.453	−2.414	0.96

[a]Sum of the three 1979 fiscal stress indicators (Z-scored) using 1960 as a base (that is, using 1960 mean and standard deviation).

[b]Sum of the three 1960 fiscal stress indicators (Z-scored).

[c]Standard-deviation-unit change between 1960–79. A positive score indicates that the city became more distressed, while a negative score indicates the fiscal base of the city improved. This column is derived by subtracting 1960 from 1979 scores.

given its position in 1960.[5] First, we might look at some of the extreme cases for 1960. Nashville, unexpectedly, was the most stressed for 1960 followed by New York, Jacksonville, and Boston. By 1979 several changes had occurred. Boston now is in greatest difficulty, with New York and Newark close behind. Relatively speaking, the greatest change toward more hardship over the two decades is found in Atlanta, Boston, and Birmingham.

On the positive side Omaha, Tucson, and San Diego were best off in 1960. Twenty years later, San Diego and Omaha are still in good shape. Tucson, however, has fallen on hard times, moving 5.46 standard-deviation units toward greater stress during this period. For 1979, San Jose assumes Omaha's place as the least financially troubled community. It might also be noted that relative to 1960 considerably more cities are worse off in 1979. Only four municipalities improved their position between 1960 and 1979; all are Southern communities, and two (Nashville and Jacksonville) underwent some form of metropolitan consolidation during this period.

The model tested here begins with the basic premise that cities with certain environmental characteristics are more likely than others to end up in financial trouble. In particular, large, old, Northern industrial cities are the ones most commonly identified as experiencing socioeconomic hardship. This condition will be assessed, using a group of environmental variables to include region (with South and West together), manufacturing, density, age of city, and total population.[6] Such characteristics frequently coexist. Indeed, principal components analysis yields a single dimension that captures more than 58 percent of the common variance among the five variables.[7] This factor will be used to represent the potential for socioeconomic decline in the analysis to follow.

Cities with adverse conditions are expected to lose crucial resources, population and employment in particular. These two developments are closely related, of course. Population change (1960–77) and employment change (1960–70) are correlated at .99. Since the loss of people seems the more inclusive indicator, a choice was made to use this measure alone to signify the decline both in population and employment. Diminishing economic resources should contribute to a reduction in the tax base, which is represented by the change in assessed property values between 1961 and 1976.

How might such cities suffering a loss of human and capital resources react? How might such conditions lead more directly to financial trouble? First, older manufacturing cities with declining populations tend to find themselves saddled with large dependent populations. As suggested above, to the extent the city responds to the perceived objective needs of such groups or to political pressure emanating from them, greater spending is the likely result. Since little comparative data on the actual political effects of dependent groups are available, we use a measure of minority population (percentage of black change between 1960 and 1970) as one measure of the potential for increased spending and fiscal burden.

Nivola (1982) insists that the socioeconomic-decline model should be supplemented in other ways. In particular, he contends that the most immediate determinant of fiscal stress is expanding city payrolls. In the analysis to follow a measure of city payroll change (1960-78)[8] is therefore included. But what pushes payrolls up? As suggested above, cities may increase spending in response to certain groups within their boundaries, minority groups for example. Two other influences contributing to employee costs, however, might be considered. Clark (1975) has accumulated impressive evidence showing that cities with a relatively large proportion of Irish residents have higher municipal budgets, especially for police and fire. He argues that big-city politics, in particular, has been unusually influenced by the Irish political ethic. The primary effect of this political outlook has been to help legitimate and reinforce political patronage. Thus, if the percentage of Irish in a community is above average we might expect higher levels of spending for employee costs, which in turn may produce a greater fiscal burden.[9] Finally, some cities are legally obligated to provide more extensive services than others, such as education and welfare, which may contribute to financial strain. The effects of variations in functional responsibility will be tested using a school/welfare assignment variable (coded as 0 for neither; 1 for either one; 2 for both functions).

PREDICTING FISCAL STRESS

As suggested by Stonecash and McAfee (1981), a combined model of fiscal stress appears to operate in a sequential fashion, with fiscal debilitation stimulated initially by the loss of human and economic resources. These conditions weaken the municipalities' capacity (for example, tax base) to respond to the service needs or demands of an increasingly politically active minority population. Additional pressure may result from the presence of a traditional patronage-oriented political culture. To test these assumptions for the 54 large cities, path analysis will be employed. This technique requires the calculation of several multiple-regression equations, following the specification of a causal order among predictor variables.

Figure 2.1 shows the hypothesized relationships among all eight variables. Initially we assume that the environmental context affects fiscal stress change only indirectly; it should operate only through more proximate influences. Indeed, this variable rather prominently influences the initial set of intervening variables (population change, percentage of Irish, and school/welfare function). The second set of intermediate effects (property value change, black population change, and city payroll change) is reasonably well explained by the three immediately preceding variables (payroll change is least well accounted for). Finally, the figure depicts the direct causal connections between the six predictors and FS change. Clearly, the most powerful direct influences come from just two forces--payroll change (.45) and black change (.39).

Path models yield indirect as well as direct effects. Table 2.2, which is based on Figure 2.1, shows direct, indirect, and total causal effects on fiscal stress change. Because change in black population is posited to exert an indirect effect (through payroll change) as well as a direct effect, it has the largest total effect (.48) on change in fiscal stress. Municipal payroll increase, with no indirect effects, is a close second (.45). Population change, with powerful indirect connections, ranks third for total effects (-.43). The cluster of environmental characteristics, operating solely through other influences, is not inconsequential, with total effects of .30. So, age, density, manufacturing base, and region do matter, but only indirectly. More significantly, if such cities are losing total population, gaining in proportion minority, and have growing municipal payrolls, they are especially likely to reflect a deteriorating fiscal condition.

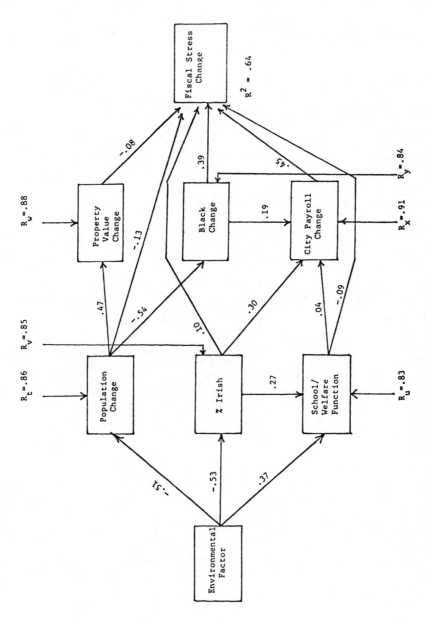

FIGURE 2.1. Path models to explain fiscal stress change (1960–79).

TABLE 2.2

Direct, Indirect, and Total Effects of
Independent Variables on Fiscal Stress[a]

	Direct	Indirect	Total Causal
Environment factor	--	.30	.30
Population change	-.13	-.30	-.43
Percentage of Irish	.10	.12	.22
School/welfare function	-.09	.02	-.07
Property-value change	-.08	--	-.08
Black change	.39	.09	.48
City payroll change	.45	--	.45

[a]Total causal effects are the sum of the direct and indirect effects. Spurious effects, those noncausal connections resulting from a common dependence on prior variables in the equation, have not been reported, since as noncausal effects, their interpretation is ambiguous.

DISCUSSION AND IMPLICATIONS

The results of this systematic assessment of urban fiscal stress among 54 large U.S. cities confirms the usefulness of an approach that combines the socioeconomic model of stress with one that emphasizes the importance of intervening political forces. In brief, a sequential pattern seems to occur in which adverse social and economic conditions give rise to a set of influences leading to increased fiscal strain. Above all, if declining cities have growing minority populations and expanding payrolls, serious fiscal problems seem likely.

That a prominent linkage exists between a growing black population and fiscal stringency comes as no surprise. We might add quickly that we do not intend to blame the victim. Whether one considers racism as a principal reason or merely that blacks have been the last deprived immigrant group to reach America's big cities, which are themselves undergoing economic transition, the rapid growth in this minority population can impose a considerable financial burden on city hall.

Can anything be done about the other immediate contributor to fiscal decline--growing city payrolls? Nivola (1982) insists that indeed this is controllable, and evidence does suggest that the payroll boom is over; lay-offs and cutbacks are the order of the day in many places. Perhaps we may see more concessions by labor in the public sector to match some of the labor-management agreements recently achieved in the private sector.

A final question to be addressed here concerns public-policy alternatives that cities might pursue as they contend with financial adversity. What actions can national, state, and city officials take in an effort to ward off or more effectively deal with fiscal stress? A number of proposals have been advanced. First, at the micro, or local, level, two basic approaches have been identified for dealing with fiscal strain--strengthening general and financial-management capacity and cutback/retrenchment strategies.

Clark and Ferguson (1983:255-61), in support of the first approach, contend that many financial difficulties could be avoided if municipal government in general were strengthened. They believe that if local officials were given adequate authority, municipalities would be less vulnerable to organized groups and thus could more effectively respond to citizen preferences. In particular they recommend that (1) federal funds be made available in more unrestricted form, (2) federal and state regulations (for example, mandated costs) and state limits on city spending and debt should be simplified and reduced, (3) more technical assistance in fiscal matters be made available, and (4) states facilitate municipal-bond market access.

Similarly, Martin's study (1982) of Boston and Detroit suggests that the root of fiscal stress is not over-spending or even socioeconomic or demographic factors, but archaic accounting and legal practices, which cause officials to overestimate municipal income. She recommends that the city budget be disaggregated into major revenue and expense accounts (for example, three basic revenue components--tax, transfer, and debt) as a way of giving officials better information and control over their finances.

A second basic approach city officials may follow to deal with fiscal pressures is to engage in cutback management and retrenchment strategies. Indeed, research suggests that many severely troubled cities respond initially by cutting costs and reducing service levels. These

communities apparently are forced to cut first and seek
new resources or new service delivery arrangements later
(Greiner and Hatry, 1982:122). Other options may be possible in time, of course, including privatizing, improving
productivity, developing closer cooperation between public
and private sectors, and soliciting more assistance from
individual citizens. A variety of cities, regardless of the
level of fiscal hardship, are also increasing user fees and
charges as a way of handling the need for increased revenue. Most research suggests that achieving significant
increases in productivity among municipal governments is
difficult indeed. The jury is still out on privatizing. For
some services (for example, solid-waste collection) contracting to the private sector may work well if real competition
can be achieved, but it inevitably generates opposition
among municipal employees and there is no unanimity
among city officials that real cost savings can be achieved
(see Florestano and Gordon, 1981). Some real success
stories of public-private cooperation can be found, but how
much of this success owes to special conditions within a
given community is often difficult to determine. Perhaps
greater citizen involvement in service delivery (that is, coproduction) may help cities cope with retrenchment, but
there are still too few successful examples of this strategy
to be overly sanguine about its potential.

    Local government officials can and should attempt
to strengthen general and financial management capacity
and employ cutback/retrenchment strategies, but this may
not be enough. For example, local governments are at the
mercy of higher-level governments with respect to mandated
costs and spending and debt limitations. In addition, to
impose restrictions on the in-migration of persons contributing to the dependent population of the city would be
constitutional suicide. In short, urban policy must be
viewed as inextricably linked with federal and state policymaking.

    In order to combat urban fiscal decline, the Com-
mittee on National Urban Policy argues for a "rethinking
of urban policy (Hanson, 1983)." The central thesis of the
committee is that a national urban policy is necessary to
guide the new urban system which has emerged as a result
of the shift from an industrial/manufacturing to a service-
oriented economy. The policy agenda for those areas of
the nation hardest hit by this economic transition includes:

1. Planning by firms and worker organizations, in cooperation with federal, state, and local governments, to help workers in declining industries, occupations, and communities prepare for more rapid and smooth transitions to other jobs, whether in their communities or elsewhere.

2. Particular attention to education and training for urban minorities and the economically disadvantaged so that more of them can move into the economic mainstream.

3. Gradual restructuring of fiscal transfers within the federal system to equalize the fiscal capacities of states . . . and to encourage states to reduce urban-suburban fiscal disparities.

4. Development of community-based centers that employ and train minorities and other economically disadvantaged workers.

5. Selective use of public employment as part of a general strategy of improving the quality of local labor forces and the quality of public services in support of economic development (Hanson, 1983:2-3).

The acceptance and implementation of this policy agenda largely depends, of course, upon its political appeal. For example, the ideas of greater cooperation between private-sector firms and worker organizations to retrain workers, community-based centers that employ and train minorities (as long as it is a function of state and local governments), and the restructuring of fiscal transfers within the federal system are, for the most part, consistent with the Reagan administration's Program for Economic Recovery. On the other hand, proposals for education and training programs for minorities and the economically disadvantaged as well as the use of public employment to improve the quality of local labor forces should expect to receive little fiscal support from the national executive branch. Under the Reagan administration, the guaranteed student-loan subsidy, Job Corps, compensatory education for disadvantaged children, and CETA have already been reduced, some substantially (Palmer and Sawhill, 1982:17-19). Moreover, the notion of an urban policy in which the national government plays a significant role seems inconsistent with Reagan's state-centered federalism.

In conclusion, two things seem apparent. First, considerable ferment, experimentation, and trial and error are likely to be required as fiscally troubled cities struggle to find the most appropriate strategies to fit their specific needs. Second, given current political winds, cities should look to the states for political leadership, technical assistance, and fiscal help. The degree to which the states respond to the needs of their intergovernmental partners will be of critical importance to the future of urban America.

NOTES

1. Irene Rubin (1982:5-9) offers a fine review of the various theoretical approaches to understanding urban fiscal stress, complete with extensive references to the appropriate literature. She identifies three different but related approaches: the migration/tax base erosion argument, the growth-of-bureaucracy argument, and the political-vulnerability model. The latter two political models are clearly similar--both posit that burdensome municipal spending results from enlarged payroll and/or programmatic commitments arising from bureaucratic imperialism or pressures from external interest groups.

2. Honolulu and Washington, D.C., are not included in the analysis.

3. The nine common functions are police, fire, sewerage, sanitation, highways, parks and recreation, financial administration, general control, general building (all excluding itemized capital outlays).

4. The 1979 measure was created using the 1960 mean and standard deviation so as to permit a direct comparison of the scores for the two time periods.

5. The residualized change measure actually analyzed is merely a linear transformation of the change in standard-deviation units shown in Table 2.1 (r=.99). The change measure shown in Table 2.1 is easier to interpret than the residuals obtained from regressing 1979 FS on 1960 FS.

6. Environmental measures used in the analysis are for 1960 because each such measure represents a kind of threshold effect or base position for the early period that should better predict the trends of the following two decades than would a measure for a later period.

The environmental variables are operationalized as follows: region (0/1; 0 = South and West; 1 = Northeast and North Central; age of city (in decades, since the city reached 50,000 population; manufacturing (value added per capita); <u>density</u> (natural log); <u>population</u> (natural log). All come from standard census sources.

    7. The common factor solution uses Kaiser's criterion (eigenvalue > 1) to determine the number of factors. The single dimension explains 58.3 percent of the common variance (eigenvalue = 2.48).

    8. City payroll for 1960 is full-time payroll for city government employment; for 1979 the data are total expenditures for salaries and wages. All are from Bureau of Census sources.

    9. Percentage of Irish is operationalized as total Irish foreign-born, plus total foreign or mixed parentage, divided by city population, from Table 81, U.S. Bureau of the Census (1970). Data for this measure for 1960 were not available.

REFERENCES

Chinitz, Benjamin. 1979. "Toward a National Urban Policy." In <u>Central City Economic Development</u>, edited by B. Chinitz. Cambridge, Mass.: Abt Books.

Clark, Terry N. 1975. "The Irish Ethic and the Spirit of Patronage." <u>Ethnicity</u> 2: 305-59.

_____. 1976. "How Many More New Yorks?" <u>New York Affairs</u> 3: 18-27.

Clark, Terry N., and Lorna C. Ferguson. 1983. <u>City Money: Political Processes, Fiscal Strain, and Retrenchment</u>. New York: Columbia University Press.

Donnelly, Harrison. 1982. "Reagan Changes Focus with Federalism Plan." <u>Congressional Quarterly Weekly Report</u> 40: 147-54.

Florestano, Patricia, and Stephen B. Gordon. 1981. "A Survey of City and County Use of Contracting." <u>Urban Interest</u> 3: 22-29.

Garn, Harvey, Thomas Muller, John Tilney, John Kordalewski, and Jacqueline Swingle. 1977. <u>A Framework for National Urban Policy: Urban Distress, Decline and Growth</u>. Vol. 2. Washington, D.C.: Urban Institute.

Greiner, John, and Harry Hatry. 1982. Coping with Cut-backs: Initial Agency-Level Responses in 17 Local Governments to Massachusetts' Proposition 2½. Report to the U.S. Department of Housing and Urban Development. Washington, D.C.: Urban Institute.

Hanson, Royce, ed. 1983. Rethinking Urban Policy: Urban Development in an Advanced Economy. Washington, D.C.: National Academy Press.

Herbers, John. 1981. "Shift to Block Grants Raising Issue of States' Competence." New York Times, October 1.

Howell, James M., and Charles Stamm. 1979. Urban Fiscal Stress: A Computer Analysis of 66 U.S. Cities. Lexington, Mass.: D.C. Heath.

Katznelson, Ira. 1981. City Trenches. Chicago: University of Chicago Press.

Martin, Joan K. 1982. Urban Financial Stress: Why Cities Go Broke. Boston: Auburn House.

Muller, Thomas. 1975. Growing and Declining Urban Areas: A Fiscal Comparison. Washington, D.C.: Urban Institute.

Nivola, Pietro. 1982. "Apocalypse Now? Whither the Urban Fiscal Crisis." Polity 14 (Spring): 371-94.

Palmer, John L., and Isabel V. Sawhill, eds. 1982. The Reagan Experiment. Washington, D.C.: Urban Institute.

Pelissero, John P. 1983. "How Well Do States Respond to City Needs?" Paper presented at the annual meeting of the Midwest Political Science Association, April 20-23, Chicago.

Peterson, George E. 1982. "The State and Local Sector." In The Reagan Experiment, edited by John L. Palmer and Isabel V. Sawhill. Washington, D.C.: Urban Institute.

Piven, Frances Fox. 1976. "The Urban Crisis: Who Got What, and Why." In Urban Politics and Public Policy, 2d ed., edited by Stephen David and Paul Peterson. New York: Praeger Publishers.

Rubin, Irene S. 1982. Running in the Red: The Political Dynamics of Urban Fiscal Stress. Albany, N.Y.: State University of New York Press.

Stanley, David R. 1976. Cities in Trouble. Columbus, Ohio: Academy for Contemporary Problems.

Stonecash, Jeff, and Patrick McAfee. 1981. "The Ambiguities and Limits of Fiscal Strain Indicators." Policy Studies Journal 10 (December): 379-95.

U.S., Bureau of the Census. 1970. Census of Population: General Social and Economic Characteristics. Washington, D.C.: Government Printing Office.

3

Social-Welfare Policy and Privatization: Theory and Reality in Policymaking

James C. Musselwhite, Jr. and
Lester M. Salamon

A major issue in public policymaking is the usefulness of social-science research and analysis in promoting
better decision making. Does social science provide information that enables decision-makers and those who influence them to make policies that are more likely to work?
Is social science actually used in public policymaking,
and used appropriately? Are policies that are based on
social science better than those that are not?

Past research on these questions is not encouraging.
This research indicates that policymakers often use social
science to support existing convictions and beliefs rather

This chapter is based primarily on work carried
out by the Urban Institute's Nonprofit Sector Project, an
inquiry into the scope, structure, and roles of the private,
nonprofit sector, changes in government policy affecting
the sector, and the way nonprofit organizations are responding. Lester M. Salamon is director of this project;
James C. Musselwhite, Jr., has directed project work dealing with government spending and use of nonprofits in 16
communities across the nation. The project is supported
by more than 40 grant makers, including community foundations, national foundations, and corporations and corporate
foundations. The authors wish to express their apprecia-
tion to Alan Abramson, Michael Gutowski, Lauren Saunders,
and Lori Marczak, as well as to the Local Associates of
the Urban Institute Nonprofit Sector Project for help in developing the data.

than to evaluate government policy or public problems objectively (Aaron, 1978). Because social-science research often speaks with more than one voice or changes over time, policymakers have a large menu from which to choose. Finally, researchers themselves can suffer from blind spots that obscure crucial elements of the reality they are observing.

These features of the relationship between social science and public policymaking are illustrated all too clearly in the debate over privatization stimulated by the Reagan administration's assault on the social-welfare policies of the New Deal and Great Society. Underlying that assault was not simply a difference in budgetary priorities, but also a more fundamental theoretical challenge to the perceived liberal approach to social and economic problems, and to the social-science research on which this approach rested.

It is the argument of this chapter, however, that the conservative attack on the social-welfare policies of the New Deal and Great Society has been, in part at least, misdirected because of a failure to recognize how social-welfare programs have actually operated in this country, and in particular how extensive a role they have left for private, voluntary agencies. What is more, this failure is shared by many of the liberal analyses of current social-welfare policies as well. One of the ironic consequences of the Reagan attack on prevailing social-welfare programs, therefore, may be to stimulate a better comprehension in both liberal and conservative camps of how these programs work.

To document these points, we briefly assess the conservative critique of the welfare policies of the New Deal and Great Society, compare this critique with the liberal image of the American welfare state, and then bring to bear a new body of data we have assembled that challenge key elements of the conservative critique and clarify the liberal understanding of current realities as well.

THE CONSERVATIVE CRITIQUE

The conservative critique of the welfare policies of the past five decades is rooted in two basic premises: First, that problems of poverty and dependency are best handled by private, voluntary organizations rather than

public bureaucracies; and second, that to the extent government has a role to play in social-welfare policy, authority should be exercised at the local level, close to the
problems being addressed.

These premises reflect long-standing conservative
fears about big government and about social interventions
that might disrupt the workings of the labor market and
the economic incentives to work. But these sentiments
have been buttressed in recent years by social-science
findings stressing the value of such "mediating institutions"
as the family, the church, the neighborhood, and the voluntary association as mechanisms to protect individuals
from feelings of anomie and alienation (Nisbet, 1962).
What is more, some research has shown that individuals
and families tend to turn to these types of institutions
first in times of need, and only to government agencies as
a last resort. Reliance on such private, voluntary institutions is thus viewed as a more promising, less bureaucratic, and more effective way to solve social problems
(Berger and Neuhaus, 1977; Woodson, 1981; and Egan,
Carr, Mott, and Roos, 1981).[1]

From the conservative perspective, the policy developments of the past several decades violated these basic
premises. According to the conservative critique, the expansion of the federal role in social-welfare policy that
began with the New Deal has had at least two harmful
consequences: First, it has undermined the position of
state and local government in the social welfare field; and
second, it has weakened private, voluntary institutions by
substituting governmental bureaucracies for them. As
President Reagan put it in 1981: "We have let government
take away many of the things that were once ours to do
voluntarily. . . ." In the process, this line of argument
holds, the costs of service have increased, the quality of
service has declined, and the capacity for self-reliance on
the part of the poor has been weakened (Nisbet, 1962; and
Berger and Neuhaus, 1977).

While it has usefully called attention to the importance of private, voluntary organizations in the solution of
human problems, the conservative critique of existing
social-welfare programs has failed to take account of the
way the welfare state evolved in the United States (Salamon,
Musselwhite, and Abramson, 1984). In particular, it has
failed to acknowledge the tremendous role that state and
local governments and private, voluntary organizations

continue to play despite the growth of federal involvement. In point of fact, the federal government does very little itself in the domestic field. What it does, it does largely through third parties--among them state and local governments and private, voluntary groups (Salamon, 1981). As a consequence of this pattern of "third-party government," the expansion of the federal role has not displaced these institutions, as the conservative critique contends. On the contrary, there is some evidence that expanded federal social-welfare activity helped to extend the activities of local governments and private organizations in the welfare field, enabling them to take on new functions and to serve larger numbers of people (Salamon and Abramson, 1982a; and Salamon, 1984a).

Interestingly, the important role that voluntary organizations play in the U.S. version of the welfare state has been overlooked in liberal analyses as well. Eager to build a case for federal involvement in the social-welfare field, liberals have tended to downplay the contribution of the voluntary sector and ignore the extent to which liberal social-welfare policies are actually being implemented by private nonprofit groups. As a consequence, little systematic information has existed to document the role that voluntary agencies play in the U.S. welfare state.[2] And because of this, conservative critics of the New Deal and Great Society could advance a program of budget cuts as a policy for stimulating the nonprofit sector without realizing the extent to which these cuts would jeopardize the ability of this sector to function.

THE REALITY OF PARTNERSHIP

To remedy this situation and provide a firmer base of knowledge on which to design policy, we launched a major national project in 1982 to document the roles of federal, state, and local governments in financing and administering social-welfare policy, and to assess as well the extent to which governmental resources are used to finance service delivery by private nonprofit groups. This work focused on six major program areas--social services, health care, housing and community development, employment and training, arts and culture, and income assistance-- and involved data collection at the national level and in 16 field sites of varying sizes and characteristics located in all parts of the country (see Table 3.1).[3]

TABLE 3.1

Field Sites for the Urban Institute
Nonprofit Sector Project

Northeast
  New York City
  Allegheny County (Pittsburgh) Pa.
  Rhode Island (Providence)
  Fayette County (Uniontown) Pa.[a]

Midwest
  Cook County (Chicago) Ill.
  Hennepin County (Minneapolis) Minn.[b]
  Ramsey County (St. Paul) Minn.[b]
  Genesee County (Flint) Mich.
  Tuscola County (Caro) Mich.

West
  San Francisco County (San Francisco) Calif.
  Maricopa County (Phoenix) Ariz.
  Ada County (Boise) Idaho
  Pinal County (Casa Grande) Ariz.

South
  Dallas County (Dallas) Tex.
  Fulton County (Atlanta) Ga.
  Hinds County (Jackson) Miss.
  Warren County (Vicksburg) Miss.

Note: We used the entire metropolitan area as the geographic focus of the work for most parts of the Nonprofit Sector Project, but for the budget analysis reported here, only the central-city county was covered, as shown.

[a]Data on government spending not complete for this site.

[b]Minneapolis and St. Paul were treated as two sites for purposes of the government-spending work.

The central conclusion that emerges from this work is that the image of inherent conflict between federal and local governments, and between government and voluntary organizations, which is stressed in the conservative critique of New Deal/Great Society policy, is greatly overdrawn. In practice, at the operational level, the prevailing relationship among the levels of government, and among public and private institutions, is one of partnership—a point stressed by Morton Grodzins and Daniel Elazar in their work on federalism two decades ago, but applicable to public-private relations as well (Grodzins, 1965; and Elazar, 1972). The data we have collected on the division of responsibilities among levels of government, and between public and private institutions, illustrate this point well.[4]

Federal/State/Local Roles

While conservative theories emphasize the extent to which the growth of federal social-welfare spending has displaced state and local governments, our data suggest that state and local governments have preserved a substantial role in the social-welfare area. In the first place, state and local governments provide a significant share of the resources. As shown in Table 3.2, nearly three-tenths of total government spending in the six program areas we examined originates with state and local government, most of it from state sources.

Moreover, state/local funds are particularly signifi-cant in four of the six program areas of concern, includ-ing social services and health care, where the debate over relative federal and state roles has been particularly heated. There is considerable variation in the share of state/local government spending by community, however, ranging from a high of 44 percent to a low of 9 percent in the 16 study sites. In general, the state/local share of government spending in these fields is higher in more populous communities, and in the Northeast and Midwest. Smaller communities and communities in the South and West are likely to be more dependent on federal funds in these fields.

In addition to providing almost $3 of every $10 spent by government in the social-welfare area, state and local governments also play a major role in administering many of the programs paid for by federal dollars. For example, state and local governments administered such major federal programs as Medicaid, Title XX (now the Social Services Block Grant), the Community Development Block Grant, the Comprehensive Employment and Training Act (CETA), and the Aid to Families with Dependent Chil-dren (AFDC) program. In FY 1982, state and local gov-ernments in our study sites typically administered about

TABLE 3.2

Share of Government Spending in Selected Fields from
State and Local Own Source Revenues in 16 Sites FY 1982*

Median Program Area	Percentage State	Percentage Local
Health care	21%	6%
Social services	30	9
Housing and community development	0[a]	1
Employment and training	1	0
Arts and culture	9	78
Subtotal (without income assistance)	20%	10%
Income assistance	19	0
Total (with income assistance)	20%	8%

*These data reflect the median value for the 16 sites in each program area. In each community the local budget year was used to define the fiscal year.

[a]Less than 0.5 percent. This reflects in part the restrictive definition of housing and community development used in this research.

Source: Data compiled and estimated by The Urban Institure Nonprofit Sector Project from federal, state, and local-government sources.

43 percent of all federal spending, or 68 percent if the large Medicare program is excluded. Again, these figures varied greatly by community, ranging from 71 to 29 percent with Medicare included, and from 91 to 50 percent with Medicare excluded.

Taken together these findings suggest that state and local governments administer about 60 percent of all government spending for social-welfare programs. Half of this represents spending that originates with state and local government, and the other half spending that originates at the federal level but is administered by state and local authorities. Therefore, even though the federal government is the primary source of publicly generated spending for

social-welfare services, state and local governments play a
major role in deciding how government funds are finally
spent, as well as a significant role in funding the services themselves.[5]

Public/Private Partnership

In addition to casting doubt on the conservative
claim that increased federal involvement has significantly
undermined the role of state and local governments in the
social-welfare area, the data we have assembled also raise
questions about the conservative contention that government
social-welfare activity has displaced private, nonprofit
groups. Rather, these data make clear that the tremendous expansion of government activity in social welfare
over the last several decades was made possible in large
part by government reliance on private, nonprofit and
for-profit organizations to deliver publicly funded services.
As shown in Table 3.3, more than a third of all federal,
state, and local government spending on social-welfare services exclusive of income assistance in 1982 went to support service provision by nonprofit organizations. Another
20 percent went to support service provision by for-profit
firms. This means that government actually carries out
less than one-half of the social-welfare services it funds.
In fact, in about a third of the sites examined, nonprofit
organizations delivered more publicly funded services than
government itself. This pattern varies, of course, by program area, and by community. For example, the median
value of government reliance on nonprofits is highest in
social services (47 percent) and lowest in housing and
community development (9 percent). In Allegheny County/
Pittsburgh nonprofits receive 50 percent of all government
spending in these fields, while in Tuscola County/Caro,
Michigan, the figure is only 12 percent. State and local
government administrative discretion, the location of major
health facilities, and different nonprofit traditions are
largely responsible for these variations. Yet overall, the
nonprofit sector has played almost as large a role as government agencies themselves in delivering the services
paid for through public programs. Reflecting this, government has emerged as the single most important source of
revenue for nonprofit service organizations and the nonprofit sector has retained or increased its vitality during

TABLE 3.3

Share of Public Spending by Type of Provider,
in 16 Sites, FY 1982

Program Area	Median Share of Public Spending* Spent by		
	Nonprofits	For-Profit	Government
Health care	38%	23%	38%
Social services	47	3	47
Housing and community development	9	16	70
Employment and training	24	5	49
Arts and culture	20	0	80
Total (of all spending)	36%	20%	41%

*Shares may not total 100 percent since each value rep-
resents the median of the 16 sites.
    Source: Data compiled and estimated by The Urban Insti-
tute Nonprofit Sector Project from federal, state, and local-
government sources.

the last two decades at the same time that government has
greatly increased its spending in the social-welfare field
(Salamon, 1984c).[6]
    These data make clear that extensive public/private
partnerships were already in place before the New Federalism initiatives of the Reagan era arrived on the scene (for
more detail on the early history, see: Nielsen, 1980; and
Salamon, 1984a). Nonprofit organizations rely on government funding to carry out much of their operations, and
government relies on nonprofits to deliver many of the
social-welfare services it funds. The extent and complexity of this interdependent relationship is only now being
documented, but understanding this relationship is fundamental to informed debate and decision making on the future course of the welfare state.

GOVERNMENT RETRENCHMENT AND PRIVATIZATION

    The ssingle most important action the Reagan admin-
istration has taken to achieve its New Federalism agenda

has been the reduction of federal spending for social-welfare programs. Though federal spending cuts were not as great as originally proposed for many programs, the fact that they occurred during a severe recession broke the pattern of cyclical increase so long associated with social-welfare programs. The architects of these spending reductions hailed the new course as one that would revitalize the nonprofit sector and lead to the building of substantial public/private partnerships. The results of these new policies have not always worked out that way, however, in large part because of the faulty premises on which they were based (Musselwhite, forthcoming; Salamon, 1984b and Salamon, 1984c).

Federal Spending Cuts

Though federal social-welfare spending had begun to decline in some program areas under the Carter administration, as Table 3.4 shows, a major decline occurred from 1981 to 1982 when the New Federalism initiatives were translated into policy at the national level. With the passage of the Omnibus Budget Reconciliation Act in late 1981, the Reagan administration not only reduced federal spending for social welfare, but did so during a period of severe recession when federal spending typically rises to meet increased needs. In addition, although federal spending increased in most program areas between 1982 and 1983, it did not regain the levels it had achieved as of 1980, except in health care, where steady increases in Medicare persisted throughout the early 1980s.

The implications of these spending cuts for nonprofits were twofold. First, decreased government provision of services increased the service demands on nonprofits, particularly since these changes took place against the backdrop of a severe recession. In the second place, however, these same reductions in federal spending reduced federal funding of nonprofit organizations. As shown in Table 3.5, federal reductions in funding to nonprofits were particularly severe in the program areas of employment and training, housing and community development, and social services. Although the situation improved somewhat in the 1982–83 period, nonprofit revenues from the federal government in 1983 were substantially less than in 1980 in every program area except health care.

TABLE 3.4

Year-to-Year Changes in Overall Federal Spending in Selected Programs
of Concern to Nonprofits, in 1980 Dollars, FY 1980-83

Program Area	FY 1980 Level ($ millions)	Percentage Change in Real Value of Federal Spending			
		FY 1980-81	FY 1981-82	FY 1982-83	Total FY 1980-83
Health care	$58,133	+8%	+1%	+3%	+12%
Employment/training	9,376	-20	-48	-10	-62
Housing/community development	7,665	-1	-9	+3	-7
Social services	7,088	-2	-14	+5	-12
Arts/culture	333	-14	-11	-3	-25
Subtotal	82,595	+3	-5	+3	0
Income assistance	27,835	+10	-3	+7	+14
Total	110,430	+5	-5	+4	+3
Total, excluding health care and income assistance	$24,462	-9%	-24%	+1%	-30%

Source: Derived from December 1983, updated estimates of data in Salamon and Abramson, 1982a.

TABLE 3.5

Year-to-Year Changes in Federal Support of Nonprofit Organizations Nationally
in Selected Programs in Real Dollars, FY 1980–83

Program Area	FY 1980 Level ($ millions)	Percentage Change in Real Value of Federal Spending			
		FY 1980–81	FY 1981–82	FY 1982–83	Total FY 1980–83
Health care	$24,644.7	+9%	+3%	+3%	+16%
Employment/training	3,341.6	-19	-51	-7	-63
Housing/community development	768.4	-5	-24	-6	-32
Social services	3,445.9	-2	-11	+1	-12
Arts/culture	152.5	-17	-2	-8	-25
Total	$32,353.1	-6	+7	+3	+4
Total, excluding health care	$7,708.4	-10%	-28%	-2%	-36%

Source: Derived from December 1983, updated estimates of data in Salamon and Abramson, 1982a.

This left the nonprofit sector with a greater demand for its service, but substantially less government resources, than it has had in recent years. In other words, the federal program shift that was designed to encourage nonprofit service provision and public/private partnerships seemed to be weakening the nonprofit sector and damaging existing public/private partnerships.

Nonprofit Response to Cuts

Were nonprofits able to take up the slack left by cuts in government spending? As Table 3.6 shows, for the sector as a whole, the answer to this question is a partial yes. At a minimum, the sector's overall revenues managed to keep pace with inflation despite the reductions in government support. The sector was not, however, able to expand in real terms enough to take on service burdens that government was shedding. What is more, most of the increased revenue the sector gained between 1981 and 1982 came not from private charitable contributions, but from service fees and charges. Reflecting this, the types of agencies that did the best were those with the greatest access to fee income--namely those serving a clientele able to pay for their services. By contrast, agencies serving the poor not only failed to grow, but ended this period with overall net losses in total revenue (Salamon, 1984b; Salamon, 1984c).

What this seems to suggest is that the New Federalism initiatives may be forcing nonprofit organizations into a tough choice between organizational survival and continued service to those in greatest need. The trend to date has been toward an expansion of those services for which a paying clientele is available, and a contraction of those portions of the sector serving those in greatest need. This raises the central question of whether the reduction in government support that has been the hallmark of the Reagan approach to the voluntary sector will have the effect of pricing the poor out of nonprofit-sector service provision and changing the basic character of this sector in the process.

TABLE 3.6

Sources of Nonprofit Revenues and Inflation–Adjusted
Changes in Revenues by Source of Funding, 1981–82

Source	Percentage of Revenues 1981[a]	Inflation–Adjusted Change 1981–82
Government	41.2%	−6.3%
Service fees/ charges/dues	27.9	+6.6
Direct individual giving	6.0	+7.9
Sales/special events, etc.	5.6	+2.2
United Way	5.3	+1.9
Endowment/ investment income	4.5	+4.1
Foundation gifts	3.4	+5.2
Corporate gifts	3.0	+5.8
Religious/other federated charities	2.7	+3.6
Unallocated	0.4	na
Total funding	100.0%	+0.5

Note: Data exclude hospitals, colleges, and universities.
N = 2,304.

[a]Numbers total slightly less than 100 percent because of rounding.

Source: The Urban Institute Nonprofit Sector Project Survey, 1982.

PUBLIC/PRIVATE PARTNERSHIP AND THE FUTURE

New Federalism advocates have usefully emphasized
the role that the private, nonprofit sector can play in re-
solving some of the key problems facing American social-
welfare programs in the 1980s. Making this point has
served a very useful purpose because the importance of
nonprofit organizations in providing social-welfare services
has been ignored or grossly underestimated by most policy

actors prior to this. The New Federalism strategy of privatization is flawed, however, because it has failed to
recognize the extensive role already played by nonprofit
organizations in social welfare, and the damage that its
policy initiatives have thus done to the amazingly large
and diverse set of public/private partnerships already in
place in this field.

Whatever perspectives or objectives policymakers may
have regarding the future of social-welfare policy in
America, they must come to grips with the private, nonprofit sector and public/private partnerships. The sheer
size of the nonprofit sector and the major interdependency
relationship existing between government and the nonprofit
sector guarantee that nonprofits will continue to be major
actors in social-welfare policy in the 1980s. Moreover,
nonprofit organizations offer significant social-welfare service alternatives which may be instrumental in solving
some of the major problems faced in the field. In one form
or another, then, policymakers will have to deal with the
role of nonprofit organizations in social welfare.

The Role of Social-science Analysis

Social-science analysis has an important role to play
in the debate and decision making concerning privatization
and the future of social-welfare policy. Few areas of public policy have been so poorly documented or understood as
the private, nonprofit sector and its relations with government. Even the most basic data have been unavailable
until recently. For this reason, many different types of
data collection and analysis are needed. For the sake of
discussion, however, three research priorities can be identified:

- Analysis of the financing and provision of social-welfare
  services, including the role played by government, the
  nonprofit sector, and the for-profit sector; interdependency; the level of resources; the kinds of services provided; and who receives the services;
- Assessment of the impact of changing policies and economic conditions on the levels of social-welfare services
  available and on the division of responsibilities among
  governments, nonprofits, and for-profit institutions;

–Analysis of the rationale for government use of nonprofit organizations to provide services, and of the advantages and disadvantages of this mode of service delivery.

Analysis of Current Social-Welfare Provision

Analysis of the institutions that finance and deliver social-welfare services has advanced considerably over the last several years. A significant body of data and reports, much of it generated by The Urban Institute Nonprofit Sector Project, are now beginning to address the size of government and nonprofit service, the structure of these sectors, and their interrelationships. This research is also providing basic information on how much money is spent for social-welfare services, the activities for which this money is spent, the sources of funding, who provides the service, and who receives the service. This body of work has already demonstrated that the nonprofit sector is a major actor in the social-welfare field and that it has extensive and diverse interdependency relations with government. Yet much work remains to be done to document and clarify the relationships that result and to assess the impact they have had both on the nonprofit sector and on government.

Impact of Changing Policies and Economic Conditions

A second major task of social-science analysis is to measure and assess the impact of changing social-welfare policies and economic conditions on the availability of social-welfare services. This work includes consideration of the following kinds of questions. Has the level of resources changed, and have the sources of these funds changed? Are there differential impacts by sector? Are there changes in who receives services? What are the implications of these changes and coping strategies for the quality and quantity of services provided, for the roles of different institutions, and for the efficiency, effectiveness, and fairness of the human-service delivery system?

Government Use of Nonprofits

The final and perhaps most difficult task of policy analysis is to find out when and why governments use nonprofit organizations to provide services, and to assess when they are most useful to achieve public purposes.

What data exist on this question suggest that the principal reason governments turn to nonprofits to assist in the delivery of publicly funded services is expediency. In many fields, nonprofits are used simply because they are there, with a ready-made delivery system. This is especially important where start-up time is short, or where the continuation of a function is in question. What is more, nonprofits sometimes exert political pressure to gain a "piece of the action." For all these reasons, government use of nonprofits is typically most extensive where the nonprofit sector has traditionally been most active, in fields such as hospital care, nursing-home care, child care, and adoption services. By the same token, the principal source of changes in government use of nonprofits is change in the spending levels of the programs where use of nonprofits is already established.

Whether this pattern of reliance and nonreliance on nonprofits makes sense in terms of program costs and effectiveness, however, is a far more open question. Advocates of the nonprofit sector point to the greater flexibility and responsiveness of these organizations, their professional commitment to quality care and their access to volunteer labor and charitable contributions and thus their ability to offer services at reduced cost. Critics complain, however, that nonprofits are poorly managed, that professionalization has undermined their supposed informal character, and that the absence of a market test leads to a loss of touch with client needs.

Given the emphasis that is now being placed on privatization as a way to improve public services and reduce their costs, it seems clear that an effort to clarify the advantages and disadvantages of reliance on nonprofits as service providers is a high priority for policy research, albeit one that will be exceedingly difficult to carry out.

CONCLUSION

The Reagan administration embarked on its New Federalism and private initiative strategy in the social-welfare field with little apparent regard for the operating realities of existing programs. Because the administration largely ignored what social-science research could tell it about these realities, its strategy for reducing the federal government's role in the social-welfare field and increasing the roles of state and local governments and private institutions turned out to be flawed in at least two major respects. First, it failed to take account of the role that state and local governments already play in existing social-welfare activities, both as providers of funds and as administrators of funds provided by the federal government. And second, it failed to acknowledge the extent to which existing programs already relied on private nonprofit groups to deliver services.

As a result of these flaws, the administration's initiatives have had effects quite different from those intended. Rather than strengthening the voluntary sector, the administration's budget cuts have reduced nonprofit revenues while increasing the service demands on these organizations. Thus far, nonprofits as a group have managed to replace the government funds they lost, but only by turning more extensively to service fees and charges. Little progress has been made, however, in expanding the sector to fill in for the reduction in government service. What is more, agencies serving the poor have generally not been able to offset their losses of government funds. As a result, there is some question about whether the current national policy changes may be altering some of the very characteristics that make the nonprofit sector so valuable.

To ensure that the private, nonprofit sector contributes to its full potential in the resolution of social-welfare problems in the future, it is essential that social-science research focus more on the role of the sector to provide informed debate and decision making. It is just as essential that public officials seriously consider this information in their decision making and encourage further research where it appears to be most useful and cost-effective. The large size of the nonprofit sector and the extensive and diverse interdependency relationships between the nonprofit sector and government guarantee that the nonprofit sector will play a major role in social-welfare programs in the 1980s and beyond. Effective policy making in this sector requires a clearer understanding of what the nonprofit role is now, what is happening to it as a result of policy and economic changes, and ultimately when and how the use of nonprofits best serves public purposes. These questions must be more systematically addressed in policy making if decision makers are to deal knowledgeably with the whole array of public/private partnership issues now before them.

NOTES

1.   For a fuller summary of the conservative position on the role of voluntary organizations, see Salamon
and Abramson, 1982b; and Salamon, 1984b.

2.   One notable exception is Kramer, 1980.

3.   These six policy areas were chosen because government activity in them affects either the demand for nonprofit services or the revenues of nonprofit organizations.
Education is one policy area that could be construed as
meeting this test but was not included.   At the local level,
however, most education money goes to support primary and
secondary education.   Nonprofit primary and secondary
schools receive very little government support.   Rather
than bring the entire local education budget into the analysis, therefore, we decided to exclude it and to include only
subsidized training for the unemployed or underemployed.

For purposes of this work, attention focused on the
central city county within each metropolitan area, except
for Rhode Island and New York City, where the entire state,
and the entire city, respectively, were covered.   The 16
sites covered have median values quite close to national
averages along with a number of key socioeconomic dimensions, such as percentage of population in poverty, percentage of population age 60 and over, per-capita income,
percentage of workers in manufacturing jobs, and percentage
unemployed.   The 16-site median differs most from the national averages in percentage of population in poverty and
per-capita income, primarily because of a slight overrepre-
sentation of larger metropolitan areas, where incomes are
generally higher.

4.   For further detail, see the individual site reports published to date, including: Gronbjerg, Musselwhite,
and Salamon, 1984; Harder, Musselwhite, and Salamon,
1984; Disney, Kimmich, and Musselwhite, 1984; Rozman and
Musselwhite, 1985; Musselwhite and Saunders, 1984; Johnson
and Musselwhite, 1984; Musselwhite, Hawkins, and Salamon,
1985.

5.   State and local discretion in administering federal programs varies from program to program.   This discretion has been expanded under the Reagan administration
through the use of more block grants.   For a discussion of
the changes under Reagan, see Nathan and Doolittle, 1984;
and Peterson, 1984.

6. Data from a survey we conducted of 3,400 non-profit service organizations, exclusive of hospitals and higher-education institutions, reveal that 40 percent of total nonprofit income came from government as of 1981 and that two-thirds of the organizations in existence as of 1982 had been formed since 1960. For more detail, see the individual site reports published to date. These include: Lukermann, Kimmich, and Salamon, 1984; Gutowski, Salamon, and Pittman, 1984; Lippert, Gutowski, and Salamon, 1984; Disney, Kimmich, and Musselwhite, 1984; and Gronbjerg, Kimmich, and Salamon, 1985.

REFERENCES

Aaron, H. J. 1978. Politics and the Professors: The Great Society in Perspective. Washington, D.C.: Brookings Institution.

Berger, P. L., and R. J. Neuhaus. 1977. To Empower People: The Role of Mediating Structures in Public Policy. Washington, D.C.: American Enterprise Institute.

Disney, D., M. Kimmich, and J. C. Musselwhite, Jr. 1984. Partners in Public Service: Government and the Nonprofit Sector in Rhode Island. Washington, D.C.: Urban Institute Press.

Egan, J., J. Carr, A. Mott, and J. Roos. 1981. Housing and Public Policy: A Role for Mediating Structures. Cambridge, Mass.: Ballinger.

Elazar, D. 1972. American Federalism: The View from the States. New York: Thomas Y. Crowell.

Grodzins, M. 1965. The American System. Chicago: Rand-McNally.

Gronbjerg, K., M. Kimmich, and L. M. Salamon. 1985. The Chicago Nonprofit Sector. Washington, D.C.: Urban Institute Press.

Gronbjerg, K., J. C. Musselwhite, Jr., and L. M. Salamon. 1984. Government Spending and the Nonprofit Sector in

Cook County/Chicago. Washington, D.C.: Urban Institute Press.

Gutowski, M., L. M. Salamon, and K. Pittman. 1984. The Pittsburgh Nonprofit Sector in a Time of Government Retrenchment. Washington, D.C.: Urban Institute Press.

Harder, P., J. C. Musselwhite, Jr., and L. M. Salamon. 1984. Government Spending and the Nonprofit Sector in San Francisco. Washington, D.C.: Urban Institute Press.

Johnson, D. A., and J. C. Musselwhite, Jr. 1984. Government Spending and the Nonprofit Sector in Boise/Ada County, Idaho. Washington, D.C.: Urban Institute Press.

Kramer, R. 1980. Voluntary Agencies in the Welfare State. Berkeley, Calif.: University of California Press.

Lippert, P. C., M. Gutowski, and L. M. Salamon. 1984. The Atlanta Nonprofit Sector in a Time of Government Retrenchment. Washington, D.C.: Urban Institute Press.

Lukermann, B., M. Kimmich, and L. M. Salamon. 1984. The Twin Cities Nonprofit Sector in a Time of Government Retrenchment. Washington, D.C.: Urban Institute Press.

Musselwhite, J. C. "The Impacts of New Federalism on Public/Private Partnerships." Publius. (Forthcoming.)

Musselwhite, J., W. Hawkins, and L. Salamon. 1985. Government Spending and the Nonprofit Sector in Fulton County (Atlanta). Washington, D.C.: Urban Institute Press.

Musselwhite, J. C., and L. K. Saunders. 1984. Government Spending and the Nonprofit Sector in Two Michigan Communities: Flint/Genessee County and Tuscola County. Washington, D.C.: Urban Institute Press.

Nathan, R. P., and F. C. Doolittle. 1984. "The Untold Story of Reagan's 'New Federalism.'" Public Interest 77 (Fall).

Nielsen, W. 1980. The Endangered Sector. New York: Columbia University Press.

Nisbet, R. A. 1962. Community and Power. New York: Oxford University Press.

Peterson, G. E. 1984. "Federalism and the States: An Experiment in Decentralization." In The Reagan Record, edited by J. L. Palmer and I. V. Sawhill. Cambridge, Mass.: Ballinger.

Rozman, S., and J. C. Musselwhite, Jr. 1985. Government Spending and the Nonprofit Sector in Two Mississippi Communities: Jackson/Hinds County and Vicksburg/Warren County. Washington, D.C.: Urban Institute Press.

Salamon, L. 1981. "Rethinking Public Management: Third Party Government and the Changing Forms of Government Action." Public Policy 29(3) (Summer): 255-75.

_____. 1984a. "The Invisible Partnership: Government and the Nonprofit Sector." Bell Atlantic Quarterly 1: 1 (Summer).

_____. 1984b. "The Nonprofit Sector: The Lost Opportunity." In The Reagan Record, edited by J. L. Palmer and I. Sawhill, pp. 261-85. Cambridge, Mass.: Ballinger.

_____. 1984c. "Nonprofits: The Results Are Coming in." Foundation News (August/September): 16-23.

Salamon, L., and A. Abramson. 1982a. The Federal Budget and the Nonprofit Sector. Washington, D.C.: Urban Institute Press.

_____. 1982b. "The Nonprofit Sector." In The Reagan Experiment, edited by J. L. Palmer and I. Sawhill, pp. 219-43. Washington, D.C.: Urban Institute Press.

Salamon, L., J. Musselwhite, and A. Abramson. 1984. "Voluntary Organizations and the Crisis of the Welfare State." New England Journal of Human Services 4 (Winter).

Woodson, R. 1981. A Summons to Life. Washington, D.C.: American Enterprise Institute.

Part II

Domestic Policy and Institutional Reactions

4

Changes in White: Health-Delivery Options in a Time of High Cost

Myrna R. Pickard

Measures to contain and reduce the costs associated with health care are now so common that using terms like crisis and emergency situations seems to obscure the real dimensions of the health-care problems faced by Americans and America. Health-care costs continue to take a larger share of the consumer and employer dollar, as reflected by numerous indicators. For example, since 1967 the Consumer Price Index increased by 297 percent, health-care costs have increased 366 percent (Monthly Labor Review, 1982 and 1983).

Health-care costs have increased for a variety of reasons and the emphasis applied to each reason is often a function of the values of the reviewers or researchers studying the problem. For example, those wishing to blame doctors point to an increase in the average salary of physicians that far exceeds the changes in income for other groups of professionals. Between 1970 and 1983 physicians' services have risen by 22 percent as compared with 6 percent for dental services (Monthly Labor Review 1982 and 1983).

The antihospital advocates have produced a large amount of data to illustrate the added costs of hospital stays, such as the extra days spent in hospitals, and the number of tests ordered for patients. Freeland et al. (1979) suggest that 65 percent of the increase in hospital expenditures between 1970 and 1978 was due to inflation, while another 6 percent was due to population growth and the remaining 29 percent was due to increased intensity of hospital service. There was a doubling of laboratory tests, an 18 percent increase in surgical operations, and a 24 percent increase in outpatient visits. In-patient days increased 8 percent in the same period. Finally, there are critics who, from a more traditional class-oriented or Marxian perspective, identify an environment not unlike the "great American health empire" of the Ehrenreichs (1966), which exists both to collect and transfer wealth to the owners of hospitals, drug companies, and the producers of medical-technology equipment.

The impressive array of researchers, each arguing that certain elements of the health industry are at fault for the high cost of health care, might convince many readers that, indeed, the problems with financing health care does indeed rest with the providers of health care. There is, however, another side of the story. For example, Davis (1983) found that food, equipment, and energy-price increases are primarily responsible for 58 percent of the increase in personal health-care expenditures. Probably the largest factor responsible for rising health care, some argue, has been the changing demographic characteristics of the U.S. population. The number of citizens over 65 years of age grew to more than 10 percent of the total population in 1978, and this percentage will increase as the life-span of Americans lengthens. The economic result is that fewer people will be in the total workforce contributing to a tax base and the older citizens will need long-term care facilities, home-help agencies, or geriatric day-care centers to meet their needs. According to Davis (1983), older individuals spend three times as much on health care as the rest of the population and they account for approximately 10 percent of the increase in health-care costs. Schulz and Johnson (1983) found that the elderly represented less than 11 percent of the population in 1977, and used nearly 30 percent of all health-care resources; therefore, the aging population must be considered an important factor in rising costs. The increased precision in diagnoses, a function of technological advancements, has also raised costs as many of these new machines and techniques are still extremely costly. Almost 35 percent of the rise in cost can be attributed to our increased ability to treat disease with greater use of technology and more services per capita (Davis, 1983). Unfortunately, there are some cases in which the high costs of technology may exceed the benefits. For example, Russell (1979) found no difference between home care and hospital intensive-care mortality rates for heart-attack victims. She also found no significant relationship between cancer deaths and hospital use of cobalt-radiation therapy. It appears that in some cases the costs outweigh the benefits. Lastly, with physicians increasingly concerned with malpractice suits, a tendency has emerged to apply a battery of tests to patients to cover all possible alternatives and to avoid the possibility of litigation. Some patients also demand these tests and change physicians if the request is not granted. Physicians then pressure hospital administrators to offer the most advanced technologies (Block and Pupp, 1985).

A reading of this varied and extensive debate on health-care costs can be quite confusing if the goal is to identify guilt and responsibility as part of any cost-reduction program. Indeed, that seems to be the thrust of many major policies and programs. For example, the Reagan administration's much-publicized DRG (diagnostically related groupings) program is designed to reduce excessive hospital stays critics believe are the fault of physicians and hospitals seeking to either increase profits or decrease the likelihood of malpractice suits. This legislation initiated a new system of payments to hospitals for inpatient care under the Medicare program. It was a change from retrospective cost reimbursement to prospective cost reimbursement. Under this new prospective system, a fixed predetermined price is paid to the hospital for each Medicare patient. The number of services, laboratory tests, or length of stay are not considered; the diagnosis is the only factor in reference to payment. Thus the DRGs became the system of payment to hospitals for inpatient care under Medicare (Campbell, 1984). Other Reagan administration proposals also seem designed to place the blame for rising costs on consumers. A controversial proposal is to limit the amount of employer-paid health benefits that are tax-free to the employee. The purpose of this proposal is to encourage individuals to select lower-cost plans with larger deductibles and coinsurance provisions. The consumer will become more aware of the price of health services and there should be a reduction of unnecessary expenses. This proposal would make health plans such as HMOs more attractive and more competitive.

Griffith (1984) has pointed out that, generally, an increase in out-of-pocket price to consumers leads to a decrease in demand. Demand in health care is used in referring to utilization and it should not be confused with need for health care. Need is defined as the care which a person should have to remain or become healthy. Third-party payors have used reduced payments to decrease the demand for services. If the consumers have to pay more, it logically follows that they will begin to shop around for the best health-care buy. It also follows that some will not be able to buy what they need to remain well.

In terms of reforming the health-care industry and its costs, this chapter is less interested in assessing guilt than in considering the organization of the health-care industry itself. Indeed, all industries seem to develop, over time, an inertia of sorts which keeps production styles and techniques locked into existing methods of operation. These methods of production are only changed when the system is shocked by competition or bankruptcy. The automobile industry is certainly an example where outmoded methods of production were shocked into change by foreign competition. Such a shock is less likely in the health-care industry, but there are important options in terms of the production of health care that could dramatically affect the cost of health. A consideration of one of these options is the goal of this chapter.

The inadequacy of primary health-care services in rural areas and inner cities resulted in governmental mandates during the 1970s to develop nontraditional responses to these problems. While there has been some research to look at other issues in changing delivery systems, this chapter will focus specifically on responses made by schools of nursing and the efforts to lower costs through the use of nursing as an alternative to high-cost care.

ACADEMIC POLICY RESEARCH AND HEALTH-CARE REFORM

The Role of Schools of Nursing in Practice and Policy Formation

There are more than 1.3 million registered nurses employed in the United States today; this is the largest single professional component of the U.S. health-care system. The Institute of Medicine Study recognized nursing as the prime group to work with the health-care delivery problems. Their responsibilities are diverse and there has been a growth in specialties, such as nurse practitioners, nurse midwives, and a variety of clinical nurses. Schools of nursing have the responsibility of educating professionals for future service in society. Universities also have the responsibility of preparing the kinds of practitioners who can first determine the health needs and then develop programs to meet those needs.

A Nursing-policy Perspective

Griffith (1984) proposes that nursing services could be seen as substitutes for physician services, and as the cost of health care increases there is greater incentive to use substitute products. Midwives, nurse practitioners, nurse anesthetists, and psychiatric nurse specialists could be substituted when the services are within the scope of nursing practice. Home health-care services could be a substitute for certain hospital services, and if physicians' prices increase while the out-of-pocket expense for the consumer increases, it follows that there would be an increase in the demand for nursing services.

Griffith states that there are five major groups whose perceptions regarding health policy should be considered. They are: consumers, insurers, physicians, nurses, and legislators. According to a survey conducted by the New York Times, consumers are expressing more willingness to accept expanded services from nurses. That study indicated that nearly six out of every ten consumers would be willing to have routine illness treated by nurses rather than doctors (Reinhold, 1982).

Insurers have been hesitant to consider health promotion and preventive-health treatment because it would drive up health-care costs, but if nursing services can substitute for physician services the insurers may be more willing to negotiate for insurance coverage of nursing. Physicians have been willing to work with nurses in expanded roles if they are under physician supervision and do not have independent practices. The physician prefers to pay the nurse's salary, which is less than the amount collected for his or her services. Nurses have attempted to define their practice as health promotion, counseling, and health prevention. It was believed that this kept them from competing with the physician. The physician is now expanding into the same roles and the nurse may have to look at the right to assess, diagnose, and treat illness to the extent that they are prepared and credentialed. Avoiding competition with the physician may not be possible, but collaborative relationships can continue (Griffith, 1984).

Legislators are very interested when nurses claim that they can decrease expenditures for health care. Nurses' requests for additional services which may cost more when they are added to the third-party system as reimbursable services do not receive such positive attention. Legal mandates for nursing, direct third-party reimbursement, and securing hospital privileges are needed to permit the nurse to serve as a substitute for physician services (Griffith, 1984).

Nurse midwives have demonstrated their ability to deliver safe and less-expensive maternity care than that of the traditional hospital. Charges for nurse midwifery services at a New York City Child Bearing Center are 37.6 percent of in-hospital care. An audit report noted that the cost to Blue Cross for families who used the center is 66 percent of the cost of the plan if they had gone to a hospital.

A survey by the American College of Nurse-Midwives in 1982 found that the number of nurse-midwives in clinical practice had increased dramatically since 1968. As of July 1, 1982, there were 2,550 certified nurse-midwives, a 67 percent increase since 1968.

Maternal and child health-care delivery are changing as a result of the new federal policy and reduced health budget. States have a greater discretion in the use of federal money, but can the states provide the health services for mothers and children? State maternal and child-health and crippled-children's programs report reductions for services for almost 15 million mothers and children. The 1982 budget for maternal and child services was $50 million less than in 1981. States are expected to use their resources to make up for this loss (Free, 1983).

The importance of primary-care nurses in reducing maternal and infant mortality and especially in working with low-income mothers and children cannot be underestimated. Free (1983) has pointed out that primary-care nurses composed the largest employed group in rural and urban maternal and child clinics in the early 1980s. Unfortunately, many of these nurses lost their positions with the federal cuts and allocations to programs and clinics. This is a clear indication that the nursing profession has become dependent on the federal government, not only for funding education and research, but for services as well.

Health Care for the Elderly

Another major concern is the health care of the aged, but what are the health goals for this population? O'Neal (1983) identified the broad goal as improved health and quality of life. There is the need to assist older adults in functioning independently and to reduce premature death from influenza and pneumonia. Since the nation's concept of health is changing, nursing has the knowledge base and the track record to meet the needs of our elderly public. Nurses are in a position to organize informal support networks of family members and neighbors and provide the overall coordination of a support system.

Several issues have been identified by O'Neal (1983) which relate specifically to the aging population and health-care needs. The response of the government to the health-care needs for the aged has been categorical funding, such as services to people with certain diseases, but this doesn't help the aged person who is simply frail. Another issue is the need for interdisciplinary practice, since the problems of the aged are so complex and require the input of many disciplines. Traditionally, the physician has had the final authority and responsibility.

A third issue has to do with the requirements of the health-service agencies which become constraints to the consumer. Each program has its own eligibility requirements and it presents an incomprehensible maze for the older person to find out what programs might be available. There is a wide array of services but the consumer needs assistance in matching the services to the specific needs. The need is for a large, coordinative role in the design of health in social-service delivery systems and the nurse is the ideal person to provide that role (O'Neal, 1983).

Aiken (1982) has discussed a need to remove financial barriers to health care by expanding nurses' individual roles, developing new roles outside the hospital setting, improving the quality of nursing care available, and improving economic rewards for nurses. The American Nurses Association has suggested altering the reimbursement mechanism for currently covered community-based services. Free-standing community nursing centers could be established and financed by a predetermined payment system. On-site and in-home services for three major population groups could be provided: (1) the Medicare home health population groups, (2) Medicaid and child health-service recipients,

and (3) previously hospitalized and at-risk rehospitaliza-
tion, chronically ill, Medicare, or Medicaid populations.
The nursing agency would have to demonstrate that the
services are cost-effective at or below the average cost of
similar services from other agencies in order to qualify as
a community nursing center (McKiblin, 1982).

Procompetitive health models continue to surface as a
possible solution, but there are questions which need to be
considered.

1. Will competition for patients between physicians
and nurses increase if nurses receive reimbursement for
their services?

2. Could nurses form independent organizations to
contract with employers or others for the delivery of primary health-care services?

3. Will legal barriers become more relaxed to promote nursing services (McKiblin, 1982)?

NURSING AS AN ALTERNATIVE TO HIGH-COST CARE

The nurse practitioner role shows a lot of possibility
for solving some of the health-care dilemmas. These are
nurses who have received additional education and training
for the purpose of providing primary care to the consumer.
Kutait and Busby (1980) found an increase in nurse practitioners in this country to 9,634 from 1965 to 1979, and
500 of them are self-employed. There are approximately
180 nurse-practitioner programs in the United States.

The nurse-practitioner movement gained impetus in
the 1960s because of several social phenomena. There were
health-manpower shortages, especially of pediatricians and
family practice physicians, escalating health-care costs,
and a need for primary health care for the rural and urban
poor populations. Initially the nurse practitioner was expected to provide primary care for those who did not have
access to care through private means; to provide health
maintenance and prevention of illness for more people for
less cost; and to permit nurses to expand their skills
through health appraisals (Marchione and Garland, 1980).
More recently nurse practitioners have added to their role
total client assessment, follow-up, and health promotion.
The focus of practice has been changed from a disease
orientation to health promotion, health maintenance, and responsibility for continuity of care (Archer, 1976).

The American Nurses Association defines the nurse practitioner as one who

> provides direct care to individuals, fami-
> lies, and other groups in a variety of set-
> tings. . . . The service provided . . .
> is aimed at the delivery of primary, acute,
> and chronic care which focuses on the
> achievement, maintenance, or restoration
> of optimal function of the population. The
> advanced nurse practitioner engages in
> independent decision-making about the
> nursing care needs of clients and collabo-
> rates with other health professionals, such
> as physicians, social workers, and nutri-
> tionists in making decisions about other
> health care needs . . . . plans and insti-
> tures health care programs as a member of
> the health care team (A.N.A. Statement,
> 1978).

Health promotion is a major emphasis in the role of the nurse practitioner, and much expense and illness can be prevented through health teaching. Murray and Zentner (1975) found accidents to be a leading cause of death and disability for young adults. Safety education should be a prime concern in occupational and school settings. Defensive driving and safety rules involved in swimming and boating need to be encouraged. Life-style influences health and illness and healthy life-styles can be taught. Suicide is the tenth leading cause for death in the United States, and students, faculty, and administration need to be aware of advance signs of suicide so that high-risk students can be identified. Who is going to assume this responsibility?

Another major role for the nurse practitioner and professional nursing in general is the consumer advocate. It is now recognized that consumer knowledge and involvement can save dollars in care, but the bureaucratic structure of the health-care system creates barriers. Bureaucracies tend to be middle-class and reflect the rules of that class.

Hamilton (1982) described the six issues of consumerism in health care today as:

1. the consumer's role in the marketplace, in which there is no longer consumer sovereignty;

2. the high cost of health care, which makes it unavailable to consumers;

3. the quality of health care, which is not determined by the consumer who buys it, but rather by the profession;

4. the patient's and consumer's rights, which are often jeopardized upon entering the health-care system;

5. the availability of accessible grievance mechanisms in health care for the consumer; and

6. the desire/need for more involvement with consumer participation in health policymaking.

The nurse can assist the consumer in dealing with each of those issues by assuming an advocacy role.

Initially, there were many objections to the new role of the nurse practitioner. A common statement was: "Nobody will see the nurse if they have a chance to see the doctor." A number of studies have now documented the satisfaction of patients with care provided by the nurse practitioners and their ability to deliver equivalent primary care, when compared with physicians. Patients have indicated that nurse practitioners perform adequate examinations; were easy to communicate with and offered adequate explanations regarding the illness and care; did not have long wiating periods before seeing the patients; did not rush the patients during the visits. Many indicated that they would return to see a nurse practitioner and that this provider was an asset to the present health-care practice (Henry, 1978; Levine et al., 1978; Linn, 1976; Spitzer et al., 1974). Particularly impressive was the study described by Dunn and Chard (1980) in which nurse practitioners and physicians' assistants were used as providers in a health-maintenance organization and the cost of the average visit decreased by 20 percent. Other studies have documented a decrease in the use of medication by patients and a 27 percent decrease in laboratory and prescription costs when services are provided by the nurse practitioner/physician team.

The team concept of physicians and nurse practitioners is common in the HMO, and this seems to have some effect on giving quality care at affordable prices. Fewer hospital days of care are used by HMOs as they are able to utilize home health-care services and again

the nurse takes the major role. Another example in a recent report indicated that elderly patients given home
health care by a physician, geriatric nurse, and social
worker team spent 38 percent fewer days in the hospital
and 59 percent fewer days in nursing homes than patients
receiving traditional home care. Overall treatment costs
both in and out of the home were nearly 9 percent lower
("Home Health Care . . .," 1983). Hospitals are also realizing the need to offer home health-care services to decrease the length of stay. This trend works extremely
well with nursing and the goal to assist people to maintain their health since nurses can work with the consumer
to become partners in health care. The one concern is
that the public or layperson may not understand that the
nurse can provide this service. The consumer's preference for a health practitioner must be a consideration,
regardless of cost. The consumer wants to know that there
is access to care 24 hours a day, seven days a week, and
that the practitioner has the competence to deal with the
problem and the wisdom to refer problems outside of his or
her competence. With adequate consumer knowledge and
understanding of the new health professional such as the
nurse practitioner, consumers can decide through their influence on legislation whether or not they wish to receive
health care from these new health professionals. The issue
of hospital privileges also must be confronted. If the
nurse practitioner is granted staff privileges, the functions
that may be carried out in the hospital must be specified.
Also, policies are needed for referral of patients to nurse
practitioners (Bliss and Cohen, 1977).

Nurse-managed Clinics

Projects to provide cost-effective kinds of primary-
care nursing are being tried in 63 nursing centers in the
United States. The original purpose of the centers was to
serve as model teaching centers for students where the
best of nursing practice could be observed and tested.
These centers may have to shift their focus from the educational concerns of nursing faculty and students to the
clinical care of clients and looking at productivity and
efficiency, as well as access and comprehensiveness of
services (Lang, 1983).

What are some examples of what is done in the nurse-managed centers?

Ogle County, Ill.: This nursing center was set up by faculty from the University of Illinois who wanted practice sites for registered nurses and graduate students. They were most interested in offering health-promotion and health-maintenance services. Eventually, they provided fee-based services for chronic diseases and health promotion. They developed a contract with the Visiting Nurses Association, which helped with some reimbursement mechanisms for home-care service.

Scottsdale, Ariz.: This center is an example of service for low-income groups. The center was developed in 1977 by the College of Nursing at Arizona State University and was originally funded by a federal grant. It is an outpatient treatment center and it offers adult and child-health services, maternity care, immunization, and referral to other community sources for acute illnesses. It is open five days a week and three evenings. The staff includes three full-time nurse practitioners, a part-time physician, a clinic nurse, a coordinator, and clerical support staff. In addition, nurse faculty and students give direct patient care, make home visits, and conduct screening programs, health-education classes, and community projects. More than 70 percent of the clients live within four miles of the center, and it is made up mainly of women and children with incomes below $10,000.

Chicago, Ill.: Another center which serves primarily a low-income neighborhood is Chicago, offering prenatal, family-planning services and mental-health care. The staff consists of six full-time master's-level nurse clinicians in different specialties and a full-time family physician. The operating budget was just over $700,000 and the funds came from six private foundations, institutional support, fees, third-party reimbursement, government contracts, and contributions.

Mansfield, Conn.: This center is called a wellness center and it is located next to the town's senior center; thus most of the clients are 55 years of age and older. Clients receive a great deal of preventive screening and health maintenance, counseling, and health education. The center is open 4.5 days a week and staffed by full-time nurse practitioners, a half-time secretary, two senior volunteers, and nursing students. They do not charge fees, but they take donations.

Funding of these centers still remains the central problem. Third-party reimbursement is most likely the potential funding source. Currently, there are approximately 180 nurse-practitioner programs in the country and 37 states provide some legislation for expanded nurse practice (Lang, 1983).

It has been said that the nurse practitioner puts the glue to the entire health-care system. The primary-care role involves three functions: assessment, direct patient care, and case management. The assessment involves not only the illness and physical health status, but also the resources and levels of community functioning. Nurses may provide direct treatment as well as planning of care and discharge. Case management is the part that keeps patients from falling between the cracks of the health-care system. The case management function includes: continuity of care, patient advocacy, coordination of care, preventive education, resource development, and accountability (Slavinsky, 1984). Accountability is the key to the success of the role. Through delegating accountability to a single person there is the responsibility for patients 24 hours a day, seven days a week, and there is coordination of care and communication.

THE FUTURE OF HEALTH CARE AND NURSING

Several predictions about the future of health care were described in an eight-month survey conducted by the American College of Hospital Administration and Arthur Anderson and Co. Some of the trends predicted were:

- Congress will define life and death by 1990 in dealing with life-support systems.
- A multilevel system will provide a minimum of care for all, and extras will be available only to those who can pay.
- The eligibility age for Medicare patients will be raised.
- Patients will seek second opinions and challenge doctors more.
- An increasing number of elderly people will spur growth in the health-care industry.
- Hospitals will feel the competition of outpatient clinics, birth centers, hospices, and minor emergency centers.

-Physicians will work for salaries and earn smaller incomes. They will have less power and feel diminished
satisfaction.

The changes in the physician's power will be affected by a 130,000-doctor glut by the year 2000 as predicted by the Graduate Medical Education National Advisory
Committee in a report to the federal government in 1980.

As we plan for the year 2000, we have to address
three health areas: preventive-health services, health
protection, and health promotion. Preventive-health services include immunization, screening tests for newborns,
and a vast array of procedures and services designed to
prevent disease. Health protection, such as regulations to
provide safe air and water, will be directed at population
groups more than individuals. There will be increased
enforcement of health and safety regulations for industrial
and consumer products and practices.

Health promotion will be accomplished through health-
education programs and efforts to promote lifestyles to reduce the risk of death from chronic disease or injury.
Emphasis will be placed on unhealthy behaviors such as
smoking, alcohol, poor nutrition, or drug abuse. Health
education will also be focused on expectant mothers, im-
pressing on them the importance of care in the early months
of pregnancy.

Research must continue on alternatives in dealing
with our elderly and providing some options for financing
their health care. Lanahan (1983) has described a developing concept called the "Life Care Retirement Center,"
which offers the elderly a living arrangement to meet their
social and medical needs. Such a center could be supported by revenues from entrance fees and monthly maintenance fees, as well as interest earned on invested funds.
Tax-exempt revenue bonds have become a primary source
of financing these facilities in the past few years. A
registered nurse is usually on call for 24 hours, and
transportation, recreation areas, cleaning and laundry
services, and a central dining room would normally be
provided.

Scholen (1983) discussed another option for the elderly to finance home care by converting home equity into
income while remaining at home. This idea is still in the
testing stage, but the potential for providing income from
equity to purchase home care is attractive, since three out

of four households of elderly persons own homes and four out of five are mortgage free. The total amount of elderly-owned home equity in 1980 was approximately $500 billion. Through the plan homeowners sell some of their ownership rights but they continue to live in the home. Since the elderly strongly prefer to remain in their homes as long as possible, it appears that this plan would promote better use of the public health dollars by increasing the ability to pay.

A discussion of changes in the health-care delivery system would not be complete without considering the fast development of the hospice. Hospices provide care for dying patients and many are limited to cancer cases. The emphasis is on palliative care and the involvement of the total family. Hospice care has been added to Medicare and Railroad Retirement programs.

The future may hold additional changes in payment mechanisms. One possibility is a generalized prospective payment arranged in which organizations would arrange for the total health service requirements of the enrolled population. That would include hospital care, physician visits, long-term home or institutionally based nursing care, etc. There would be competition for members and the members would be entitled to a federal annual contribution for the health-services requirements. This would be a very major change but it could be accomplished as early as 1990 (Brimmer, 1984). Other reforms in payment mechanisms have been considered and it seems likely that prospective payment may be used for physician services, nursing homes, home-health services, and services in other ambulatory-care settings.

All the changes discussed will present new economic challenges and employment opportunities for the professional nurse. Computer-controlled robotics will assume more and more importance in the delivery of health care. They can deliver water, medications to the patients' bedside, dietary support service, and routine monitoring of temperature, pulse, and blood pressure (Brimmer, 1984). New opportunities may be available for the nurse to be freed to spend more time in nurse/patient relationships. Innovative discharge planning, health-education programs, and contract services for short-term and long-term patient care in the community are possible new roles for nurses. Nurses as well as all health-care workers will feel an increased responsibility for cost control. Only the most productive workers will remain in the system. The greatest challenge will remain to deliver necessary health-care services to the public regardless of modifications in health-care financing.

SUMMARY

The dilemma of public-policy issues in health care can be summarized in terms of the concern with efficiency and supply and with containment of costs of medical services. The nation cannot continue to institute new programs and continue current medical benefits unless some method is found to contain medical costs. Professions and organizations affected by any recommended cuts in federal assistance are immediately up in arms and they are also very powerful political entities. The question of how much health care should be redistributed to the different population groups continues to haunt policymakers. A successful mechanism for redistributing health care to underserved populations has not been found. If we continue to have subsidy programs for specific populations, they must be administered more efficiently so that the most needy receive help. This certainly provides a challenge of how to provide quality care at an affordable price.

REFERENCES

Aiken, L. H. 1982. The Impact of Federal Health in the 1980s: Crises, Opportunities and Challenges. Philadelphia: J. B. Lippincott.

American Nurses Association. 1978. A Position Statement on the Advanced Nurse Practitioner. Austin, Tex.: Texas Nurses Association.

Archer, S. E. 1976. "Community Nurse Practitioners, Another Assessment." Nursing Outlook 24(8): 499-503.
Baurnecht, V. 1981. "A.N.A. Testifies on Proposed Budget Cuts." American Nurse 13(5): 1-2.

Bliss, A. A., and E. D. Cohen, eds. 1977. The New Health Professionals. Germantown, Md.: Aspen Systems Corp.

Block, H., and R. Pupp. 1985. "Supply, Demand, and Rising Health-Care Costs." Nursing Economics 3(2): 119-23.

Blum, H. L. 1974. Planning for Health: Development and Application of Social Change Theory, p. 3. New York: Human Science Press.

Brimmer, P. F. 1984. The Economic and Employment Environment: Recent Developments and Future Opportunities. Kansas City, Mo.: American Nurses Association.

Campbell, J. 1984. "DRG's: An Administrative Perspective." Travis County Medical 4: 12.

Carney, K. 1982. Health Care, p. 6. Dallas, Tex.: League of Women Voters.

Cashin, J. 1978. The Impact of the Advent of Medicare on Hospital Costs. Hempstead, N.Y.: Hofstra University.

Congressional Budget Office. 1982. Containing Medical Care Costs through Market Forces. Nos. 9, 11 (May). Washington, D.C.: Government Printing Office.

Davis, C. K. 1983. "The Federal Role in Changing Health Care Financing." Nursing Economics 1(1): 10-17.

Dunn, B. H., and M. A. Chard, eds. 1980. Nurse Practitioners: A Review of Literature, 1965-1979. Kansas City, Mo.: American Nurses Association.

Free, T. A. 1983. "The States' Challenge to Provide Maternal and Child Care." Nurse Practitioner 8(5): 46-51.

Freeland, M. S., G. Anderson, and C. E. Schendler. 1979. "National Hospital Input Price Index." Health Care Financing Review, Summary.

Geitgey, D. 1983. "Financing Nursing Education--A Public Perspective." Economics of Higher Education in Nursing 83(1): 14. Washington, D.C.: American Association of Colleges of Nursing.

Griffith, H. 1984. "Nursing Practice: Substitute or Complement According to Economics Theory. Nursing Economics 2(2): 105–12.

Hamilton, P. 1982. Health Care Consumerism, p. 13. St. Louis: C. V. Mosby.

Heckler, M. 1983. Paper presented at American Hospital Association. Houston. August.

Henry, O. M. 1978. "Progress of the Nurse Practitioner Movement." Nurse Practitioner 3 (May–June): 4.

"Home Health Care Team Cuts Costs for Elderly." 1983. Hospitals 57 (13): 25.

Johnson, K. A. 1983. "Hospital Economic Forecast." Hospitals 57 (7): 65, 68.

Kalisch, P., and B. Kalisch. 1978. The Advance of American Nursing. Boston: Little, Brown.

Kane, R. L., J. M. Kasteler, and R. M. Gray, eds. 1976. The Health Gap. New York: Springer.

Kutait, K., and D. Busby. 1980. "New Health Practitioners and Arkansas." J. of Arkansas Medical Society 76 (February): 353–60.

Lanahan, M. B. 1983. "Life Care Retirement Centers: A Concept in Development." Pride Institute J. of Long Term Home Health Care 2 (2): 41–42.

Lang, N. M. 1983. "Nurse Managed Centers: Will They Thrive?" American J. of Nursing 83: 1290–96.

Levine, J. I., S. T. Orr, D. W. Sheatsley, J. A. Lohr, and B. S. Brodie. 1978. "The Nurse Practitioner Role, Physician Utilization, Patient Acceptance." Nursing Research 27 (July–August): 245–54.

Linn, L. S. 1976. "Patient Acceptance of the Family Nurse Practitioner." Medical Care 14 (April): 357–63.

Luce, B., and S. Schweitzer. 1978. "Smoking and Alcohol Abuse: A Comparison of Their Economic Consequences." New England J. of Medicine 298 (10): 569-71.

Marchione, J., and T. N. Garland. 1980. "An Emerging Profession? The Case of the Nurse Practitioner." Image 12 (June) 2: 37-40.

McKiblin, R. C. 1982. Nursing in the 80's: Key Economic and Employment Issues. Monograph. Kansas City, Mo.: American Nurses Association.

Monthly Labor Review. 1982 and 1983. Washington, D.C.: U.S. Department of Labor, Bureau of Labor Statistics.

Murray, R., and J. Zentner. 1975. Nursing Assessment and Health Promotion through the Life Span. Englewood Cliffs, N.J.: Prentice-Hall.

Nurse-Midwifery in the United States: 1982. 1984. A project of the Research and Statistics Committee of the American College of Nurse-Midwives. Washington, D.C.

Nursing and Health Care in the 80's. 1982. A document prepared by the Interdivision Coordinating Committee. December. New York: National League of Nursing.

O'Neal, D. J., III. 1983. "The Aging Society and Nursing Education: A National Perspective." The Aging Society: A Challenge for Nursing Education. Papers presented at Fall 1981 meeting of Southern Council on Collegiate Education for Nursing, pp. 1-28. Atlanta, Ga.: Southern Regional Education Board.

Reinhold, R. 1982. "Majority in Survey on Health Care Are Open to Change to Cut Costs." New York Times, March 29.

Rosen, H., J. M. Metsch, and S. Levy. 1977. The Consumer and the Health Care System: Social and Managerial Perspectives, pp. 237, 243. New York: Spectrum.

Russell, L. 1979. Technology in Hospitals. Washington, D.C.: Brookings Institution.

Salamon, L. M., and A. J. Abramson. 1982. The Federal Budget and the Nonprofit Sector, p. xvii. Washington, D.C.: Urban Institute Press.

Scholen, K. 1983. "Financing Home Care with Home Equity." Pride Institute J. of Long Term Health Care 21(2): 43–45.

Schulz, R., and A. C. Johnson. 1983. Management of Hospitals, 2d ed. New York: McGraw-Hill.

Slavinsky, A. T. 1984. "Psychiatric Nursing in the Year 2000: From a Nonsystem of Care to a Caring System." Image: The J. of Nursing Scholarships 16(1): 17–20.

Spitzer, W. O., D. L. Sackett, J. C. Sibley, R. S. Roberts, M. Gent, D. J. Kergin, B. C. Hackett, and A. Olynick. 1974. "The Burlington Randomized Trial of the Nurse Practitioner." New England J. of Medicine 290 (January 31): 251–56.

"Study on Health Professionals: Highlights, Problems Facing South's Policyholders." 1983. Regional Action 32(2): 4. Atlanta, Ga.: Southern Regional Education Board.

"The Times Are Changing: A Report of a National Conference on Economic and Strategic Outlook for Hospitals." 1983. Hospitals 57(14/July 16): 101–8.

5

Changers and the Changed: Affirmative Action and Local Governments

Patricia A. Huckle

INTRODUCTION

This is a period of assessment and rethinking of
national policy direction, stimulated by renewed debate
over the preferred roles of the federal government. The
Republican view of federalism initiated by President Richard
Nixon has a different flavor in the Reagan administration
of the 1980s. The initial emphasis on decentralization of
funding and decision making from the central government
to states has been expanded dramatically to include at-
tacks on the regulatory role of federal government, reduction in funding for social programs, and a move toward a
passive, least-government ideology. Two questions often
overlap: What do we mean by equity, or equality of opportunity, and to what extent should or can the federal
government regulate? The debate, and current efforts to
implement the passive approach to government, represent
what Walt Williams calls a "great leap" rather than an
incremental change in the way the federal government is to
be viewed (1984). That is, rather than accepting modest
alterations in policy over extended periods of time, the
Reagan administration has attempted to bring about major
shifts rather quickly.

Nowhere has the change and debate been more evident than in the area of civil rights (if one omits discussion of defense spending). After more than two decades
in which the federal government took a primary role in
stimulating increased employment opportunities for women

and minorities, the Reagan approach has crystallized in fierce resistance to affirmative action in its evolved form. My purpose here is to describe the parameters of the debate over the role of the federal government in the implementation of civil-rights legislation on employment, and to set that conflict in the context of the actual implementation process as it occurred in a local government setting. One question is whether or not the various federal regulations and messages about equal opportunity have been effective. Another is whether the current administration's efforts to dismantle the enforcement relationship between employers and the federal government are likely to succeed, and what that dismantling might mean to local government and to women and minorities.

THE CHANGERS: GOVERNMENT OFF OUR BACKS

In fulfillment of campaign promises in 1980, President Reagan moved to alter federal civil-rights enforcement activities. Budget reductions were only a part of the strategy, and activists included representatives from the Justice Department as well as other segments of the federal bureaucracy and members of Congress. Three strategies became central: (1) dismantle and reorganize the Civil Rights Commission; (2) eliminate or modify the scope of action for the Equal Employment Opportunities Commission (EEOC) and the Office of Federal Contract Compliance Programs (OFCCP); and (3) challenge the use of numerical goals and timetables and shift focus from effects to intent, in analysis of discrimination.

Civil Rights Commission

By 1982, President Reagan had replaced the chair of the U.S. Civil Rights Commission with Clarence Pendleton, former head of the San Diego Urban League. The new chair agreed with the president that "anytime one gives preference to one group over another, discrimination takes place" (1983, Firing Line, p. 10). He further agreed that numerical remedies (always called quotas) are, as Nathan Glazer said, "affirmative discrimination." The next year, when the president moved to fire three other incumbents on the CRC, and replace them with his own nominations, a battle broke out. The president believed that the CRC had overstepped its bounds, both in its posture supporting affirmative action and in its series of publications of research on both enforcement efforts and discrimination problems.[1] In his view, the CRC had become too partisan in supporting equity goals. The battle over renewal of the CRC continued in Congress and the press over the next several months. Several civil-rights groups participated in the debate. William L. Taylor, Center for National Policy Review in Washington, D.C., noted: "A basic bipartisan consensus was built up beginning in 1964. . . . I think the administration has been acting outside that bipartisan consensus, and every time the president does, he loses." Ralph Neas, executive director of the coalition group, Leadership Conference on Civil Rights, in opposing the president's attempts to modify the direction of the CRC, remarked: "The civil rights agenda has moved from doing away with segregation to the more complex area of ensuring equal economic opportunity." (Both statements reported in Congressional Quarterly, September 17, 1983, p. 1932.)

By November 1983, Congress had approved legislation extending the life of the Civil Rights Commission by six years. New provisions provided for appointment of four members each by Congress and the president, with removal from the commission only for cause. The president was able to reshape the current CRC more nearly to his own perspective, but Congress reinforced the intended independence of the commission.

In addition, the public debate re-energized a coalition of civil rights and women's organizations. They criticized Reagan's delay in appointing a new head for the Equal Employment Opportunities Commission, and have continued to bring public attention to budget cuts and changing priorities in enforcement. The practical effect of the new Reagan approach to civil rights is reflected in the 9 percent decline in real outlays from FY 1981 to FY 1983. Bawden and Palmer (1984) point out that there was a 10 percent reduction in the EEOC budget and a 24 percent reduction in OFCCP during this time, resulting in staff cuts for both agencies. Although the number of complaint investigations by OFCCP went up from 1980 to 1983, the number of actions taken dropped, and backpay awards dropped. While the number of complaints was up, the employment discrimination cases brought by the EEOC and the Justice Department declined by half in the two years.

Congressional Hearings

The president was not alone in his attack on the structure of civil-rights enforcement. Critics of affirmative action have also been busy in Congress. While always careful to express their belief in equal opportunity for all Americans, and sometimes acknowledging a historical pattern of discrimination against blacks and women, critics focused on two challenges. One was not new with the Reagan administration: Management inefficiency or runaway bureaucracy is a recurrent theme of government critics. The second challenge focused on the weaknesses of enforcement strategies used to implement civil-rights legislation passed in the 1960s.

The oversight hearings in 1981 reflected both concerns. With respect to the EEOC, the Senate committee chaired by Sen. Orin Hatch solicited testimony on the operation of the EEOC from its newly appointed director. His focus was on the disorderly state of records, and possible misuse of federal funds. The new director's criticism of the agency was rebutted in the published testimony by a former EEOC director, Eleanor Holmes Norton. Contrary to his view, she pointed out the ways in which the EEOC had been reorganized effectively to meet criticisms in an earlier review.

The 1981 oversight hearings on the Office of Federal Contract Compliance Programs generated more than 1,000 pages of testimony. Critics focused on perceived bureaucratic inefficiency. Employers complained of voluminous data collection requirements and short deadlines. Several brought their stacks of reports (one more than five feet tall) and complained of heavy costs in preparation for and negotiation with OFCCP. In his opening comments, Senator Hatch noted: "People are just sick of the federal government, and they are sick of this kind of authority" (U.S. Congress, 1981b, p. 38). A representative from Prudential Insurance Co. estimated that the company's costs related to OFCCP exceeded $5 million a year. He estimated also that the annual cost for all federal contractors exceeded $1 billion. Speaking on the cost issue, another witness cited the Business Round Table survey, "banks spend only one one-hundredth of their gross revenues in establishing and operating their affirmative action programs; OFCCP spends $1.26 in federal revenues to cover each of 40 million workers" (U.S. Congress, 1981b, p. 53).

In a more serious tone, employers noted an adversarial relationship with staff from OFCCP. They complained that they were assumed to be guilty at the beginning of an audit, and that hostile and abrasive attitudes characterized regional staff. They were generally very unhappy with OFCCP, and suggested that compliance might best be accomplished on a voluntary, internal basis unless there were significant evidence of discrimination.

Every witness stressed, as did Senator Hatch, firm belief in the principles of equal opportunity, and most employers testified to their own company's progress in increasing opportunities for women and minorities. They objected to bureaucratic inefficiencies, but beyond that they were deeply offended by what they called "preferential treatment." Most of that concern centers on the use of numerical goals and timetables. This debate over the consequences of compensatory treatment is not new, and has been renewed with vigor in the past few years. Supporters argue that there would be no compliance without sanctions and monitoring by the federal government. They believe that the history of systemic discrimination in the United States indicates the need for more than an "open door" approach. Here the focus shifts from equality of opportunity to equality of results. Do people deserve a "fair shake" or a "fair share" in this society? Will discrimination be remedied according to the level of intent, or by the results of action?

Justice Department, Amicus Curiae

The debate continues in the courts over use of goals and timetables and intent versus effects. The Justice Department articulated the Reagan perspective on limits of civil-rights legislation through media statements and "friend of the court" briefs. William Bradford Reynolds stated: "Where unlawful discrimination exists, the civil rights laws are being enforced to their maximum extent. . . . But we will continue to challenge . . . the remedies of overreaction. Racial quotas in the work force or the schoolroom will not be sought, nor will they be accepted" (Congressional Quarterly . . ., September 17, 1983, p. 1925).

The Justice Department has supported a series of recent challenges to police- and fire-department affirmative action decisions. In one case it was stated: "The federal judge in this case exceeded his authority under the 1964 civil rights law. By so doing, the administration contends, he created a new class of victims, completely innocent of any wrongdoing, by depriving them of their rights under a valid seniority system" (Congressional Quarterly . . ., April 18, 1983, p. 755). The Justice Department has suggested that affirmative-action programs that benefit individuals who themselves were not direct victims of discrimination are unconstitutional. Following that line of reasoning, Senator Hatch proposed a constitutional amendment to prohibit any distinctions based on race, color, or national origin. That amendment would specifically prohibit use of "goals, quotas, timetables, ratios, numerical objectives which make distinctions on account of race, color, or national origin" (U.S. Congress, 1981a, p. 4).

Thus, Reagan's views on affirmative action have permeated all branches of government. His strategy can be outlined as follows. First, get rid of the burdensome paperwork and reporting requirements and shift to voluntary compliance by employers. Second, where an individual is discriminated against, use the full remedies of law to make that individual whole in the legal sense; and in the process eliminate the use of statistics to demonstrate discriminatory effects. Third, eliminate use of goals and timetables, or any mandated numerical approach to increasing employment of women and minorities. These reflect the Reagan ideology: reduce the role for the federal government, narrow the scope of enforcement efforts, and simplify the definition of equality by focusing on access rather than system change.

THE CHANGED: A LOCAL GOVERNMENT CASE STUDY

Reducing the involvement of the federal government in enforcement has an effect on local governments. While the consequences are not as easy to observe as is the case with shifts in direct federal funding, a shift in federal civil rights policy is reflected at the local level. In addition, the articulation of new directions generates a climate for change: As the challenges are made to affirmative action, the perception of what is required may change to follow policy shifts or to anticipate changes in enforcement methods and/or guidelines. Just as reporting requirements and federal court decisions influenced the earlier development of affirmative-action programs, the current administration's efforts to restrict civil-rights enforcement are seen as a message to employers.

Selected for presentation here are the results of a study of Los Angeles city government carried out in 1973–75, with a follow-up in 1983. The passage of ten years provides an opportunity to study the implementation process and raises several questions. The first section displays representation of women and minorities in Los Angeles city employment in 1973 and in 1982. Next is presented the process of policy change over the decade. A final section summarizes the results of two sets of structured interviews with midlevel managers for their views of affirmative action then and now.2

Representation of Women and Minorities: Los Angeles

California not only sent its former governor to the White House, it has led the nation in citizen tax revolts. By the late 1970s, local governments were no longer expanding and were concerned about their fiscal ability to provide basic services. In the nine years between 1973 (the first year that state and local governments were covered by the Civil Rights Act, Title VII) and 1982, there was an overall drop of 9 percent in Los Angeles city employment.3 Table 5.1 illustrates who bore the greatest burden of overall reductions, and also shows the change in representation by race and sex. In 1973, men held 84 percent of the city's jobs, and 64 percent of the total employees were Caucasian. The percentage of women employees went up from 16 percent in 1973 to 20 percent in 1982, while the percentage of men dropped to 80 percent. This decade showed a 14 percent reduction in representation of men, with a 12 percent increase for women. Many more men left (4,875) than women gained jobs (951).

Even greater changes are evident for minorities over this same period. Table 5.1 shows that the percentage of Caucasians went from 64 in 1973 down to 53 percent in 1982, slightly lower than population parity for Caucasians at 58.8 percent. In every category except Caucasian there were increases. With a 9 percent reduction in overall workforce, the City of Los Angeles increased representation of Hispanics by 29 percent, or an increase of 1,611. Their numbers went from 3,879 in 1973 to 5,490 in 1982. The change for blacks in this same period was much less dramatic, with only 97 additional blacks employed, for a 1 percent change over 1973. But in 1973 there were 9,135 blacks employed, more than twice the number of Hispanics in a city population where the percentage of blacks and Hispanics is nearly even. The overall distribution of minorities in the city's workforce has increased substantially.

TABLE 5.1

Los Angeles City Representation of Women and Minorities, 1973 and 1982

| | 1973 | | 1982 | | Change | |
	Number	Percent	Number	Percent	Number	Percent
Citywide totals*	41,621	100	37,956	100	−3,665	−9
Caucasians	26,681	64	20,185	53	−6,496	−24
Blacks	9,135	22	9,232	24	+97	+1
Hispanics	3,879	9	5,490	14	+1,611	+29
Asian Americans	1,659	4	2,185	6	+526	+24
American Indians	267	0.6	376	0.9	+109	+29
Women	6,660	16	7,611	20	+951	+12
Men	34,961	84	30,086	80	−4,875	−14

*Number of employees includes those people who have not identified themselves by race and/or sex.

Source: Derived from Los Angeles City Affirmative Action Program, Appendix F, Numerical Progress 1973–1980, and City of Los Angeles Affirmative Action Audit Report for Fiscal Year 1981–82.

However, these minority employees are not evenly distributed across occupational categories. The vast majority of blacks and Hispanics were concentrated in four categories in 1982: service/maintenance (3,196 blacks and 1,066 Hispanics); skilled crafts (1,492 blacks, 1,092 Hispanics); protective services (1,224 blacks and 1,169 His-

panics); and office/clerical (2,186 blacks and 1,120 Hispanics). Eighty-eight percent of blacks (8,098) and 81
percent of Hispanics (4,447) were employed in these four
categories. In addition, blacks and Hispanics were represented as paraprofessionals, in positions which can feed
into administrative and professional career ladders. Although there are few of these jobs, and minorities hold
less than 40 percent of the positions, these jobs are considered an important part of the city's efforts to increase
opportunities. Fewer than 10 percent of blacks or Hispanics
are employed as administrators, professionals, or techni-
cians. A similar concentration occurs in the employment
of women, and they are employed in an even smaller range
of job titles (Huckle, 1985). Neither women nor minorities
are employed in significant numbers in high-paying or
more powerful levels of this local government.

What Changed? Legal Action and Reaction

The increases did not result from voluntary efforts.
The city's reports on employees was initially required by
the California Fair Employment Practices Commission (CFEPC)
as the result of a discrimination complaint in the late
1960s. Los Angeles city also had the dubious distinction
of being the first city to be sued for discrimination after
the Civil Rights Act was amended to cover state and local
governments in 1972. That case, Los Angeles Department
of Water and Power v. Manhart et al. (1978, 98 S.Ct. 1370)
ended sex discriminatory provisions of the city's retirement
program and challenged the use of sex-based averaging.
Three court-ordered consent decrees also affected
the city's employment practices in the 1970s. All mandate
a numerical remedy of the kind least favored by the Reagan
administration. Imposed in 1977 and in operation through
1987, the Dennison consent decree mandates special examinations for blacks and Hispanics who took a test for
skilled-craft classifications and either failed or scored too
low to be appointed. More than 300 appointments of minorities have been made. The other two consent decrees affect
the police and fire departments. Fifty percent of newly
hired persons for fire-fighter positions must be minorities.
Since the imposition of this numerical remedy in 1975,
minorities have made up about 47 percent of new trainees.

The police department consent decree, agreed to in 1980, covers both women and minorities. The decree requires that 25 percent of each new police officer training class be composed of women, and that 45 percent be composed of blacks and Hispanics, with double counting of minority women permitted. Unlike the Dennison decree, which involved individuals who had been "damaged" and were to be compensated, the fire and police decrees dealt with women and minorities in general. The decrees were based on the assumption of systematic exclusion over time of women and minorities which required compensatory treatment of a class of people, rather than compensation for injured individuals. Given the Justice Department trend away from class-action suits and toward compensation for individuals, it is likely that the two class-based consent decrees will be appealed.

Several factors have affected the institutionalization of affirmative action by Los Angeles. There have been a series of employee complaints, most resolved internally, but a few resulting in court cases. Reporting requirements from several antidiscrimination agencies have become increasingly sophisticated and detailed. During the late 1960s and 1970s, civil-rights and women's organizations became increasingly vocal and the national climate seemed supportive of civil-rights legislation. As agencies clarified expectations on reporting, and the courts spelled out acceptable remedies, the city gradually reviewed its own policies and practices and put in place the structure of affirmative action.

After issuing the now-standard nondiscrimination policy statement, the city moved to review possible barriers. In spite of some initial resistance, the city changed to sex-neutral job titles. EEOC guidelines on treatment of pregnant employees were implemented. Training classes and bridge positions were used to encourage women to enter nontraditional fields. Recruitment efforts in minority communities were intensified, and contacts established with minority and women's organizations. Methods of testing and selection were reviewed to eliminate bias. Orientation sessions for new employees included affirmative-action information, and in-house bulletin boards were used to advertise opportunities.

This was an expensive and long-term process. There were almost no resources allocated to affirmative action prior to 1972. At that time all reporting, investigation of complaints, or attempts at resolution were handled by one full-time employee and several part-timers in the city's Personnel Department. Over the next decade, resources were increased, both in budget and in staff. Nationally, of course, a new field of affirmative-action specialists developed. City staff were assigned to affirmative-action responsibilities, both in the Personnel Department and throughout the workforce as EEO specialists. By the mid-1970s, there was an extensive literature and network of civil-rights specialists with whom to share strategies and strengthen programs.

While support for affirmative action was provided by the courts and guidelines, and staff expertise tended to institutionalize requirements, there were other actors who affected the city's practices. Local minority and women's groups maintained pressure. Participants on various commissions raised questions, criticized practices, undertook independent studies and monitored progress. On an informal basis they required a certain amount of accountability which tended to support affirmative action.

ATTITUDES OF MANAGERS

While the general methodology for this study was open-ended, relying on limited participant/observation, review of historical and current documents and internal reports and interviews with staff, a more structured approach was designed to assess the views of midlevel managers toward affirmative action. Adapted from Kathleen Archibald's study on the Canadian civil service (1970), these interviews were designed to get a perspective on how managers responded to affirmative-action requirements. The results of the two sets of interviews conducted ten years apart are discussed in Huckle (1983). What follows is a summary of comments related to implementation.

In 1973 a selected group of 50 midlevel managers were interviewed, and a similar group interviewed in 1983. Not surprisingly, the samples in both time periods were overwhelmingly white males in their early 50s. In both time periods the majority supervised fewer than 30 employees, although several reported indirect supervision of hundreds. Responses in the two time periods differed in some respects. In 1973 only 30 percent of the managers had attended any training on affirmative action, though all had been invited to do so. Several did not seem to understand legal requirements, and two thought affirmative action related to federal programs such as the street and sewer plan. They responded briefly, indicating that they thought the program would probably increase opportunities for minorities (not mentioning women).[4]

By 1983, a much higher level of sophistication was evident. Not only were the managers able to describe basic provisions in much greater detail, but they also emphasized their own responsibilities as managers for implementation. The 1983 interviewees all stated their belief that affirmative action would have an impact within their own departments; in 1973 they were much less certain.

Two kinds of comments were consistent over the ten years. First, managers in both sets of interviews expressed concern that affirmative-action hiring would conflict with principles of merit. They also connected affirmative action with the likelihood of hiring the "unqualified." Second, both groups expressed their dislike for preferential hiring, even while some acknowledged it might be desirable in order to correct past practices. Comments like these were typical in 1973: "This discriminates against WASP males," ". . . penalizes nonminorities," "I don't like to see it . . . there's so much hanky-panky if it's not civil service." In 1983 the managers responded in a similar way: "Preferences undermine quality and merit," and "You can't rectify the sins of the past overnight."

Overall, the managers in the 1983 interviews seem to have much greater understanding of the affirmative-action provisions and accept its provisions. They, like their colleagues in 1973, resent the implications of "reverse discrimination" against white males and continue to fear possible undermining of the civil service system. The major change observed over the decade is that current supervisors accept their own responsibility for implementation within their particular job sphere.

CONCLUSIONS

There is solace for both sides in this case study. Supporters of affirmative action can point to the three court-ordered consent decrees and annual affirmative-action audits as incentives for increased hiring of women and minorities. Those increases over the decade suggest that the city has internalized equal-opportunity goals, in spite of reductions in overall workforce size. Federal regulation has effected changes in practices and policies. Although women and minorities remain concentrated in a few occupational categories, supporters could claim general progress.

But opponents can take solace from the situation in the Los Angeles study as well. First, it is evident that white males have lost numerical ground as a group. They have dropped in overall capture of jobs. This certainly reflects a cost to some individual white males even where attrition underlies the figures. The competitive pool for hiring has expanded more rapidly for minorities than it has expanded for white males. The latter no longer have a corner on city employment, except in some occupational categories. More than that, we can see confirmation of President Reagan's views in the attitudes of the managers. They too resist affirmative action in their concern about "merit" and fears that the program will lead to hiring of the "unqualified." Like the president, the managers don't like the idea of preferential hiring. They echo his view that compensatory treatment is somehow un-American.

These city managers don't seriously challenge the current use of goals and timetables, nor do they openly resist compliance with reporting requirements. Maybe this just reflects the ease with which bureaucrats adapt to new regulations. If so, affirmative action has been institutionalized by the city in the same way that other new approaches have been adopted. While employees might not like some aspects of a new policy, over time they get used to it or absorb it into their other employment tasks. After a decade of practice, and structural incentives to comply, the managers take the affirmative-action program for granted.

This apparent institutionalization raises the interesting question of how the city might respond to the Reagan administration's efforts to eliminate or restrict the federal role in civil-rights enforcement. As the message transmitted from the national level changes, how will local government respond? Will local governments eliminate affirmative-action programs and move to the Reagan equal access is enough point of view?

It is too early to be certain about the future of affirmative action. Implementation of controversial policies is always a slippery process, marked by constant adjustment and modification (Edwards, 1980; Bardach, 1977).

Changes in the city's workforce are similar to those reported elsewhere: Women and minorities have increased
overall representation but continue to be concentrated in a
few occupational categories (see Cayer and Schaefer, 1981;
Clynch and Gaudin, 1982; Hall and Saltzstein, 1977; Eribes
et al., 1984, among others). Policies and practices have
been changed; EEO staff have a professional, vested interest in retention of the programs; local groups continue to
monitor and pressure for increased opportunities. These
would suggest that affirmative action will not easily be
eliminated at this point.

The range of structural changes, slowly implemented,
is now very much part of "business as usual." To the extent that reporting systems are computerized and perceived
as useful tools to both managers and personnel department
analysts, they are likely to be retained. The only sign
of response to the president's new agenda is in the challenge to use of numerical remedies reflected in the city's
consent decrees. If the Justice Department is successful
in its attempts to eliminate their use, or severely limit
their use to cases of individual harm from discrimination,
the city is likely to appeal their current consent decrees.
If that appeal is successful, it would effectively close
down that particular affirmative-action strategy.

The federal/local government interaction is always
complicated. If President Reagan is successful in neutral-
izing affirmative action, employers are likely to respond
unevenly. Where equal-opportunity goals have been internalized and structured into the bureaucracy, they will
be difficult to eliminate quickly. In the case of local
governments, the likelihood of change is also affected by
the local political climate. In a city like Los Angeles,
with a large and organized minority community, political
pressure can be brought on the city to continue affirmative-
action programs in spite of changes at the federal level.
The question is whether that set of local pressures, coupled
with structural changes within the bureaucracy, plus
raised expectations of women and minorities, will be sufficient to overcome the backward swing of the equal-
opportunity pendulum. It would be naive to believe that
affirmative action in its present form is immutable, but
there are a series of forces at work in addition to a national administration which wishes to turn back the clock.
If the national climate changes enough, or is perceived to
have changed drastically, then affirmative action as we

have come to understand it over the past 15 years will no longer exist. At the moment, there seems to be an uneasy balance of forces.

NOTES

1. In addition to the Civil Rights Commission's oversight reports on the federal government's civil-rights efforts (1971, 1972, 1973, and 1977), the CRC has published a series of general reports on discrimination. Two have been criticized by opponents as examples of overreach: Affirmative Action in the 1980's: Dismantling the Process of Discrimination (November 1981) and Women: Still in Poverty (July 1979).

2. Funding for the 1973–75 research was provided by the University of Southern California Center for Urban Affairs and the Ford Foundation. San Diego State University provided financial support in 1983.

3. Most of this reduction was accomplished through "managed attrition," through voluntary departures from city employment, terminations, and retirements. (L.A. Audit Report 1981–82)

4. The more than hour-long interviews with the midlevel managers were conducted by M. St. Germaine and J. Short in 1983, and by M. Rosentraub and F. Bish in 1974.

REFERENCES

Archibald, K. 1970. Sex and the Public Service. Ottawa, Canada: Queen's Printer.

Bardach, E. 1977. The Implementation Game. Cambridge, Mass.: MIT Press.

Bawden, D., and J. Palmer. 1984. "Social Policy: Challenging the Welfare State." In The Reagan Record, edited by J. Palmer and I. Sawhill. Washington, D.C.: Urban Institute.

Cayer, N. Joseph, and Roger C. Schaefer. 1981. "Affirmative Action and Municipal Employees." Social Science Quarterly 62 (September): 487–94.

Clynch, E. J., and Carol A. Gaudin. 1982. "Sex in the Shipyards: An Assessment of Affirmative Action Policy." Public Administration Review 42 (March/April): 114-21.

Congressional Quarterly Weekly Review. April 18, 1983, September 17, 1983, and December 10, 1983. Washington, D.C.

Edwards, G. 1980. Implementing Public Policy. Washington, D.C.: Congressional Quarterly Press.

Eribes, R. A., A. Karnig, N. J. Cayer, and S. Welch. 1984. "Women in Municipal Bureaucracies." Paper presented at the annual Western Political Science Conference. Sacramento, Calif.

Firing Line. 1983. "Debate: Resolved: That Affirmative Action Goals for Women and Minorities Should Be Abolished." Southern Educational Communications Association.

Hall, Grace, and Alan Saltzstein. 1977. "Equal Employment Opportunity for Minorities in Municipal Government." Social Science Quarterly 57 (March): 874-72.

Huckle, Patricia. 1975. "Local Government Employment of Women: Opportunities, Policies and Practices." Ph.D. dissertation, University of Southern California.

_____. 1983. "A Decade's Difference: Mid-Level Managers and Affirmative Action." Public Personnel Management 12(3) (Fall): 249-57.

_____. 1985. "Whatever Happened to Affirmative Action? Employment of Women, L.A. City, Dept. Water & Power, 1973-83." Review of Public Personnel Administration (Fall).

U.S., Congress, Senate. 1981a. "Affirmative Action and Equal Protection." Hearings before the Subcommittee on the Constitution of the Committee on the Judiciary, Serial No. J-97-24.

_____. 1981b. "Oversight of the Activities of the Office of Federal Contract Compliance Programs of the Department of Labor." Hearings before the Committee on Labor and Human Resources. July, October, and December.

_____. 1982. "Oversight of the Equal Employment Opportunity Commission." Hearing before the Committee on Labor and Human Resources.

_____. 1983. "Civil Rights Commission Reauthorization." Hearing before the Subcommittee on the Constitution of the Committee on the Judiciary on S. 1189, J-98-62.

Williams, Walter. 1984. "Implementation and Social Policy: The Macro/Micro Balance." Paper presented at the Annual Western Political Science Conference. Sacramento, Calif.

6

Economic Differentiation, Growth Centers, and the Failure of National Economic Policy

Lyke Thompson

INTRODUCTION

Conflict is an ever-present part of U.S. cities. Often conflict is submerged or it is channeled through the normal processes of local government. Then too there are the episodes of overt conflict that lead to confrontations in the courts or on the streets (National Advisory . . ., 1968). Some would argue that the periods of overt conflict lead to either the suppression or resolution of conflict. Then periods of increasing covert conflict lead on to periods of overt protest or violence (Piven and Clowart, 1971).

The roots of urban conflict are based in racial and ethnic differences, economic disparities, and geographical competition. Conflict is especially intense when these differences are greatest and greater still when these disparities overlap. That is, when racial groups increasingly diverge economically and occupy distinctly different communities, the conflict potential increases. This conflict potential is high and increasing now.[1]

Over the last decade, through both conservative Democratic and Republican administrations, the United States has experienced increasing economic disparities that are both racially and geographically focused.[2] No recent national administrations have designed effective policies to decrease the disparities or the distances. And the Reagan administration has actively sought to undermine the few relatively ineffective policies that benefited poor people or minority groups (Congressional . . ., 1984a, 1984b; Pear, 1983; U.S., House . . ., 1984). The Reagan administration's policies ended many social programs and decreased (in real terms) the funding of others (Congressional . . ., 1984a, 1984b). Their policies have decreased the taxes of the rich and increased the relative burden of all others. The number of poor people has increased and unemployment levels have remained high even after the end of the recession. The Reagan policymakers have probably succeeded in increasing disparities, but even more importantly they have sought to eliminate the avenues of civilized protest by undermining the legal-services movement and affirmative action. Thus, we are within an era of increasing covert conflict, conflict that may become violent if pressures continue to build.

This chapter attempts to discuss one theory about the processes that increasingly differentiate areas and groups within our cities. It attempts to show that there is no necessary stabilization of this differentiation. It also suggests that similar processes or differentiation occur between regions, and the differences between regional systems are no more stable than those in cities. These processes are dangerous to the nation, especially in a political environment where conflict is suppressed as rapidly as it is created. Therefore, considerable attention is paid to methods of undermining the differentiation, thus short-circuiting conflict before more violence emerges.

GROWTH CENTERS

The general process through which differences are increased and conflicts of interest created is the economic-growth process. Although it is not necessarily so, economic growth in the United States is increasingly differential. While one region expands, another contracts. Recently there have been stark disparities in the distribution of economic growth across industrial sectors, geographic regions, within states and even within cities. To some extent, the processes that produce these disparities are driven by the availability of natural resources combined with technological change and the resources of an area's population. Chance certainly plays a role. However, there are two sets of factors that contribute to these processes which are important, but not fully considered or accepted. One factor is the internal and cumulative nature of the economic-growth process itself, which produces a tendency for capital to converge upon successful areas or industries. This produces growth poles or growth centers. A second factor is the increasing ability of developers of regions, cities, and areas of cities to orchestrate the availability of factors of production so as to partly rationalize the achievement of economic growth. That is, there exists a rapidly increasing ability to create growth centers intentionally.

A central purpose of this chapter is to discuss how the interaction of these two growth factors leads to differentiation, inequality, and segregation. These effects will be shown within cities and across city systems. Certain commonalities are noted between growth processes at these levels and in the way the growth process is being rationalized. Finally, the chapter will suggest a new public-sector role in controlling the creation and distribution of growth so as to reduce inequalities and conflict.

Intra-city Growth Poles

One commonly accepted point from the literature on the growth of cities is that there are substantial differences in the location of industrial, commercial, and residential growth within cities (Bourne, 1971). Considering only residential growth, the physical dimension of this form of growth is typically concentrated at the periphery in the cities of the United States. This is especially so if we look at the physical construction of new dwellings. If, however, the physical aspect is controlled by removing the effect of distance from city center, a very different pattern begins to emerge (Thompson, 1981). Investment, measured as the change in value of capital stock from one period to another, can be seen to be closely related to the income and racial characteristics of neighborhoods. However, even the effects of these variables disappear if we use growth in past periods as a predictor of growth in future periods. Future investment is positively related with past investment. That is to say, that growth in housing investment appears to include a cumulative growth process, a form of growth that has been noted in other studies of cities (Oates et al., 1971). High-investment neighborhoods get ever more investment; low investment, ever less.

The dynamics of this process are not fully clear, but a body of theory called growth-pole theory is useful in explaining this phenomenon. The theory was developed by scholars who have studied growth processes in third-world countries (Kuklinski, 1972). Growth-pole theory argues that growth in regions tends to focus on certain crucial, propulsive industries, such as the microprocessor industries of Silicon Valley. Once a pattern of high investment has established itself in and around these propulsive industries, these areas act as investment magnets, drawing ever more investment from outlying regions. Negative growth poles or areas of decline are created where many investors recognize decline and choose to relocate their capital elsewhere.

In discussions about growth-center theory, there are several critical concepts which form the basis for theory. The first concept is the "kick," or initial conditions that start the cumulative process in a particular direction. In the case of François Perroux's original growth-pole model (1970), the kick was an innovation or some degree of oligopoly. Oligopolists might trigger the process as they use their power in economy to draw in their suppliers to their own location, perhaps to lower their costs. The Japanese and, now, American automakers' use of "just-in-time production" is an example. Expectations are critical. If a particular structure or set of events is to supply a kick, it will do so only to the extent that it alters investors' expectations. If expectations are altered, then investors will perceive chances of higher returns around a particular locale and the accumulation of investment will begin. Second, there is the concept of cumulative causation, which says that the advantages accrued by one area in the first time period give it a head start over other areas in attracting resources in a second or future time period. This initial advantage allows that area to draw ever more resources for its growth. The notion of cumulative causation is well established in the economic literature (Tinbergen, 1973), general-systems theory (Maruyama, 1963), and sociology (Blalock, 1969). The basis of this cumulative process lies in investors' rational reliance on past patterns of growth to structure their expectations and, thus, their investments.

The second important concept is that of externalities. What would attract resource owners to invest or people to come or businesses to locate near a growth center, if they could not benefit from the growth? It is through such externalities as agglomeration economies or linkages that most of the benefits of growth are spread. Linkages exist as networks of actors or businesses that make products which are critical to the growth process. So we would expect to find a dense network of businesses around a growth pole, which helps to generate the growth and benefits from trickle-down effects.

The third critical concept is friction. Whether thinking in terms of physical distance, economic distance, or social distance, travel across this distance implies friction, a slowing down, a narrowing of the spread of effects. An example may help. If computers are the propulsive industry in the model, then businesses tightly linked to computers are likely to benefit from the trickle-down of growth effects. Thus some businesses may be economically distant, some may be economically and physically distant, and some may be economically, physically, and socially distant. Benefits for the last will obviously be the least.

One can use growth-pole theory to offer a more comprehensive view of the policy problem of housing disinvestment as well as housing overinvestment. The alternative explanations commonly used to explain disinvestment in urban housing—racism or income differences—actually supply excellent examples of the initial conditions or kick starting the cumulative-growth process, which creates a negative growth center. If differences in incomes between whites and blacks once existed or if racist lending practices existed, though they may or may not exist now, these differences could easily have supplied the initial condition for the discounting of investments in homeownership in minority communities. After this initial discounting, minority communities would later be discounted as areas for investment, based on their past failure to attract investments.

Segregation provides the friction that separates positive centers and areas of decline. For example, in Dallas, separate professional associations still exist for black and white real-estate brokers, creating a separate real-estate sales network in the black community. The existence of such a network makes it easy for minorities to search for a home within the minority community, and less likely that they will stray outside that community. Segregation in housing has actually increased in recent decades (Farley, 1977). This segregation and the separate real-estate networks form the continuing basis of a dual housing market. This is reinforced by the relatively higher concentration of FHA than conventional mortgage lending in minority communities. Real-estate agents continue to steer minorities and whites to separate sections of town (Pearce, 1979). Individually, most white households and some black households avoided moving into integrated neighborhoods (Katzman and Chiles, 1979). Thus, residential choice processes of households helped recreate segregation. The effect of this pattern of segregation in the growth-pole model is to sever linkages to growth centers.

Racism, then, can provide initial conditions that give majority areas an advantage and minority areas a disadvantage. Segregation acts as a form of friction, increasing distance between the markets, and preventing a leveling out. A third general aspect of a growth-center theory of home investment is the real-estate network. It is through this network that externalities of growth centers are passed to linked firms. This real-estate network includes developers, builders, lenders, and brokers. These actors decide, in some cases independently, where new homeownership opportunities will occur and, in other cases, influence home buyers through suggestions and by structuring of household choices (Hempel, 1969). When these real-estate market firms make their own investment decisions or influence household investment decisions, they do so based on their perception of an area's prospects. Their best indicator of future performance is likely to be past performance. Thus, these firms and their recommendations to households focus investment around positive growth centers, creating cumulative growth.

Investment in homeownership is dependent upon the quality of the institutional network intended to deliver homeownership. If that network is absent or of low quality, it will be that much harder to produce homeownership, both because access of households to services will be reduced and because there will be fewer influential land-based interests pushing for investment in that area. To the extent that a network exists, expands, and elaborates, so will investment in that community become more institutionalized and reinforced. At the same time, however, investment in the network will also be influenced by past success that an area has had in attracting investment. Thus, investments in the network may reinforce and institutionalize the cumulative growth processes already set in motion.

There is evidence that the investment in homeownership in one urban area in the 1950s and 1960s did follow
this kind of cumulative model (Thompson, 1981). Analysis
of U.S. census data tended to indicate that racial composition of neighborhoods was strongly and independently related to investment in the 1950s. However, in the 1960s,
the effect of race disappeared if previous investment patterns were considered. That is, investment appeared to
collect around certain poles that were related to race by
past investment decisions. Relative values declined in
areas of low past investment, as predicted by a growth-
pole model. In addition, further analysis indicated that
the same pattern existed for the location of real-estate
firms during the same time periods. Thus, both investments in homeownership and real-estate market infrastructure appeared to follow cumulative growth patterns, insti-
tutionalizing the past effects of explicitly racist behavior.

Conversely, if one concentrates their focus on the
positive growth poles within modern U.S. cities, they can
be portrayed as "growth machines" (Molotch, 1976). In
these areas, tightly knit groups of businesspersons and
community boosters evolve strategies of competing for growth.
Typically, this has been portrayed as an alliance of largely self-interested actors in which leadership is either held
by private developers or is loosely distributed among the
actors. Their success is heavily dependent on innovation,
defined either as copying new approaches used elsewhere
or inventing new structures for funding development or attracting residents. Increasingly, development firms are
evolving the capability to plan, build, and market whole
residential communities on the periphery of major cities.
The significance of such new communities lies especially in
that it represents the full rationalization of the development of growth poles within particular organizations. This
represents the routinized and successful manipulation of
expectations of both homebuyer and institutional investors,
such that growth centers are created rather than evolved.

There are several reasons for the emergence of these
increasingly successful growth machines. The first and
most crucial factor is the increasing capability of the
largest developers to manage large projects by coordinating
large numbers of subcontractors. The special accomplish-
ment is the standardization of the tasks, thus controlling
the uncertainty with which each subcontractor must deal.
Second, the technology of housing construction and real-

estate development has become more automated and modular-
ized, thus permitting and demanding increasing scale.
Third, project management techniques have advanced substantially the ability of developers to handle large-scale
projects. Fourth, as the capability to increase scale expands so also does the developer's ability to capture the
positive externalities or spread effects of creating a growth
center. This fourth point provides the motivation to rationalize the process more by generating substantial sur-
plus payments to those who succeed.

Inter-city Competition

Growth-center theory was first applied to discuss
unequal growth among regions and among cities. Thus, it
seems appropriate to use the framework to discuss disparate
growth; in particular, this section will attempt to portray
both positive and negative growth centers. It will also
attempt to differentiate between those types of cumulative
growth processes which can be directed by local policy as
opposed to those that are well beyond that control.
When François Perroux originally proposed the notion of growth poles he spoke of cumulative growth around
propulsive or "motor" industries. These industries were
characterized by high levels of innovation, declining relative costs, and substantial external economies. Perroux
did not speak of growth poles in a geographical sense,
but rather as concentrations of economic activity in "economic space." Economic space is a general concept which
can encompass more particular dimensions of economic activity, such as across sectors or geography. The distinction is not trivial to the consideration of the development
of cities in a growth-center context. In fact, this is a
central point, especially in a time when physical space is
having an ever-decreasing influence upon economic activity
because of the increasing comprehensiveness and speed of
communication and transportation. Put more pointedly,
growth centers are now developing in industries and across
industries without substantial physical concentration.
These may be called sectorally centered growth poles as
opposed to physically centered growth poles. Both forms
of growth centers are emerging, but local development
policies are likely to have differing levels of influence
depending on the type of center.

SECTORAL CENTERS

The sectorally centered growth pole is especially likely to occur with regard to technological innovations. Physical technologies are likely to be tightly linked to other technologies. Changing a physical technology also requires changing the machines which produce the new technology. The ripple effects of a revolution in one technology are likely to travel through sets of related technologies, which are probably close in sectoral space, but not necessarily in terms of physical space. Even where they are concentrated in space so as to take advantage of a labor pool or information exchange, the growth process is well beyond the ability of local economic development agencies to control (Oakey, 1981). These agencies may attempt to reinforce, latch onto, or even limit these processes of growth or decline but the degree of control is not likely to be substantial.

There are clear examples of negative growth poles in the current restructuring of U.S. economy. Steel is perhaps the most obvious example of sectorally centered cumulative decline. Steel's decline probably began with disruptions in production from repeated strikes that permitted foreign competition to gain a foothold in the market. These overseas competitors, with very low labor costs relative to those of U.S. steel, could produce at lower costs. Moreover, they were producing from relatively newer facilities. However, the cumulative process of decline came in recent years as expectations of managers of leading domestic firms switched to the negative, and disinvestment began in earnest.[3] This point was driven home by the U.S. Steel Corporation's decision to begin diversifying into other industries. This decline has also been substantially insensitive to local policies, proceeding apace despite many local efforts to arrest it. Plant-closing legislation and even substantial wage cuts have not been sufficient to stop the decline. Decisions to close plants are made in central offices with limited concern for local impacts because the survival of firms or networks of linked firms are the determinant.

An example of a positive, sectorally centered growth pole is the expansion of microelectronics industry. The expansion of this industry has been the product of industrial innovations. These innovations have not occurred randomly in economic or physical space, but neither has this industry's growth been significantly affected by local industrial policies. The most dominant public influence on the development of the microelectronic industry has been concentrations of skill and capital, usually in connection with monopoly situations (Bell Laboratories) or defense contracts. Thus, the growth in semiconductors has been centered in and around firms that are closely connected with the defense establishment or large research institutions.

The real kick or takeoff for cumulative growth, however, began with the development of microcomputers for home and business. At least two factors required that this growth would also be concentrated and cumulative, though somewhat more spread. First, the complexity of these machines is immense to the uninitiated. Market entrance was difficult. Much of the knowledge was tightly held in patents and copyrights. Second, the speed of change in the market and technology was extremely high, imposing high development costs on those not already in the market. These factors constitute the friction which prevented employment benefits from trickling out to many areas.

In its early development microelectronics was structured at these two levels--chip production and microcomputer production. Both were relatively concentrated within a narrow set of firms and a narrow set of locations. Tightly held knowledge acted as a constriction on spread effects, while sudden consumer adoption of video games and microcomputers provided the kick to start the cumulative growth process. A tightly concentrated network of suppliers, producers, and marketers evolved in Silicon Valley of Cupertino, Calif., and in the Boston area and other sites. However, this occurred largely beyond the control of local economic developers. The concentration began to dissipate when the software market began to develop. Computer programming was a much more widely distributed and accessible skill than the design of integrated circuits or the interfacing of such circuits to make a microcomputer. Also, as much as half of the money spent on home or office systems is for software. The result was a profusion of packaged software disks and cartridges produced by a plethora of firms. Through this means, a network of suppliers of software was created for each of the various major microcomputers. This began to deconcentrate or spread the effects of growth in this industry. Thus, what began as a concentrated, cumulative growth process became a more deconcentrated one.

A critical point to recognize in this sectorally centered form of cumulative growth process is that an industrial innovation model provides a bandwagon that local entities can try to get aboard by persuading some leading firm to come to their city. However, innovation is not a process that can be influenced substantially at the local or even the state level. Innovation within a particular sector or industry is sufficiently random and locationally idiosyncratic that it cannot be used to produce local growth. Likewise, once this process begins it will be difficult to maneuver because of the dependencies upon locationally specific labor skills (Oakey, 1981).

The primary means by which microelectronics has achieved high rates of growth is through the technology's ability to reduce the costs of users. That is, the technology permits users to do the same task as before at substantially lower cost or do more at the same cost. This ability attracts more demand as well as more investment, which permits more research and development, leading to even greater cost reductions for users. The cycle repeats itself. Given that costs were a critical initiator of the growth cycle, if one can find other means of decreasing costs dramatically, then cumulative growth may be initiated short of hard technological innovation. This is evident, for example, in the cumulative processes that are initiated in areas surrounding a newly discovered mineral deposit. However, such windfalls are unpredictable. What is not so unpredictable and may be somewhat controllable are the linkages of firms to the local economy.

LOCAL CENTERS

Businesses commonly recognize their linkage to related firms, both those that use their products and those that produce the supplies that go into making those products. Businesses are equally, if not more dependent upon the local communities in which they reside for a supply of labor and land, for the provision of transportation facilities, and for a host of other services. Many of the costs of these services or resources are substantially beyond the control of local entities, but increasingly communities are coming to recognize their ability to structure costs in systematic ways. Since the 1930s, Southern industrial developers have tried dozens of techniques of manipulating local costs to attract industry (Cobb, 1982). The impact of these has been mixed, and much of the literature is pessimistic. However, it is becoming increasingly evident that by long-term, concerted implementation of strategies of development, states, especially, can affect rates of development and create growth centers. In particular, this is accomplished by manipulating costs, availability of crucial resources, and reduction of crucial uncertainties.

One premier example of this is the Research Triangle in North Carolina's Raleigh, Durham, and Chapel Hill areas. The Research Triangle Park is a 5,800-acre tract located close to an airport with railroad and major highway access nearby. Begun in 1957, the park now has 34 firms with an employment of more than 20,000. The park is dedicated to research and development, though there is also an element of manufacturing production in the park. The Research Triangle is especially interesting for its particular mixture of private and public action. Though not originally his idea, the late North Carolina governor, Luther Hodges, was the central force behind the formation of the park. Instead of making it a state endeavor, Hodges sought private donations, first for the purchase and then the initial development of the park. He and other initiators created a foundation to control the development of the park. Then, along with the traditional industrial development incentives of lowered land prices, industrial-development bonds, and tax abatement, the promoters took two other approaches. First, they built relationships among three area universities and the firms locating at the park. This permitted firms to externalize large portions of the risk of research, while also creating access to pools of skills that would not otherwise be available. Second, the proponents, especially Hodges, sought out federal research laboratories to reinforce and cement the research focus of the park. Finally, by landing a major IBM research facility, they were able to get the critical mass or trigger for the cumulative growth process. Since then, the growth in jobs has roughly followed an exponential curve.

The Dallas–Fort Worth Airport provides a second example. The airport is owned jointly by the cities of Dallas and Fort Worth. The airport as a piece of land is vastly larger than is necessary for the airport as a facility. This is ostensibly because of the need for future expansion and for noise protection. Regardless of the original reason for purchasing the thousands of additional acres, they provide a huge reserve of industrial land owned by the airport. The airport board, appointed by the two cities, but substantially independent, has proceeded vigorously to develop the land. Given that it is city land, they cannot sell it, but rather must lease it. Moreover, since it remains city property, revenue-bond authority may be used to finance totally any buildings or facilities constructed there. Additionally, on one section of the airport, the administration has developed inland port facilities, where products can be brought through customs or even processed without paying duties. This is done at a location where the conjunction of airport aprons, railroads, freeways, and warehousing permit extremely rapid intermodal transfer at low cost. Again, all facilities are airport-owned, and paid for through lease arrangements.

In this case, the airport developers have made it possible for a firm to reduce intermodal transfer costs to the minimum as well as to keep all their capital in operating machinery (airplanes). They have eliminated the peripheral uncertainties associated with owning buildings. By oversizing the air-transportation facilities (runways and aprons) and highways into the airport, the uncertainties associated with congestion are minimized. Again, the airport has triggered very rapid growth both within its borders and around its periphery.

What is common to and important about these situations is the rational and intensive effort to manipulate the factors of production in ways so as to make certain locales substantially more competitive than they had any potential of being without systematic public-private intervention. In the Dallas-Fort Worth case, the airport is taking over and reducing or controlling uncertainties of transportation cost, capital cost, regulatory cost, and land cost in a systematic way that permits firms to concentrate on their core technology in a way they would not otherwise be able to do. That is, they are able to externalize onto a public entity many of the uncertainties of their operation. The same phenomenon is occurring in the Research Triangle, where the proximity to universities permits research firms to reduce a number of critical uncertainties in a dramatic way. First, research skills that are only occasionally needed can, in essence, be borrowed from the universities through consulting arrangements. Second, more frequently used skills can be developed by the universities in students who can be hired by the firms. Third, the campus environment, in which a relatively free exchange is maintained, with its synergy, is maintained both by the concentration of research firms in close proximity, but also by the proximity of the universities.

The relevance of growth-pole theory to these situations is direct. For in both the Research Triangle and the Dallas-Fort Worth Airport cases, we see intentional manipulation of economic factors to trigger a pattern of cumulative growth in an area. Though there are dozens of cases of failure for each of these cases of success, it is quite obvious that public and nonprofit entities are working with for-profit firms to create growth centers through the reduction and containment of uncertainties for firms in particular areas. In both cases we can see that major public or nonprofit investments, targeted to reduce costs of critical factors of production, triggered a process of cumulative growth.

Both in the growth competition within cities and among cities, some players have accumulated capital, skills, and knowledge that permit them to create successfully what are in essence areal combines. These combines or as Molotch called them, growth machines, are characterized by spatially sensitive uncertainties and costs. These differ by context. In housing, they are especially related to homebuyers' concerns about neighborhood quality and the availability of an easily used network of agents and lenders. In research parks, the critical uncertainties have to do with the availability of crucial skills. In the airport case, the more general uncertainties of capital investment and transportation costs were controlled. By controlling these uncertainties and by intentionally creating positive agglomeration economies through the grouping of classes of economic activity, these actors make activity less costly and potentially more effective. Once a critical mass or a trigger of the cumulative growth process occurs, it proceeds on its own pace.

The most important point to be taken from the previous two sections is that the rational creation of growth centers draws talent, resources, and wealth from other areas. Some of these other areas become centers of negative growth--that is, decline. That is to say, economic decline is partly a by-product of the rational creation of growth centers. Decline need not necessarily be the case

but it often is. This is more readily seen in the intra-
urban than in the interurban case. There is a large and
growing literature discussing drastic differences in intra-
urban mortgage investment, investment in retail and commercial networks, job creation, and provision of public
services. Though this chapter has concentrated on mortgage investment, the argument might be just as defensible
in these other areas.

The linkage of regional growth centers to regional
centers of decline is probably less direct. The original
causes of the recent regional decline in the Northeast and
Midwest were independent of those of regional growth in
the Southwest. Whatever the trigger, however, there is a
cumulative hemorrhage of resources--human, physical, and
capital--from the Northeast to the Southwest. This is
abetted by Reagan administration policies that reinforce
the defense and related industries centered in the Southwest at the expense of industries located elsewhere. It is
reinforced also by refusal to support ailing industries in
the Midwest.

The second major implication of these theories is
that encouragement of positive growth centers can become a
strategy of differentiation. The effects of growth-center
creation can be to increasingly concentrate wealth and
poverty, skill, and ignorance, along with investment and
disinvestment, in different locales. That is, it may create
the conditions that expand differences, increase economic,
physical, and social distances and, thus, exacerbate conflicts of interest. Again, this need not necessarily be the
case, but it is clearly the case in the growth encouraged
by Reagan policies.

The third implication may explain the Reagan administration's behavior. For the concentration of growth
in Southern and Western states or in suburban areas of
all major cities is a strategy that builds to Republican
strength. It may be a strategy that helps create a Republican realignment. However, the problem is that such
a strategy pits one part of a city against another, and
one region against another.

Clearly then, growth-center strategies can be conflict producing and sectional. It can create schisms that
are nation breaking. Paradoxically though, a more balanced growth-center strategy might have the opposite effects. The next section lays the groundwork for such a
strategy.

META-ENTREPRENEURSHIP

A major argument in previous sections was that public, nonprofit, and private developers have created or learned techniques to initiate cumulative growth. These developers are performing three new functions. The first is to control uncertainties to help firms thrive by concentrating on their special area of expertise. The second is to subsidize directly or make available factors of production so as to increase the opportunities for entrepreneurship. This complements the traditional local role in economic development of providing infrastructure, utilities, and roads. The third function is capturing externalities by creating larger-scale developments in which the spread effects of cumulative growth are capitalized by the initiators. This effect is strongest in the Research Triangle case, but apparent even in the suburban residential case.

Performing these new functions clarifying areas of probable success and then encouraging that success by manipulation of the growth process, these functions create the preconditions of entrepreneurship. As this occurs prior to and is necessary for entrepreneurship, it can be labeled meta-entrepreneurship. This communicates the notion that entrepreneurship itself will not exist except under conditions created by public or public-private action. However, the term also seeks to communicate that economic development in the modern context is an active function in and of itself. Further, it should be clear that this meta-entrepreneurial function is interactive with entrepreneurship, reacting and adapting to the class of possible and probable opportunities for business endeavor in a particular community.

The tasks of meta-entrepreneurship extend substantially beyond the traditional roles of entrepreneurship. First, the task is not simply one of combining resources for one business, but for a large number of them. Secondly, it involves identifying and containing crucial uncertainties for a class of firms, not for one firm. Third, it usually involves dealing with a whole set of uncertainties which other forms of entrepreneurship can treat as constant--political uncertainties. That is, the meta-entrepreneur must also have the skills of what Lewis (1980) calls public entrepreneurship. He or she must, while building programs, build constituencies, negotiate commitments, and manage public opinion. Indeed, then, the tasks of meta-entrepreneurship are both more myriad, more general, and more complex than traditional entrepreneurship. As such, their successful performance requires great skill, large financial resources, and substantial access to pools of authority.

POLICIES

In cities and regions increasingly characterized by differential cumulative growth, the skills, resources, and authority necessary to successful meta-entrepreneurship are not evenly distributed. However, if meta-entrepreneurship is a reproducible skill, this need not necessarily be the case. Rather, the patterns of success can be copied, adapted, and used to aid the very areas that are becoming negative-growth centers because of Reagan administration policies. In fact, the administration's policies are likely to provide the motivation to do so. This is because the conflict bred from policies encouraging differential growth can be suppressed only so long in the current system of government in the United States. If the general economy improves, the conflict can be abated and ignored, but a second recession which concentrates pain as specifically the same groups, areas of cities, and regions will lead to more overt conflict.

Many of the debates will no doubt center on such terms as "industrial policy" and "jobs programs." Yet it is crucial that the debate be refocused on the underlying cumulative-growth processes that produce these disparities. Further, the discussion must center on balancing the distribution of growth not by injuring areas of positive growth but by creating new growth centers in areas experiencing negative growth.

A national economic policy could be elaborated that both equalizes growth, is politically viable, and is unity creating. Such a program would use regional redistribution to create growth poles in lagging areas, using meta-entrepreneurial strategies. One conceptualization of such a program might include these elements:

-A joining of all federal economic-development grants into one program which is administered by the states as a block grant. The funds would be distributed according to a formula whereby the ten states with the

worst combined unemployment and discouraged-worker
rates are given 35 percent of the money and the next
worst ten get 20 percent. The remainder is divided
evenly among the other states.
-The money is then distributed in a similarly progres-
sive fashion within the states to counties or metropolitan areas with greatest problems. These first two
provisions would supply enough money to hardest-hit
locales to be able to significantly alter investor expectations and to create the massive doses necessary to
trigger cumulative growth.
-Each receiving entity would have to create or demonstrate the existence of a meta-entrepreneurial network
to qualify for funds.
-These actors would have to agree to training or to
qualify to a certain level of economic-development technical skill.
-The locales would have to invest in at least two growth
centers, one community-residential center in a disin-
vested neighborhood and one commercial-industrial
center.
-The locales would have to produce annual strategic
plans and schemes to leverage public investment in
each center.
-The industrial strategies would be required to center
at least 50 percent of their dollars on high-growth industrial sectors not currently dominant in the locale so
as to diversify the local economy.
-At least 60 percent of the money must be spent on persons who have qualified for unemployment in the last
year. This would prevent the oversubsidization of
capital that is now endemic to economic-development
programs.
-No area would be funded for less than four or more
than six years.
-Over 80 percent of the funds must be used to aid or
create self-sustainable economic entities that continue
to produce new employment without significant subsidies.
These may be public or private, profit or nonprofit.

Beyond these and a few other provisions localities
would be free to design their own growth machines, even
to join together to create combines. Like any other program,
this approach would have its failures. However, it could
and should create growth centers in the most distressed areas.
It could and should attract investors who will expand the

initial governmental investment. It might well take areas a few years to develop coherent meta-entrepreneurial strategies, but sunset provisions would force fast action.

Politically, this program is feasible because it does combine a redistributive dimension with a distributive one. All these states get something; and all have the assurance that if their key industry is the next to decline they will get the help needed. Finally, unlike current policies, the program is conflict reducing rather than conflict producing and nation enhancing rather than nation breaking.

NOTES

1. No major nationwide studies of segregation have been conducted of studying segregation indices since the 1980 census. Several studies have been conducted on individual cities that appear to indicate a stabilization or, in some cases, a decline in segregation indices. However, some studies based on the 1970 census indicated some declines in segregation, while others indicated increases (Van Valey et al., 1977; Farley, 1977). What is more clear, however, is that minority unemployment has remained extraordinarily high in comparison to whites through the recession and beyond. In particular, the ratio of black or minority unemployment to white unemployment has been on the rise since 1977 and throughout the Reagan administration. See Employment and Earnings, November 1984, 1982, 1980.

2. First, unemployment has impacted minority communities more heavily, and the last several administrations have seemed willing to accept increasingly higher unemployment. Second, unemployment has taken on much stronger regional disparities with the Northeast and Midwest experiencing high rates at the same time the Southwest had relatively lower rates. Third, minorities have grown poorer more rapidly than whites (U.S. Department of Commerce, 1983, p. 20).

3. The decline of the steel industry is a sad one. Recently it has been especially sad because of the obvious disinvestment syndrome that has gripped the industry. U.S. Steel has taken what profits it has had and invested them in Marathon Oil to the point where it has been financially strapped (see Business Week, September 27, 1982). Steel plants are regularly closed rather than reconstructed

(Business Week, May 31, 1982). Capital is "bled away" to pay operating costs (Business Week, August 9, 1982).

REFERENCES

Blalock, Hubert M., Jr. 1969. Theory Construction. Englewood Cliffs, N.J.: Prentice-Hall.

Bourne, Larry S., ed. 1971. Internal Structure of the City: Readings on Space and Environment. New York: Oxford University Press.

Cobb, James C. 1982. The Selling of the South. Baton Rouge, La.: Louisiana State University.

Congressional Budget Office. 1984a. Effects of Major Cuts in Individual Taxes in 1981 and 1982 for Households in Different Income Categories. Washington, D.C.: Government Printing Office. March.

_____. 1984b. The Combined Effects of Major Changes in Federal Taxes and Spending Since 1981. Washington, D.C.: Government Printing Office. April.

Farley, Reynolds. 1977. "Residential Segregation in Urbanized Areas of the United States in 1970: An Analysis of Social Class and Racial Differences." Demography 14(4): 297–518.

Hebert, Robert F., and Albert N. Link. 1982. The Entrepreneur. New York: Praeger Publishers.

Hempel, Donald J. 1969. The Role of the Real Estate Broker in the Home Buying Process. Storrs, Conn.: The Center for Real Estate and Urban Economic Studies, University of Connecticut.

Katzman, Martin, and Harold Chiles. 1979. "Black Flight: The Middle Class Black Reaction, School Integration and Metropolitan Change." Discussion paper, Department of Political Economy, University of Texas at Dallas.

Kuklinski, Antoni. 1972. Growth Poles and Growth Centers in Regional Planning. Paris: Mouton.

Lewis, Eugene. 1980. Public Entrepreneurship: Toward a Theory of Bureaucratic Political Power. Bloomington, Ind.: Indiana University Press.

Magaziner, Ira L., and Robert B. Reich. 1982. Minding America's Business. New York: Vintage.

Maruyama, Magaroh. 1963. "The Second Cybernetics: Deviation Amplifying Mutual Casual Processes." American Scientist 51(2): 164-79.

Molotch, Harvey. 1976. "The City as a Growth Machine: Toward a Political Economy of Place." American Journal of Sociology 82: 309-22.

National Advisory Commission on Civil Disorders. 1968. Report. Washington, D.C.: Government Printing Office.

Oakey, R. P. 1981. High Technology Industry and Industrial Location. Aldershot, England: Gower House.

Oates, W. E., E. P. Howrey, and W. J. Baumol. 1971. "The Analysis of Public Policy in Dynamic Urban Models." Journal of Political Economy 89(1): 142-53.

Pear, Robert. 1983. "Reagan Halted Growth in Four Non-cash Aid Plans." New York Times, September 23.

Pearce, Diana M. 1979. "Gatekeepers and Homeseekers: Institutional Patterns in Racial Steering." Social Problems 26(3): 325-42.

Perroux, François. 1970. "Note on the Concept of Growth Poles." In Regional Economics, edited by David McKee et al. New York: Free Press.

Piven, Frances Fox, and Richard A. Clowart. 1971. Regulating the Poor: The Functions of Public Welfare. New York: Pantheon.

Ripley, Randall B., and Grace A. Franklin. 1980. Congress, the Bureaucracy and Public Policy. Homewood, Ill.: Dorsey Press.

Thompson, Thomas L. 1981. "Institutional Racism in the Housing Market: A Study of Growth Poles and Investment Patterns." Ph.D. dissertation, University of Texas at Arlington, Institute of Urban Studies.

Tinbergen, Jan. 1973. An Econometric Approach to Business Cycle Problems. Paris: Mouton.

U.A., Department of Commerce. 1983. Bureau of the Census. Money Income and Poverty Status of Families and Persons in the United States: 1983. Current Population Reports, Series P-60, No. 145. Washington, D.C.: Government Printing Office, March.

U.S., Department of Labor. Bureau of Labor Statistics. 1984, 1982, 1980. Employment and Earnings. November. Washington, D.C.: Government Printing Office.

U.S., House of Representatives. 1984. Committees on Ways and Means. Subcommittee on Oversight. Effects of the Omnibus Budget Reconciliation Act of 1981 (OBRA) Welfare Changes and the Recession on Poverty. Washington, D.C.: Government Printing Office.

Van Valey, Thomas L., Wade Clark Roof, and Jerome E. Wilcox. 1977. "Trends of Residential Segregation: 1960-70." American Journal of Sociology 82(4): 826-44.

7

Urban Policy and Telecommunications Systems

Mitchell L. Moss

INTRODUCTION

The deregulation of the telecommunications industry, in conjunction with recent technological advances, poses an important challenge for urban governments in the United States. Cities have traditionally been major users of telecommunications systems for such functions as emergency services and police communications, but local governments have had relatively little involvement in planning and policymaking for communication technologies, apart from the regulation of cable television. This chapter describes the emerging telecommunications infrastructure in the United States and the implications for urban governments.

Local governments have a long and complex history in the use of information and communications technologies. Seymour Mandelbaum has noted that cities are responsible for such information-intensive services as schools and libraries, and in certain cases, urban governments control broadcast television and radio systems. Despite this active engagement with information-based activities, there has been surprisingly little public policymaking for communications systems at the local level. As Mandelbaum states, "the concept of an urban communication infrastructure was not expressed in local institutions comparable to those which realized public concerns with education, environmental quality, housing or transportation" (Mandelbaum, 1985:6).

Cities have a vital stake in the changing telecommunications environment. Although federal deregulation of the communications industry has imposed constraints on the regulatory authority of local governments over cable television, the new competitive environment in telecommunications has increased the choices and policy issues that local governments face in the planning and management of telecommunications systems. More important, private-sector initiatives in the development of new telecommunications systems has important consequences for urban economic development. Rather than restricting the role of local government, deregulation has presented new challenges to urban governments. The local-government role in communications technologies consists of four main tasks: (1) managerial, as a user of telephone systems and related computer equipment; (2) regulatory, as the governmental entity with authority over rights-of-way used for cable television systems; (3) planning, as the formulator of the city's physical development and future pattern of land use; and (4) as policymaker for local economic development, with responsibility for attracting and retaining jobs and industry.

Three basic issues will be addressed in this chapter:

1. What is the form of the emerging telecommunications infrastructure in the United States and how will it affect the growth of cities?

2. What role can local governments play in planning and managing the new telecommunications infrastructure?

3. How will the emerging telecommunications infrastructure influence economic development in cities and metropolitan regions?

THE EMERGING TELECOMMUNICATIONS INFRASTRUCTURE

There are three main components to the new telecommunications infrastructure in the United States: (1) long-distance or inter-city systems, (2) regional or local distribution systems, and (3) intra-building or intra-complex communications systems, such as local area networks or "smart building" systems. To date, there has been a great deal of speculation about each component of this

infrastructure, but relatively little research about the relationship of these communications systems to each other
and to the overall pattern of urban development. Far more
attention has been given to specific technologies than to
the interaction of technology with the fundamental organization of work, time, and space in urban society. This
intellectual gap is particularly striking, since "the size
and importance of a city is determined by the amounts and
kinds of information flowing into and out of it, and by
the way it is interconnected with other cities in the national information flow network" (Abler, 1970:12).

Long-distance Fiber-optic Systems

At the national level, competition in long-distance
service is leading to the construction of several fiber-optic
networks which will provide high-speed, long-distance
communications across the country. These networks are
supplementing the existing grid of microwave relay systems, satellites, and earth stations currently in use. The
major long-haul fiber links are remarkably urban-based;
in certain cases, the fiber routes utilize railroad rights-
of-way and follow old transportation lines. For example,
US Telecom's 23,000-mile fiber system runs parallel to the
tracks of six railroads, the Kansas Turnpike, and a Wis-
consin State bicycle path, while MCI's 18,000-mile route
runs partly along Amtrak's right-of-way. The fiber systems planned and in-place, including those of AT&T, MCI,
United Telecom, Lightnet, Fibertrak, LDX Net, Litel, and
Lasernet, are designed to serve heavy traffic and thus
must reach the large metropolitan regions that are the information hubs of modern society.

New York, Atlanta, Miami, Chicago, Kansas City,
Dallas-Fort Worth, Cleveland, Pittsburgh, Denver, Washington, D.C., San Francisco, Los Angeles, Houston, and New
Orleans are among the cities that will be served by three
or more of these fiber networks. Although many communities will have access to fiber systems, it is clear that the
new networks will, as John Goddard has stated,

> serve a restricted number of locations,
> usually the largest cities. . . . there is
> little to indicate that developments in tele-
> communications networks are likely to dis-

advantage the largest cities relative to
small towns and rural areas in any national urban system. The incremental
modernization of networks and the logic of
density will ensure that the inner parts of
large cities will have an initial advantage (Goddard).

The rush to build fiber-optic systems in the United
States resembles the rush to build railroads in the nine-
teenth century: whoever can build the first integrated
network expects to capture much of the long-distance business (Johnston, 1985). As with almost all new technologies, there will ultimately be a shake-out; only a few of
the proposed fiber-optic systems will be economically viable.
In addition to the fiber-optic systems, there are several
new long-distance services that depend upon a mix of new
technologies, such as Equatorial Communications Company's
satellite network, which links computer terminals by using
small satellite dishes that can send and receive data and
thus totally bypass telephone lines (Business Week, 1985).
The reduced cost and size of the satellite earth stations
has facilitated communications services in remote locations
of the country, at the same time that fiber systems are
improving communications between large cities.

Regional Telecommunications Systems

At the metropolitan level, the regional holding companies, created through the divestiture of AT&T, remain
the predominant communications carriers and are gradually
shifting from twisted pairs of copper wire to fiber optic
for intra-city communications. New York Telephone has
built a 48,000-circuit, Ring Around Manhattan, fiber-optic
network which links 12 major switching centers in Manhattan and has recently launched an interborough fiber network which will link adjacent counties to Manhattan.
More than one-third of all the Bell System's optical fiber
has been installed in New York Telephone's service area,
a consequence of the demand for advanced communications
systems in the New York metropolitan area (Liu and
Vaselkiv, 1984:4). In Southern California, the fiber network built for the 1984 Olympics provides an advanced regional telecommunications infrastructure.

Large firms with extensive and specialized communications needs are facing an increased set of telecommunications alternatives and are often choosing to build their own communications systems, thus bypassing the "facilities of the local telephone companies available to the general public" (Federal Communications Commission, 1984:4). Citicorp has created a metropolitan network called Micronet, which links five Manhattan sites by fiber or microwave with a connection to Citicorp's satellite network. Westinghouse has linked its plants in the Pittsburgh region with a separate network, and Boeing Corporation is considering a 70,000-line, private network in the Seattle region.

Local governments are also major users of telecommunications systems and deregulation is forcing them to consider new ways to manage their communications systems. It is no longer possible for either business or government to rely on one telephone company to provide equipment, local telephone service, and long-distance service. Most public and private organizations have, until recently, relied on the local telephone company to plan and formulate their voice-communications systems. As municipalities confront new costs for equipment and telephone lines, it will be essential that municipal planning and management of telecommunications systems be strengthened and made an integral part of local-government operations.

Until now, the emerging telecommunications infrastructure has been built through, in, and around cities, with virtually no local-government involvement in the decisions regarding the location, size, and purpose of the new information infrastructure. Cities have been acted upon, rather than being actors, in the implementation of this infrastructure. The lack of governmental involvement in the planning and development of this communications network is compounded by the absence of public information about the new telecommunications infrastructure. Unlike other critical components of the urban infrastructure, such as water supply, highways, and waste-treatment facilities, the communications infrastructure has been designed, built, and managed by the private sector. Local governments know far more about the location of water mains than about the location of satellite dishes, fiber-optic systems, and microwave transmission paths in their jurisdiction. Information about a city's telecommunications infrastructure is of importance to municipal agencies concerned with environmental hazards, emergency communications, and office-park and industrial development.

Although communications technologies do not determine locational choices of private firms, the new telecommunications infrastructure is a significant input, along
with labor, land, capital, and the quality of public services, in corporate locational decisions.   John Goddard has
said,

> such networks are a permissive factor in
> economic development--that is, a necessary
> but not sufficient condition; any shortcom-
> ings in the telecommunications infrastruc-
> ture of a particular city relative to other
> cities will inhibit its development.   But
> having these facilities will not ensure that
> development takes place if there is not the
> sufficient entrepreneurial capacity to re-
> spond to the opportunities provided by that
> infrastructure (Goddard).

Teleports: Public and Private Initiatives

Perhaps the most innovative example of public-
sector involvement in the development of regional telecommunications infrastructure is the teleport project initiated
by the Port Authority of New York and New Jersey.   The
idea for a teleport was based upon the belief that the
public sector should provide a facility, similar to airports,
but for access to communication satellites.   The large volume of electronic communications in New York City led the
Port Authority to believe that access to communication
satellites would be crucial to maintain the health of the
region's economy.   Microwave congestion within New York
City reinforced the need for an alternative local-distribu-
tion system and led to the creation of a fiber-optic network
linking the teleport on Staten Island to New York City and
New Jersey.   A 100-acre office park was incorporated into
the project, since the Staten Island site offered access to
a skilled labor force, low-cost energy sources, plus land
for back-office facilities.

Responsibility for the teleport is divided between
the City of New York, which leased the land to the Port
Authority, and the Port Authority, which developed the
land and leased the buildings on the site.   Merrill Lynch
and Western Union were brought in as partners in Teleport

Communications, to manage and market the communications systems, with the city and the port authority receiving a percentage of net profits. (Merrill Lynch initially owned 60 percent of Teleport Communications and Western Union 40 percent; today, Merrill owns 95 percent and Western Union 5 percent.)

Teleport is designed to serve ultimately 17 earth stations; two are currently operated by Merrill Lynch and one by Comsat. Several major firms, including Dow Jones, Bankers Trust, Citicorp, and SBS, are hooked into Teleport's fiber-optic cable. The provision of local telecommunications service within the New York-New Jersey region has been Teleport's most striking achievement. AT&T intends to use Teleport's fiber-optic system to provide long distance to Merrill Lynch, thus bypassing New York Telephone's local network. Teleport's fiber cable provides an important telecommunications infrastructure, at low cost, to major users in New York City and the surrounding region, which will probably emerge as the most valuable aspect of the entire project, although the initial logic of the project was based upon the need for access to communications satellites. Whether the public sector should be providing a competitor to the publicly switched telephone network is a policy issue that has yet to be fully addressed; however, it is possible that Teleport's success in the local distribution business could contribute to lower revenues for New York Telephone and eventually lead to higher rates for residential and small-business users.

The popularity of teleports can be seen in the speed with which other communities have launched efforts to build their own. In the United States, there are 20 different teleport facilities in 12 states; 11 of these are operational, two are under construction, seven are planned, and one is proposed. With the exception of the New York and Ohio teleports, which are public-private partnerships, all are privately owned projects. The diffusion of teleports is partly a result of the renaming of existing satellite antenna farms equipped with microwave transmission linkages, rather than a result of any evidence that teleports can stimulate economic development.

A variety of other telecommunications systems are also used at the local or regional level, such as microwave, coaxial cable, digital termination systems, and cellular mobile radio. In New York City, Manhattan Cable Television provides data-transmission service for banks and local government agencies over its trunk lines; however, such institutional uses of cable are rare in most cities, since cable television systems are primarily oriented to the residential market and are nonexistent in most central business districts.

"Smart Buildings" and Governmental Functions

"Smart" or "intelligent buildings" are the most localized component of the new telecommunications infrastructure. A smart building has three different meanings: (1) It can refer to an integrated management system for elevators, energy, security, and other building services; (2) It can refer to an integrated telecommunications network for local, long-distance, and enhanced services; or (3) It can provide integrated telecommunications and building services. With regard to telecommunications, a smart building provides a private branch exchange, telephone equipment, access to the public-switched network, long-distance service, and enhanced services, such as voice messaging and teleconferencing.

The growth of "shared-tenant services" provides a way to provide sophisticated telecommunications services within buildings that offer economies of scale and one-stop convenience to small and middle-sized firms. For real-estate developers, shared-tenant services can provide a service and a potential source of revenue, and many developers have formed partnerships with telecommunications firms to offer building-based communications services.

The leader in this evolving industry has been Olympia and York, the largest real-estate developer in North America. Olympia and York has formed a joint venture with United Telecommunications, Inc., to create OlympiaNet, a telecommunications network that will offer advanced data, voice, and video services to all its tenants. The development of OlympiaNet's teleconferencing network highlights the incremental way in which new telecommunications services are first offered in major urban markets. The OlympiaNet teleconferencing facilities will be initially available in New York City, Boston, and Toronto, with other cities to follow.

Although the private sector has been the pioneer in developing smart buildings, there is also a potential role for local governments, since information is at the core of so many municipal services. Libraries and schools are the traditional information-based services provided by local government, and clearly, there is a need to equip classrooms and reference rooms with sufficient telecommunications capability to allow access to computer networks and data bases. It is not sufficient to confine computers to computer laboratories in libraries and schools; eventually, all classrooms will need to be wired for computers and telecommunications links.

THE URBAN BASIS OF COMMUNICATIONS SYSTEMS

The emerging telecommunications infrastructure is a predominantly urban-based phenomenon. Although most discussions of new communications technologies emphasize the opportunities presented for decentralization, large cities are the hubs of the new telecommunications systems in the United States and are the sites for the most advanced applications of information technology. As Brooker-Gross has said, ". . . the technologies are likely to be found first in the largest markets. Advantages in communication already possessed by larger metropolises will be reinforced before the advantages diffuse to smaller places" (Brooker-Gross, 1980:7). Although new communications technologies permit geographical dispersal, the economics of the new infrastructure is oriented toward those urban regions that are major information centers.

Further, the changing regulatory framework in the United States, by modifying telecommunications pricing and investment criteria, will have profound consequences on the distribution of telecommunications facilities and the cost of telephone service for urban and rural areas. Until 1984, the principle of "universal service," in which every household was provided with low-cost telephone service, was the guiding philosophy of the Bell system. This was largely accomplished with cross-subsidies from urban to rural users and from business to residential customers. However, competition is leading to a reduction in such cross-subsidies and to user-based telephone rates and investment criteria. Just as airline deregulation has weakened air service in small towns and outlying communities, telecommunications deregulation may lead to a greater disparity in communications service between large metropolitan regions and rural areas. As Roger Noll has noted:

Some investment in rural service probably
is uneconomic. Rural residents may be unwilling to pay for telephone service that is
priced at its accounting cost. Moreover,
copper-wire technology is not the cheapest
way to serve rural areas. Instead, recent
technical advances probably make over-the-
air technologies, such as cellular radio,
cheaper in some areas than the book value
of a rural NTS [nontraffic sensitive] plant
(Noll, 1985:53).

THE CHALLENGE FOR LOCAL GOVERNMENT

Contrary to much of the popular folklore, new communications technologies have not led to the decline of
cities. Rather, new communications technologies have enhanced those cities that serve "the important function of
hosting transactional activities" (Gottmann, 1983:6). Although many so-called futurists argue that the electronic
cottage will replace the office building and that teleconferencing will replace the in-person meeting, such speculation
merely demonstrates a poor understanding of urban functions, a willingness to assume that technological feasibility
is equivalent to technological acceptability, and a disregard for the incremental and evolutionary process of technological innovation in organizations.
Public policy toward communications in large cities
has been predominantly oriented to the regulation of cable-
television systems and has largely ignored the private sector's role in the design and construction of the new urban
telecommunications infrastructure. Most local governments
have been consumed with visions of two-way cable television in every household and have focused their attention
on cable, thereby ignoring other technologies, such as
fiber optics, mobile communications, and microwave transmission, that will be far more important in shaping communications patterns in cities. After decades of predictions about the "wired city," cable television has yet to
arrive in most large U.S. cities (Moss and Warren, 1984).
The "wired city" has arrived, but it is oriented to the
office, not the home, and is based upon a diversity of
transmission systems, not just coaxial cable. It has been

built outside the domain of local regulatory and policymaking entities.

Determining the appropriate level of public involvement in development of urban telecommunications systems
will depend upon the local political environment, the performance of the private sector, and an awareness of the
dynamic state of the telecommunications industry. There
are genuine limits to public intervention in a technologi-
cally driven industry. Advances in technology are rapid,
and it is unwise for local government to become committed
to a single technology or a single type of communications
facility. The public sector does, though, have an important stake in assuring that the individuals and firms
within a city have access to advanced telecommunications
systems. To do this, local governments must improve their
knowledge of private-sector initiatives in telecommunications infrastructure development and recognize the limits,
as well as the possibilities, of direct public intervention
in telecommunications planning and policymaking. As Anne
W. Branscomb has wisely stated:

> It seems unlikely that the information in-
> frastructure for converged electronic media
> will develop its full potential solely fueled
> by private interests, entrepreneurial spirit,
> and profit-centered motives. There is
> ample room for public will to find its way
> into a full-service electronic information
> marketplace (Branscomb, 1982:171).

TELECOMMUNICATIONS AND ECONOMIC DEVELOPMENT

City officials concerned with local economic development have traditionally emphasized the availability of
labor, access to transportation arteries, and provision of
tax abatements in their efforts to foster job creation and
retention. Telecommunications infrastructure has rarely
been incorporated into urban economic-development policymaking. Yet, telecommunications systems are integral components in manufacturing and service-sector industries.
Advanced communications systems have permitted large
firms to concentrate their headquarters in one central location while dispersing manufacturing and routine information processing to suburban locations outside the central

city. Advanced telecommunications have opened up opportunities for economic development in once-remote sites while facilitating control from a single location.

Many observers suggest that "the cities of the future may cluster around satellite 'up links' rather than at the mouths of rivers. . . . The industrial parks of the future may advertise free satellite saucers rather than railroad spurs as a major attraction—especially since they are more likely to be 'communication campuses' rather than industrial parks" (Branscomb, 1982:183). It is unlikely that satellite antenna farms will replace cities. However, it is essential that cities recognize the increased use of telecommunications systems by the private sector and the need for public agencies to plan for and respond to the growing demand for a diversity of telecommunications systems. One important role is to provide access to existing public infrastructure for coaxial-cable and fiber-optic systems. For example, the public rights-of-way for mass-transit systems in cities are a valuable resource for telecommunications systems. Just as the private railways have leased their rights-of-way to new fiber systems, the public sector should seek to harness its rights-of-way for local and regional communications systems. The Massachusetts Bay Area Transportation Authority has already leased part of its right-of-way for such purposes, and the Port Authority of New York and New Jersey has used its trans-Hudson mass-transit tunnels for a teleport fiber network. These are just examples of the way in which public transportation infrastructure can be harnessed to the new communications infrastructure to achieve economic-development objectives.

CONCLUSION

The emerging telecommunications infrastructure presents a severe challenge to local governments. Although the new infrastructure is a product of the private sector, it has pervasive consequences for municipal management, planning, and economic development. Telecommunications systems will transform data-processing activities, challenge residential zoning codes that were formulated before the advent of satellite dishes, and diminish the "brick-and-mortar" approach to economic development (Kraemer and King, 1984). In formulating urban policies for telecom-

munications, it is essential that cities not become so enamored of new technologies that they adopt the "technological fix" perspective; rather policymaking should be
based on an understanding of the changing technological
infrastructure and the broad-based way in which communications technologies will influence almost all aspects of
urban-government services and economic development.

REFERENCES

Abler, Ron. 1970. "What Makes Cities Important." Bell
Telephone Magazine 49(2).

Branscomb, Anne W. 1982. "Beyond Deregulation: Designing the Information Infrastructure." Information Society Journal 1(3): 168-90.

Brooker-Gross, Susan R. 1980. "Usages of Communication
Technology and Urban Growth." In The American Metro-
politan System: Present and Future, edited by Stanley
Brunn and James Wheeler. New York: Wiley and
Sons, 145-59.

Business Week. 1985. "Tiny Satellite Dishes Are Serving
Up a Hot New Market." March 11.

Chinitz, Benjamin. 1984. "The Influence of Communications
and Data Processing Technology on Urban Form." In
Research in Urban Economics, Vol. 4, edited by Robert
D. Ebel. JAI Press, 67-77.

City of New York, Department of General Services. 1985.
A Telecommunications Policy Proposal. May.

Federal Communications Commission, Common Carrier Bureau.
1984. Bypass of the Public Switched Network. December 19.

Goddard, J. B. 1985. "The Impact of the New Information
Technology on Urban and Regional Structure in Europe."
Paper presented at Landtronics, Anglo-American Con-
ference, Westminster Center, London. June 19-21.

Gottmann, Jean. 1983. The Coming of the Transactional
City. University of Maryland: Institute for Urban
Studies.

Johnston, William B. 1985. "The Coming Glut of Phone
Lines." Fortune. January 7.

Kraemer, Kenneth L., and John Leslie King. 1984. "The
Role of Information Technology in Managing the
Metropolis: The Future of Information Systems in
Local Government." University of California: Public
Policy Research Organization.

Liu, Ernest S., and Kathryn H. Vaselkiv. 1984. NYNEX
Corporation Investment Research. December 19. New
York: Goldman Sachs.

Mandelbaum, Seymour J. 1985. "Cities and Communication:
The Limits of Community." University of Pennsylvania.

Moss, Mitchell, and Robert Warren. 1984. "Public Policy
and Community-oriented Uses of Cable Television."
Urban Affairs Quarterly 20 (2, December): 233-53.

Noll, Roger G. 1985. "Let Them Make Toll Calls: A State
Regulator's Lament." American Economic Review 75
(2, May): 52-56.

Stanback, Thomas M. 1985. "The Changing Fortunes of
Metropolitan Economies." In High Technology, Space,
and Society, edited by Manuel Castells. Urban Affairs
Annual Reviews, Vol. 28. Beverly Hills, Calif.: Sage,
122-42.

Wines, Michael. 1983. "Teleports May Be the Newest
Threat to Bell Companies' Local Dominance." National
Journal, November 12, 2348-52.

Part III

Policy Change and the Oracles

8

Urban Policy Research and the Changing Fiscal Focus of the State: Sociology's Ambiguous Legacy and Uncertain Future

Scott Cummings

REAGANOMICS AND THE SOCIAL SCIENCES

Spiraling deficits at all levels of government have severely impacted higher education. This chapter explains how the current fiscal crisis has altered program development and funding within higher education, and transformed creative activities within traditional disciplines. Special attention is given to the relationship between class inequality and the production of knowledge. Because of its unique legacy, sociology is especially vulnerable during a budget crisis. In the first section, I will describe how the changing fiscal focus of the state has enhanced selected disciplines within the academy and weakened others. In the second part are examined the political forces contributing to sociology's increasing vulnerability in the face of mounting federal deficits. In the third and fourth parts of the chapter are explained how sociology's intellectual legacy rendered it less than effective in responding to the policy challenges now confronting the discipline.

The argument developed in the chapter can be summarized by stressing the relationship between state-spending priorities and the creation of knowledge. In the present political climate, a policy market exists only for ideas endorsing Reaganomics and programs promoting private profit accumulation. Chubin and McCartney (1982) mince no words when they observe that if sociologists want to engage in policy research under current political conditions, they will have to accommodate themselves to the private agenda established by the Reagan administration:

> The new [Reagan] criterion of utility is
> what research can do for the private sec-
> tor. Thus, the effort at NSF [National
> Science Foundation] to reclaim the social
> science percentage of survey research,
> which is widely used in the private sector,
> can be seen as an effort to accommodate
> social science to new political priorities
> (p. 233).

The discipline of sociology, however, is not well equipped
to participate in Reagan's policy initiatives, a fact causing tremendous turmoil within the discipline.

Disciplines historically aligning themselves with the
poor, minorities, and the working class have faced critical
challenges over the past decade. During the Reagan presidency, sociology and related social-science fields have suffered a tremendous erosion of legitimacy and financial support. Victims of the recessionary forces ravaging the
American economy--higher education itself--has been compelled to grapple with a fiscal crisis of unprecedented
magnitude. Urban universities have been most severely
affected by spiraling public-sector deficits. Those universities located in cities and urban regions devastated by
plant closings, capital flight, and the systematic dismantling of basic industry are presently struggling to maintain
status as comprehensive educational institutions. Within
these institutions, sociology, urban affairs, social work,
and the policy sciences compete with business, science,
and engineering to maintain vitality and integrity as au-
tonomous academic programs.

Several important trends within the larger political
economy have shaped the crisis facing many social-science
disciplines within public universities. These problems
have ideological, fiscal, and organizational components.
The Reagan administration has launched a systematic attempt to privatize the public sector (Savas, 1982). Sur-
rounded and inspired by supply-side economists and advisers (Lekachman, 1982), Reagan has transformed tax laws
in a manner that simultaneously contracts public-sector
expenditures and maximizes private control over investment
capital. While designed to curb inflation and stimulate a
sagging economy, his policies have directly impacted
social-science disciplines within many universities.

Faced with severe budget cuts and deteriorating
state and local revenues, university administrators have
been compelled to make strategic fiscal decisions involving
program and disciplinary priorities. University budget
cuts are never randomly or equitably applied across departments or colleges. Consistent with the policies and
ideological orientations reflected in Reagan's economic
program, those disciplines most clearly associated with
private-sector needs and interests have not been seriously
affected by the fiscal crisis within higher education. The
social sciences, arts, and humanities, however, have not
been nearly as fortunate (Cummings, 1984). Early in the
first term, the Reagan administration politically declared
its disdain for the social sciences by launching a systematic attack on federal programs supporting policy research.
The National Science Foundation, the National Endowment
for the Arts and the Humanities, the National Institute for
Mental Health, the National Institute of Education, and
the Alcohol, Drug Abuse, and Mental Health Administration
were all slated for substantial budget reductions by Reagan
(Dynes, 1984; Himmelstein and Zald, 1984; Zuiches, 1984).
Despite Reagan's attempt to "defund the left" (Himmelstein
and Zald, 1984), the assault on federally supported research programs was only one component of the larger
crisis facing the social sciences.

In order to cope with dwindling general revenues
and declining federal support for research programs, most
public universities have been compelled to shift disciplinary
priorities in a consistent and systematic manner. Mirror-
ing the policy changes taking place within the Reagan administration, the intellectual, ideological, and programmatic
agendas of many universities have become more privatized.
Those programs and colleges most compatible with the
Reagan policy initiatives (business, science, and engineering) have been enhanced or left untouched by escalating
federal deficits (Chronicle, 1984). In order to supplement
lost public revenues, many urban university administrators
have been encouraged to launch corporate fund-drives
(Rudnick, 1983). Greater reliance on private funds,
private-foundation support, or corporate-donation programs
brings university goals and objectives into greater alliance
with business interests and ideologies (Bowles and Gintis,
1976).

Like financially troubled, private-sector firms, many
universities have also initiated labor practices designed to

reduce costs. These practices entail laying off faculty in programs deemed expendable, and reducing the quality of the work environment. Funds for secretarial-support staff, equipment and office maintenance, travel, and pursuit of research opportunities, have all been curtailed in many universities. Additionally, some universities have inaugurated the equivalent of an assembly-line "speedup" in order to cope with the fiscal crisis (Stark, 1983). This is reflected in pressure to raise student-enrollment ceilings, increase classroom contact hours, and escalate the number of course preparations that faculty are required to teach. Like blue-collar workers in the industrial sector, many university professors face escalating demands for higher productivity in tandem with lower wages and deteriorating working conditions. Most important, however, is the apparent fact that these pressures are not equitably distributed within the university community. The social and policy sciences are shouldering a major burden of these labor practices and cost-reduction measures.

In addition to implementing cost and labor-saving measures, and introducing higher standards of productivity, many administrators have chosen to save money by reducing the size of the student body. Because of the associated loss in tuition revenues, a reduction in the size of the university has been implemented through the elimination of remedial programs and open-admission policies. Tuition fees and the cost of other university services have been simultaneously increased. These policies alter the class and racial composition of the student body, thereby increasing ideological homogeneity within the university community. All of these changes contribute to the overall tendency to move universities into closer and closer alliance with the capitalist class, and those groups, agencies, and organizations promoting their interests. Under these conditions, the types of contributions made by social scientists to national urban policy are conceptually constrained and ideologically limited. Sociology has been severely impacted by these larger economic and political trends.

SOCIOLOGY, SOCIAL CRITICISM, AND POLICY ANALYSIS

Sociology, unlike political science and economics, has largely stood outside the major networks of power in

U.S. society. Very few academic sociologists have social origins within the ranks of the capitalist class, and even fewer have direct access to the inner circles of U.S. power. Sociologists are seldom consulted by those who hold the formal reins of power or recruited to serve in cabinet positions or chair important posts within federal agencies. Sociological ideas have not been particularly popular among policymakers, a fact partly explained by the activist component of the sociological tradition.

In comparison with ideas drawn from political science and economics, sociological thinking has not been as influential in shaping the national policy agenda (Rossi, 1972). This absence of influence is not surprising. Sociology has tended to assume a much more critical posture toward the state and its involvement in the perpetuation of social inequality than has the field of political science (Castells, 1977). Sociology has also adopted a strongly critical orientation toward business domination of urban policy (Faegin, 1983; Smith, 1984; Whitt, 1982), a posture not readily apparent among orthodox practitioners in the field of economics. Moreover, political activism within the academy varies dramatically among disciplines (Ladd and Lipset, 1976), the field of sociology being one of the more active (Abramson and Wences, 1971).

Because the discipline of sociology has a highly politicized and critical intellectual tradition, university sociologists are probably more sensitive to the political uses of ideas than colleagues in related social-science fields. To some degree, the absence of sociologists from the policy-formulation bodies is based upon academic idealism and belief in traditional scientific norms endorsing noninvolvement in politics. On the other hand, sociological participation in dissident political movements is not uncommon, and has earned for the discipline a reputation of being highly partisan and antiestablishment in nature (Ladd and Lipset, 1976). The discipline of sociology has never uniformly embraced Weber's conception of ethical neutrality in the research and policy-formulation process: "Almost from the beginning, some sociologists saw the field as a detached, ethically neutral scientific study of social behavior, while others saw it as a weapon in the struggle to relieve the social problems of industrial civilization" (Bates and Julian, 1975:15).

Critical sociologists have always been skeptical about the state's role in the policy process, a suspicion not encouraging active involvement in policy research or program evaluation. During the 1960s, a period marked by the civil-rights movement, student uprisings, and dissent over the war in Vietnam, many university intellectuals engaged in heated debate over who benefits from the knowledge produced by state-supported research. Some university professors insisted that colleagues cease to sell their knowledge to the military establishment, and refrain from accepting military-research contracts; many universities mobilized to block corporate and federal recruitment activities on campus (Lipset, 1976). By the late 1960s, numerous statements were made by prominent social scientists endorsing the partisan use of knowledge to promote social change, and the creation of policies capable of reducing levels of inequality in American society (Becker, 1967; Gouldner, 1968). Several professional societies were fragmented with bitter controversies over the need to develop a more critical posture toward the distribution of wealth and income, and to assist the poor and oppressed. Controversies within the American Sociological Association were especially intense. Some sociologists accused their colleagues of being handmaidens of established interests and power groups in society (Horowitz, 1963; Nicolaus, 1968), and urged a more active role in confrontational politics.

Sociological thinking about the state and the discipline's relation to it has been strongly influenced by Marxist analytical categories. Marx and Engels argued in The German Ideology that those in power are in a strategic position to structure the perceptions and ideas which influence people's lives: "The class which has the means of material production at its disposal, has control at the same time over the means of mental production, so that in consequence the ideas of those who lack the means of mental production are, in general, subject to it" (1962:74). Mannheim (1936) and Schumpeter (1954) enriched Marx's original contentions by examining the special relationship that intellectuals have to those in power.

Schumpeter observed that university intellectuals have a unique relationship to the dominant classes in society. Because of their special relationship to the upper class, individual scientists are ". . . likely to glorify the interests and activities of the classes that are in a position to assert themselves" (1954:35). The substance and form of the glorification process, however, varies according to the type of crises encountered by the state, and the utility which specific scientific paradigms have for the capitalist class. Critical sociologists have shown strong reluctance to become involved in state programs supporting the interests of the capitalist class. As a result, they are also very reluctant to engage in policy research or program evaluation.

Many academic sociologists harbor strong ambivalence toward policy research. This orientation can be partly explained by elaborating O'Connor's (1972) contention that state expenditures under capitalism are contradictory and illogical. Controversy among sociologists over policy research reflects the tension between social criticism and dependency upon the state for resources. O'Connor maintains that the state must try to create conditions under which profitable capital accumulation is possible. At the same time, it must also facilitate conditions that promote social harmony and retard the emergence of civic disorder. Since capitalism promotes inequality, which ultimately leads to dissent, the state is forced to engage in deficit spending in order to manage discord and simultaneously ensure adequate profit margins for the capital class. O'Connor contends that the state simply does not have enough money to meet legitimation and accumulation needs adequately. Permanent inflation is the ultimate result of chronic state deficits.

In O'Connor's discussion, "social-capital" expenditures or programs are necessary to continue profitability in the capital-accumulation process. Reagan's economic and tax policies clearly represent capital-accumulation priorities (Lekachman, 1982). They are designed to enhance profits and stimulate private investments. He has simultaneously contracted social-welfare expenditures. "Social expenses" are necessary to maintain the legitimacy of the social order (education, job training, unemployment insurance, Medicare, Medicaid, etc.). Those policies adopted during the New Deal and Great Society eras represent legitimation expenditures (Levitan and Taggart, 1976). When economic and political events shift expenditures from legitimation to accumulation, as Reagan has done, the vitality of social sciences is sharply eroded. When expenditures shift from capital accumulation to legitimation, on the other hand, the influence of the social-science community on national urban policy is substantially increased.

During a legitimation crisis, such as that of the 1960s and 1970s, the state must make strategic decisions

about the allocation of scarce public resources. In the
face of civil discord and social movements threatening
serious disruption in the social order, the state is often
compelled to exercise repressive measures designed to curb
dissent. Rather than exercise coercive power, most en-
lightened public officials attempt to implement social programs capable of restoring faith in established institutions
(Piven and Cloward, 1977). The kinds of public expenditures usually required during a legitimation crisis are
clearly different from those policies and programs needed
during a capital-accumulation crisis. Diesing (1982) explains the political choices faced by the state when legitimation and accumulation problems emerge simultaneously:

> While the state struggles with the accumu-
> lation problem, the legitimation problem
> also grows more serious as welfare clients
> and unemployed protest and taxpayers re-
> volt. Consequently, the state is forced to
> shift expenditures from accumulation to
> legitimation as soon as the most immediate
> profitability problems are temporarily man-
> aged (p. 254).

Because the state always hovers close to bankruptcy
in its efforts to manage legitimation and accumulation responsibilities (O'Connor, 1972), those in power must carefully choose what groups will be potentially alienated by
shifts in expenditures from one category to another.
Through policy research, intellectuals assist the state
when shifts in public expenditures occur, hopefully damp-
ening the effects of crises. Indeed, social policy itself
typically requires some type of ideological or theoretical
justification, a fact readily apparent in Reagan's effort
to recruit a large team of "supply-side" economic advisers
(Meadows, 1981), to legitimate his policies. Since the
structure of higher education is dependent upon the state
for financial support and legitimacy, its various productive activities—including teaching, research, and service—
are subject to the same political and fiscal pressures
directed toward any component of the public sector when a
shift in spending priorities takes place. The market for
various scientific models and ideas expands or contracts
depending upon the shifting fiscal focus of the state.

Sociological involvement in urban-policy analysis and development has been most active during legitimation crises. Sociological allegiance, however, has typically gone to members of the urban underclass, a fact reinforcing characterizations of the discipline as antiestablishment. During a capital-accumulation crisis, sociological thinking has little or no use value for the capitalist class, a deficiency making the discipline a prime target for budget cuts. Over and above external political events and changes in public expenditures, there are other reasons why sociology is so vulnerable during a capital-accumulation crisis. The discipline has produced a somewhat unique legacy in the area of urban studies and urban-policy analysis. Early urban sociologists promoted the idea that social scientists should avoid partisan political struggle, and developed theories consistent with this viewpoint. This legacy has given the discipline a reactionary orientation in the face of crisis.

THE LEGACY OF URBAN SOCIOLOGY: ACADEMIC IDEOLOGICAL AND SOCIAL POLICY

Positivism and classic social theory combined to form a unique ideological legacy within the field of urban sociology. Classical theory gave mainstream urban sociology a highly individualistic orientation. Positivism fostered a tendency among early social scientists to avoid political activism. Convinced that the norms of science would be compromised by direct involvement in the political process, early positivists insisted that objective research findings should be used to develop more informed social policies. This latter belief encouraged early university intellectuals to argue that science and rationality could be substituted for partisan politics, a notion still widely accepted and practiced among many sociologists.

Early urban sociology is not unique in its absence of a tradition promoting activism or in its commitment to rationalism. All branches of the sociological enterprise have typically been split between those promoting social change, and those endorsing a nonpartisan, analytical approach to social problems. Among the major exceptions to this generalization are the fields of race relations and criminology. These traditions notwithstanding, early sociologists were never very active in the formulation of national urban policy, nor did they assume an influential role in urban and neighborhood planning. The absence of a substantial legacy in this area reflects several unique features of the sociological tradition. Sociological perspectives on cities and city life have their origins in the writings of Robert Park and Ernest Burgess (1925), and what came to be known as the Chicago School of urban social theory (Faris, 1970). Based primarily upon ecological concepts and drawing heavily from biological models of human behavior, this intellectual viewpoint has strongly influenced sociological analyses of urban life and culture for the past several decades.

Social Ecology and Social Darwinism

The conservative underpinnings of the Chicago tradition are recognized by many contemporary sociologists. Abramson (1980:362) argues that sociological thinking has not found its way into the urban-policy and planning arena for several reasons.

> The lack of more serious sociological analyses reflects the historic tendency of urban sociologists not to be interested or involved in planning. This relative neglect of planning, which lasted until quite recently, was not due to an antipublic service orientation. To the contrary, Park, McKenzie, and others actively participated on many commissions. However, the ecological approach--dominant in the early period of urban sociology--played down both the desirability and efficacy of rational planning. This antipathy was clearly formulated by Park, Burgess, and other pioneering writers in their descriptions of natural areas within the city. The most distinguishing feature attributed to those areas was that although they were unplanned they very effectively met the needs of the residents.

Because early urban theory was so strongly influenced by biological models of plant and animal life, it was easy for

practitioners to disregard or downplay the importance of
deliberate intervention into human affairs. Indeed, urban
planning itself, as well as the numerous urban social programs which emerged during the 1960s and 1970s, are antithetical to notions that presume that cities and city life
are simply by-products of natural or evolutionary processes.

Despite the fact that the problems of industrial
civilization reveal themselves most fully in cities, early
urban sociology did little to resolve the potential relationship between theory and practice, or define the interface
between social problems, social policy, and political activism. As a result, a predominant legacy within urban
sociology is a neutral attitude toward planned social
change and policy formation. The absence of an activist
tradition can be partly explained through a closer look at
the Chicago School and the bioecological traditions which
shaped it.

During the 1920s and 1930s the intellectual foundations of urban social theory were constructed. For two
decades, scholars at the University of Chicago identified
and described the characteristics found within isolated and
distinct geographical areas of the city. These characteristics included the physical and environmental elements of
urban neighborhoods, the racial, ethnic, socioeconomic,
and age composition of the residents, the commercial or
residential nature of land use, and the types of behaviors
mostly commonly exhibited in what they called <u>natural
areas</u>. The Chicago researchers attempted to explain why
selected demographic and behavioral traits seemed to cluster in certain areas of the city but not in others. They
attempted to discover the underlying social processes that
shaped urban land use, and to formulate sociological laws
explaining why various spatial enclaves expanded or contracted, changed or remained stable. Arguing that a larger "moral order" shaped the urban landscape and regulated
behavior and land use within the city, Park (1925) and his
associates concluded that the industrial division of labor
was a major force patterning urban life and culture. At
base, however, human behavior, like plant and animal life,
represented an adaptive response to larger environmental
forces.

Practitioners within the Chicago School produced
numerous case studies describing the unique behavioral
and ecological adaptations found in natural areas of the

city (Anderson, 1923; Cressey, 1932; McKenzie, 1933; Shaw 1930; Thrasher, 1927; Wirth, 1928; and Zorbaugh, 1929). The research generated by Chicago's early practitioners, and those who carried on their traditions (Suttles, 1968, 1972; Fischer, 1976), established an intellectual and ideological tradition within urban sociology. The influence of the Chicago tradition has been so pervasive that most contemporary textbooks in urban sociology are dominated by an approach rooted in social ecology.

Within three of the most influential texts in the field, Urban Society by Gist and Fava (1974), Urban Society by Amos Hawley (1971), and Urban Structure by Ralph Thomlinson (1969), one finds a heavy intellectual debt to social-ecology theory. Even among the more recent texts, the influence of the Chicago School is unmistakable (for example, Bardo and Hartman, 1982; Butler, 1976; Cousins and Nagpaul, 1979; Palen, 1975; Schwab, 1982; and Taylor, 1980). Despite the longevity of early urban theory, there exist numerous assumptions within the model which make it less than useful as a policy paradigm for the 1980s. Reflecting a weak interface between sociology and social policy, none of the major contemporary texts on urban sociology contain chapters dealing with the discipline's contribution to urban policy analysis. While some texts display concluding statements dealing with the urban future or city planning, these chapters are usually very brief and underdeveloped.

More strikingly, none of the modern texts develop a critical orientation toward the state and its involvement in the creation of urban policy. Furthermore, none of the contemporary texts critically examine business domination over national urban policy. This is not surprising since the social ecology paradigm is explicitly deficient in its consideration of the state's influence in shaping the urban landscape. The perspective is also sorely inadequate in its reference to the role of corporate elites and wealthy class interests in structuring city life. These two conceptual imperfections are major reasons why the Chicago framework has not been useful in the analysis and development of urban social policy. Political and economic elements are simply absent from the paradigm. Critics contend the perspective is useful only as an ideological justification of the status quo.

Smith (1979) recently identified the ideological biases which comprise social-ecology theory. He contends that social-ecology theory was strongly influenced by nineteenth-century thinkers attempting to understand the impact of industrialization on rural life and culture (Cooley, 1902; Durkheim, 1947; Maine, 1870; and Toennies, 1956). Industrialization had uprooted rural peasants and transformed the nature of life in small villages and hamlets. The fundamental institutions of rural life had been fragmented and structurally altered by the factory system; social relationships had become increasingly impersonal and secondary. Like the classical theorists, the social ecologists were alarmed over the shift from folk to urban society, and concerned about its impact on the human personality.

Benefiting from the insights of the French sociologist, Emile Durkheim, the ecologists agreed that social order in urban society was made possible by the interdependence engendered by an increasingly complex division of labor. Durkheim (1947), foreshadowing terminology which later flourished among social ecologists, referred to this type of societal cohesion as organic solidarity. Drawing from early evolutionary theories, the Chicago researchers equated organic solidarity with ecosystems found in nature. Based on biological assumptions and metaphors, the Chicago practitioners viewed themselves as "human" ecologists. As Smith (1979) explains, the human ecologists tended to view the city as a symbiotic community, a collection of interdependent parts comprised of spatially distinct social forms and behaviors.

These varied city behaviors and peoples were not unlike the varieties of plant and animal life found in nature. Like their plant and animal counterparts, human organisms could also be found in a specialized and spatially separate environmental niche (neighborhoods, boweries, suburbs, and other "nature areas"). Also similar to plants and animals competing to dominate physical space, life in the city reflected the struggle to survive in nature. This perspective enabled the social ecologists to view the city as

> an aggregation of living forms bound to-
> gether in a web of interdependence. From
> the ecological perspective, the struggle for
> survival in a particular milieu creates a
> special pecking order and a place for each
> member and species of organism in the
> overall division of labor (Smith, 1979:3).

The logic of social ecology is strikingly similar to social Darwinism. Additionally, the laissez-faire assumptions embodied in social-ecology theory closely parallel an unreconstructed version of neoclassical economics in which individuals compete in pursuit of self-interest. The social ecologists argued that while human social life was grounded in competition and conflict, parasitic and exploitative social relationships were regulated by a higher order of morality. Included among these "higher-order" mechanisms of social control were economic and political institutions, cultural and moral bonds, and human consciousness. Despite the attempt to rescue the ecological viewpoint from its Darwinistic and laissez-faire origins, the Chicago practitioners promoted a world view which did little or nothing to challenge the existing distribution of scarce resources in society. Nor did they alter the idea that wealth and poverty, slums and suburbs, were simple reflections of the "natural" workings of the social world. From this vantage point, social ecology directly endorsed and legitimated structured social inequality in urban America, a fact making the perspective very unpopular among sociologists committed to political activism. The ideological assumptions within social ecology can be illustrated further by examining Park's theory of race-relation cycles, and early ecological theories of urban land use.

Developing the ecological viewpoint, Park (1925) reasoned that ethnic and racial enclaves in U.S. cities could be explained as spatial manifestations of conflict and competition. Similar to the invasion of new plants and animals into an ecological niche dominated by other species and life forms, Park suggested that all new immigrants to U.S. cities encountered an irreversible process. This chain of sequential events included contact, competition, conflict, accommodation, and acculturation. When a new group "invaded" a geographical area of the city, they inevitably encountered conflict and competition with established residents.

Ultimately, however, new groups displaced older residents, and occupied the space vacated by them. Park called this transaction from one group to another the invasion and succession process. The process applied not only to residential areas of the city, but conflict and competition over jobs and city services as well. Park's formulation, according to critics, ideologically legitimated ethnic stratification and ghetto formation in U.S. cities by equating structured social inequality with inevitable laws of nature.

Lyman (1972) captures the essence of Park's ideological position when he observes that social ecology detoured many urban sociologists around a critical examination of racial and ethnic inequality in this nation's society:

> . . . Park's cycle could be employed to justify the status quo and oppose moves to change it. History here is perceived as moving according to its own unchangeable and secret dynamic: Whatever state of affairs exists does so because it cannot be otherwise. Attempts to change the present situation can only result in failure because those changes that are meant to come about will do so when and because they are meant to. Men cannot change or hasten the fate intended for man (p. 68).

Ecological interpretations of the forces shaping urban land use also illustrate the Chicago School's penchant for equating power and privilege with inevitable laws of nature. Early researchers attempted to understand the spatial organization of U.S. cities through application of the ecological analogy. Among the better-known models of urban land use, most texts identify Park and Burgess' (1925) concentric zone theory, the sector model of urban growth developed by Hoyt (1939), and the multiple-nuclei theory deduced by Harris and Ullman (1945) as most influential. While most contemporary social ecologists acknowledge that no city conforms exactly to the various descriptive models developed, they do insist that ecological principles are at work in shaping the structure of urban areas.

Contemporary social ecologists have attempted to expand the number of factors included in early, biosystems models. Nonetheless, the emphasis on an ecological metaphor has been retained. The ecosystem has been enlarged to include not only environmental factors, but also population variables, organizational considerations, technological impacts, and social psychological influences. These five elements (grouped by neoecologists under the acronym POETS), allegedly combine to shape the structure of cities:

> Environment, population, technology, organi-
> zation, and social-psychological elements
> all mutually modify one another, . . . the
> systematic interrelationships underlying
> the ecological community are in a constant
> cycle of adaptation and readaptation (Gist
> and Fava, 1974:159-60).

Thus, while important changes have been made in the early ecological approach to urban land use, it is clear that biological metaphors and analogies still dominate thinking about the city. And even among the more recent advances-- social-area analysis (Shevsky and Bell, 1949) and factorial analysis (Abu-Lughod, 1971)--a biosystems approach still predominates.

Neo-Marxist Urban Theory and Social Ecology

It was not until the 1960s that serious challenges to social-ecology theory were mounted within sociology. Initially inspired by Castells's The Urban Question (1977), a treatise introducing the thinking of French structuralist Althusser (1979) to U.S. urbanists, contemporary urban sociologists launched a research agenda which radically departed from the traditions of social ecology. The emerging neo-Marxist urban research has displayed four interrelated themes over the past decade, all quite distinct from social-ecology theory (Jaret, 1983): (1) a focus on the relationship between local land-use decisions and national and international sources of capital (Cummings and Snider, 1984; Fainstein and Fainstein, 1972; Faegin, 1983); (2) a concern over how the capitalist mode of production shapes the urban landscape, and impacts local class structure, political activities, and cultural practices (Fainstein and Fainstein, 1974; Smith, 1984; Tabb and Sawers, 1978); (3) an emphasis on how deindustrialization and reindustrialization influence local land use, and the delivery of urban social services (Bluestone and Harrison, 1982); and (4) an examination of how the capitalist mode of production shapes the culture and everyday lives of the urban working class (Aronowitz, 1973; Boyte, 1980; Sennett and Cobbs, 1972; Rubin, 1976).

Drawing from Marx and Engels, especially the latter's description of land use in Liverpool, radical urbanists

countered the ecologists by reasoning that changes in technology and population transformations were simple reflections of the basic requirements of the capitalist mode of
production (Jaret, 1983). Traditional urban analysts were
also criticized for their finding that ghetto formation was
an inevitable response to the complex division of labor,
population growth, and cultural predispositions. In contrast, the new urban theorists argued that cities were
fragmented by the dictates of industrial capitalism, and
that competition and conflict between class and racial enclaves were inevitable by-products of the quest for private
profit. Jaret (1983) summarizes a major theme appearing
in recent neo-Marxist urban analysis by observing that:

> The urban complex is understood as the
> field in which inherent conflicts between
> classes and class factions are played out.
> Capitalists attempt to construct an urban
> environment that allows for efficient pro-
> duction and distribution of goods and ser-
> vices, profitable investments, and for con-
> tinuous reproduction of a disunited but
> reliable workforce (p. 50).

Basically, neo-Marxist urban theorists contend that class
conflict and struggle has been displaced from the shop
floor to city streets. The organization of urban space is
viewed by neo-Marxists as the manifestation of capital accumulation and a reflection of the labor-market needs of
the capitalist class.

The neo-Marxists view classical urban theory as
little more than bourgeois ideology glorifying the interests
of the capitalist class. Social-ecology theory, according
to them, incorrectly portrays ethnic and racial ghettos,
inequalities in the urban labor market, and inadequacies
in the delivering of urban services as the result of technological, cultural, and environmental processes. In developing a counterposition, the neo-Marxists have given
primacy to the two forces most clearly absent in classical
urban theory: (1) the state's role in promoting policies
consistent with the needs of the capitalist class, and (2)
the role of the capitalist class itself in shaping the urban
landscape.

In elaborating these two emphases, Castells (1977)
observes that the "urban question" is a crisis in capitalist

production and distribution, and reflects the state's attempt to alleviate that crisis through management of collective consumption. By collective consumption, he means state expenditures in social programs (education, housing, transportation, and health care). Similar to the position developed by O'Connor (1972), Castells argues that because of crises in capital accumulation, state policies must socialize the costs of production and reproduction through expansion of social-welfare programs. Simultaneously, however, the state must leave profits in private hands. Because the state is perpetually caught between the everyday needs of the urban working class and the profit margin requirements of the capitalist class, social policy is a matter of political debate and class conflict. According to the neo-Marxist urbanists, state policy in a capitalist society ". . . sets the course for expanding city budgets, fiscal crises, retrenchment, and urban social protest movements" (Jaret, 1983:503).

Despite changing the substance and nature of urban social theory, neo-Marxist innovations have not enhanced the ability of sociology to contribute more effectively to the development and analysis of urban policy. It is apparent that neo-Marxist interpretations of cities and city life do not glorify the interests of the capitalist class. It is also obvious that neo-Marxist theory represents the activist tradition within sociology, a fact not elevating the appeal of the discipline to those in power. Recognizing this, Himmelstein and Zald (1984) contend that political activism within the social sciences, especially those disciplines branded as "leftist," inspired the Reagan administration to curtail federal funding for social-policy research. Although some university intellectuals think that neo-Marxist scholarship represents the most important conceptual breakthrough in urban sociology in the past several decades (Jaret, 1983), its popularity within the discipline is antithetical to the private-sector agenda being promoted by the Reagan administration. As a result, sociology has become less active in the policy-formation process over the past five years.

On the methodological front, similar divisions have emerged between those urbanists schooled in social ecology and those subscribing to the neo-Marxist viewpoint. Like observations about the Darwinian underpinnings of social ecology, radical critics argue that positivism impacted early perspectives in a markedly conservative manner.

Traditional urban theorists strongly endorsed a rational and scientific approach to the resolution of urban problems. Science, they alleged, held the secrets to development of reasonable urban policies. Wirth (1964) advocated a metropolitan approach to urban planning because localism and neighborhood politics catered to irrational and parochial interests. He endorsed central planning implemented by scientific experts.

Kologowski (1968) maintains that early positivists expressed a utopian idealism based on the premise that rational, scientific thinking should dominate the way in which intellectuals view the social and physical world. One of the visions promoted by early positivists was consolidation of all knowledge into a single science. The positivists were convinced that research, planning, development, and evaluation represented procedures within the physical sciences which were directly transferable to the social sciences. For traditional urban theorists, this latter contention was uncritically accepted.

If the goal of science was to predict and control natural and biological phenomena, social ecologists reasoned that the same objectives could be applied to human activities. Further, if it could be assumed that human behavior was at base bioecological in nature, then rationality and positivism could function to modify human actions along more rational lines (Habermas, 1978). Reflecting the marriage of bioecology and positivism, early urban theorists urged social scientists to become involved in reorganizing society along more rational lines. Their vision of proper social policy, however, was strikingly conservative in nature.

Most early urbanists believed that intellectuals should play an independent and objective role in shaping social policy. Viewing themselves as technical, unbiased experts, they believed that planners should educate policy-makers and illuminate a path leading toward more rational urban policy. Wirth and other early urban theorists were especially insistent that politics and science be separated. He recommended that planners discredit policies forged in the heat of interest-group politics. Local and neighborhood political struggles typically produced partisan policies without meaningful scientific or rational merit. Urban planners, as objective social scientists, were professionally obligated to avoid compromising their methodological integrity by immersing themselves in local political struggles.

Local communities or urban neighborhoods, according to early urbanists, represented the overall breakdown of traditional social order, and the erosion of conventional social bonds. The job of urban planning was to devise and implement policies capable of achieving a more rational social order. Early urban scholars believed that social scientists could help develop policies transcending the fragmentation of urban life produced by the industrialization and population growth. In essence, early urban theorists such as Wirth were suggesting that science and rational planning could be substituted for partisan political struggle. They further suggested that policy formation and analysis could be depoliticized by technical experts, a role specially tailored for social scientists.

Needless to say, many contemporary sociologists question the desirability of substituting science for politics. Neo-Marxist theorists such as Habermas (1971, 1978) argue that the capitalist class has become increasingly dependent upon science and technology. As a result, faith in technological and scientific thinking merely serve as ideologies underwriting the existing distribution of social power and wealth. Science, maintains Habermas (1978), promotes legitimation and contributes to a "depoliticized" existence among the masses. Technical experts simply provide justification for policies supporting the interests of the capitalist class.

In advanced capitalist societies, the application of technical rationality has clouded class interests and masked business domination over the policy-formation process (Habermas, 1978). "Scientific mystification" of the policy process enables the state to control policy formation behind a veil of technical efficiency and professionalism. Through a process of technical rationalization, the class-based origins of most social policies can be obscured and camouflaged. Because science can be used to distort class-based interests and actions, it can serve as a powerful tool of legitimation. As such, science can promote the interests of the capitalist class rather than be used as a tool to liberate the masses. Connerton explains this observation:

> There is a growing awareness in the Western world as a whole that it is necessary to distinguish between the truly liberating effects of natural science, and the use of scientific empiricism, together with the use

of pseudo-science, to underwrite particular distributions of social power (1978:38).

Drawing from these more global criticisms of positivism, neo-Marxist urbanists find the idea of substituting planning for interest-group politics a particularly abhorrent notion. They characterize urban planning as a manipulative tool of the capitalist class (Jaret, 1983). Fainstein and Fainstein (1974) contend that urban planning can be employed by the capitalist class to maintain social control and assist capital accumulation. They see urban planning as an attempt to manage and mask the myriad of urban problems created by the contradictions of capitalism.

Neo-Marxist critics of urban planning also contend that it can be used to move the urban poor from one location to another (Cummings and Snider, 1984; Hartman, 1978), or provide legitimacy for redevelopment decisions made by the capitalist class (Faegin, 1983). Planners promote legitimacy by co-opting the urban underclass through citizen-participation programs (Boyte, 1980; Coit, 1978), or through the provision of a technical and scientific rationale which mystifies and obfuscates the policy process itself (Evans-Andris, 1982). While contemporary critics do not maintain that classical urbanists consciously served the interests of the capitalist class, they do insist that traditional theory and methods subtly endorsed the interests of the rich and powerful. Simply stated, radical critics maintain that classical theory and methods were formulated in a manner that failed to recognize the inherently political nature of the policy process.

THE FISCAL CRISIS, UNIVERSITY INTELLECTUALS, AND THE FUTURE OF THE POLICY SCIENCES

A major issue addressed by this book is what various social-science disciplines must do to meet the public-policy and research needs of U.S. cities in the 1980s. The contemporary needs of cities are largely shaped by the economic problems of the larger society. The economy is deep in the throes of a capital-accumulation crisis and deindustrialization; basic industry is being dismantled. Employment opportunities within the industrial sector are contracting while the lower-paying, service sector is expanding (Bluestone and Harrison, 1982). The urban working class faces a future filled with uncertainty. Many cities in the industrial belts have been devastated by plant closings and the flight of capital to other regions or overseas. Sun-belt cities have been ravaged by chaotic growth and unplanned urban development (Faegin, 1983; Perry and Watkins, 1977). Public services in many cities have been substantially reduced by the fiscal uncertainty accompanying the capital-accumulation crisis.

Academic sociologists find themselves in a very vulnerable position in the 1980s. Universities do not exist in isolation from the political and economic forces shaping the national agenda. Universities themselves are part of the public sector, and as such are extensions of the state. The knowledge that intellectuals produce is dependent upon a financial infrastructure consisting of a physical plant, supplies, computer hardware, and related research equipment, support staff, and the entire institutional apparatus comprising higher education. Political and economic events directly impact the production of knowledge within the university, and influence the kinds of ideas that intellectuals generate. As a result of the fiscal crisis under Reagan and the shift of public investments from legitimation to accumulation functions, many universities have been forced to balance their budgets through elimination of selected teaching and research programs.

Under Reagan, the market for social-science knowledge has been destabilized in both the public and private sectors. And when a market becomes unstable, either a new product line must be created or the firm itself must face bankruptcy. The production of knowledge that is useful to business and industry stimulates the possibility of profit. During a capital-accumulation crisis, the value of knowledge is gauged primarily in business and commercial terms. Social scientists, by and large, do not produce knowledge that assists capital accumulation. The production of knowledge that is useful to the working class or to political dissidents promotes neither capital accumulation nor legitimacy. As a result, disciplines most closely aligned with the poor and working-class elements of society are expendable during a capital-accumulation crisis. Herein resides a political and moral dilemma potentially influencing the future of sociology as a policy science.

Radical sociologists contend that the capitalist class influences the production of knowledge and the flow of information within the public sector in several ways. The

wealthy attempt to influence public policy directly by staff-
ing government positions with individuals sympathetic to
their interests, by extensive lobbying activities, and by
dominating and monitoring the flow of ideas to public agencies and government committees. Domhoff (1970) maintains
that elite universities, major foundations, and upper-class
thinktanks dominate the transmission of ideas and knowledge upon which the several branches and levels of government make key decisions. At the municipal level, the
local elite typically establish the ideological parameters
defining the limits of community and neighborhood-reform
programs. Local bankers, developers, and real-estate
brokers are usually enlisted to oversee revitalization or
redevelopment schemes. Public moneys are usually spent
in a way that benefits local financial and real-estate interests. City managers typically avoid implementing or
endorsing social programs inconsistent with the ideological
persuasions of the local business elite. In comparison with
working-class organizations or agencies representing the
interests of minorities, the wealthy also have much greater
access to the knowledge produced by university intellectuals.

The structure of higher education often plays a key
role in stratifying the information produced by and available to the public sector. As Szymanski (1978) observed,
despite the fact that about 40 percent of the approximately
2,000 institutions of higher education in America are owned
by the state,

> a handful of elite institutions set the aca-
> demic standards and tone for the rest.
> Twenty-five universities grant 75 percent
> of all Ph.D.'s in the United States. Ten
> receive 38 percent of all federal funds. In
> many academic fields members of the top
> ten departments write over 50 percent of
> all the articles appearing in each field's
> major professional journals. Foundation
> grants are also concentrated in several
> leading institutions (in economics and busi-
> ness ten universities and research institu-
> tions received 78 percent of all Ford Founda-
> tion grants from 1951 to 1965) (pp. 248-49).

The relationship among the monopolization of knowledge, social-class interests, and higher education is de-

scribed by David Horowitz (1969) and Ridgeway (1968).
Generally, they argue that knowledge and information produced by universities are at the disposal of large corporations and the wealthy elements of society. Ideas that may
further the interests of working-class groups and organizations are often not produced by universities at all or
left unrewarded and unrecognized by the university incentive system. While public universities have the potential
to serve as information and data-referral systems for
working-class community groups, they seldom do so (Cummings and Lee, 1982).

In the face of the recent incentives to align more
closely with the needs of the capitalist class, university
intellectuals have responded in a manner similar to rank-
and-file workers in severely depressed sectors of the economy. They have become more docile and unable to combat
effectively managerial pressure for increased productivity
and lower wages. Under Reagan, it is clear that a serious
political struggle is taking place within U.S. society, and
it directly affects those employed within the public sector.
Within the academic community, however, those programs
and disciplines furthest removed from the immediate interests of business and industry are destined to suffer more
than those contributing to their agenda.

In order to participate more fully in the policy-
formation process in the 1980s, sociologists will have to
accept and endorse the capital-accumulation agenda being
promoted by the Reagan administration. It is unlikely
that such an endorsement will be forthcoming. On the
other hand, political idealism must be tempered by the
realities of survival within the academy. Between 1970
and 1980, social science showed a steady decline in the
number of bachelor's degrees awarded (Abel, 1981). Conversely, national data showed that substantial increases
were registered in undergraduate majors matriculating from
the fields of business and management, computer and information sciences, and health professions. In addition to
social science, similar declines in enrollment and matricu-
lation appeared in the fields of education, arts and letters,
humanities, and foreign languages. These trends undoubted-
ly reflect the shifting priorities of those in power, and
the recession which has devastated the U.S. economy over
the past decade.

In the wake of the present economic malaise, sociologists come to the policy arena armed with a peculiar theo-

retical and methodological arsenal. It is surely utopian
for university sociologists to disregard the immediate problems which emerge during a capital-accumulation crisis.
While classic urban theory has tended to legitimate the
status quo, and positivism has contributed to political
noninvolvement among many social scientists, these two
postures have not ensured the durability of the sociological
enterprise in the jaws of economic crisis. And while the
neo-Marxists have made important contributions to urban
social theory, it is obvious that the radical viewpoint has
no appeal to the capitalist class, either as a paradigm
promoting legitimacy or as a set of theoretical ideas encouraging capital accumulation.

   As a result, it is unlikely that either type of sociology will be a strong contributor to the actual development of urban policy during the 1980s. And because of
declining student enrollments, it is very likely that research based on either radical or traditional paradigms
will find a very small academic market. University courses
dealing with urban sociology, race and ethnic relations,
and social inequality have encountered very small enrollments over the past few years. A decade ago, these
courses were filled to capacity or overenrolled. Yet sociology and other branches of the social sciences have a long-
standing interest in the problems of the urban working
class, the poor, women, and minorities. Despite the conservative tendencies within early urban theory, sociology--
perhaps more than any other social-science discipline--
raised profound questions about the problems accompanying
the shift from rural to urban society. In the face of the
present fiscal crisis, however, it is becoming more and
more difficult for sociologists to raise critical questions
about social inequality and public policy.

   C. Wright Mills (1959:193), over two decades ago,
identified the political and moral dilemmas facing social
scientists who wish to deal with social problems in a
critical manner:

> To appeal to the powerful, on the basis of
> any knowledge we now have is utopian in
> the foolish sense of that term. Our rela-
> tions with them are more likely to be only
> such relations as they find useful, which
> is to say that we become technicians ac-
> cepting their problems and aims, or ideolo-

gists promoting their prestige and authority. To be more than that, so far as our political role is concerned, we must first of all re-consider the nature of our collective endeavor as social scientists. It is not at all utopian for one social scientist to appeal to his colleagues to undertake such a re-consideration. Any social scientist who is aware of what he is about must confront the major moral dilemma I have implied . . . the difference between what men are interested in and what is [in] men's interest.

Advocating the interests of the urban poor and working class through critical policy research, however, is laced with practical and political hazards. The poor and the powerless are not strong contributors to the market economy. Their purchasing power is modest. They cannot purchase the books and articles published by social scientists or enroll in college classrooms. Nor can they lobby in behalf of academic programs that fall to the budget ax. A sociology, or more generally a social science, that enhances the interests of workingmen and -women as well as the business and professional classes is destined to collide. Further, the self-interest of the poor and intellectual classes is not easily reconciled. When self-interest is not mutual, a political relationship is fair-weather at best. On the other hand, it is much easier to create a social science that enhances and glorifies those classes in a position to assert their interests. While it was possible to mobilize the social-science community to restore budget cuts to federal research programs (Dynes, 1984), few efforts were made to lobby in behalf of saving programs supporting the poor, minorities, and the unemployed. Despite the fact that many social scientists have made a career of studying the poor and the dispossessed, they offered little political assistance to them when Reagan's budget ax swung in their direction.

As the several essays in this volume indicate, the nature of urban problems has shifted dramatically over the past decade. Sociology's future influence on urban-policy analysis and development will be shaped by its ability to apply its unique tradition to these shifting concerns. In the final analysis, academic participation in the development of urban policy can be best accomplished through political activism. I am inclined to agree with radical criticisms of classical urban theory, and the observation that positivism has encouraged the substitution of science for politics. Social scientists, including sociologists, can no longer afford to view themselves as detached, objective observers of social phenomena. Nor should sociology, in the face of mounting pressures to serve the interests of the business classes, abandon its allegiance with those groups and classes most severely impacted by the problems of industrial society. Knowledge has political uses; social policy is by definition formulated through the political process. Policies that glorify the interests of one class over another do little to promote the public good. A social science capable of enhancing the human condition is a vision worthy of preservation. In preserving that vision, university social scientists have a special responsibility to recognize and unmask the class-based priorities of social policies, and realize their own potential to be used as ideologists promoting class domination and conflict.

REFERENCES

Abel, Robert. 1981. "Degrees Awarded in the Nation and the South, by Sex, 1979-80." Atlanta: Southern Regional Educational Board.

Abramson, Harold, and Rosalie Wences. 1971. "Faculty Opinion on the Issues of Job Placement and Dissent in the University." Social Problems 18 (Summer): 27-38.

Abramson, Mark. 1980. Urban Sociology. Englewood Cliffs, N.J.: Prentice-Hall.

Abu-Lughod, Jave F. 1971. Cairo: 1001 Years of the City. Princeton, N.J.: Princeton University Press.

Althusser, Louis. 1979. For Marx. London: Verso.

Anderson, Nels. 1923. The Hobo. Chicago: University of Chicago Press.

Aronowitz, Stanley. 1973. False Promises. New York: McGraw-Hill.

Bardo, John W., and John J. Hartman. 1982. Urban Sociology. Itasca, Ill.: Peacock.

Bates, Allan P., and Joseph Julian. 1975. Sociology, Understanding Social Behavior. Boston: Houghton Mifflin.

Becker, Howard. 1967. "Whose Side Are We On?" Social Problems 14 (Winter): 239-47.

Bluestone, Barry, and Bennett Harrison. 1982. The De-industrialization of America. New York: Basic Books.

Bowles, Samuel, and Herbert Gintis. 1976. Schooling in Capitalist America. New York: Basic Books.

Boyte, Harry. 1980. The Backyard Revolution. Philadel-phia: Temple University Press.

Butler, Edgar. 1976. Urban Sociology. New York: Harper and Row.

Castells, Manual M. 1977. The Urban Question: A Marx-ist Approach. Cambridge, Mass.: MIT Press.

Chronicle of Higher Education. 1984. "G. E. Foundation Adds $11 Million to Aid Program." July 11.

Chubin, Darly, and James L. McCartney. 1982. "Financing Sociological Research: A Future Only Dimly Perceived." The American Sociologist 17 (November): 226-35.

Coit, Katherine. 1978. "Local Action, Not Citizen Partici-pation." In Marxism and the Metropolis, edited by William Tabb and Larry Sawers. New York: Oxford University Press, 297-311.

Connerton, Paul. 1978. Critical Sociology. New York: Penguin.

Cooley, Charles H. 1902. Social Organization. New York: Scribner's.

Cousins, Albert, and Hans Nagpaul. 1979. Urban Life. New York: Wiley.

Cressey, Paul. 1932. The Taxi Dance Hall. Chicago: University of Chicago Press.

Cummings, Scott. 1984. "The Political Economy of Social Science Funding." Sociological Inquiry 54 (Spring): 154-70.

Cummings, Scott, and E. Snider. 1984. "Municipal Code Enforcement and Urban Redevelopment: Private Decisions and Public Policy in an American City." Review of Radical Political Economy 16: 129-50.

Cummings, Scott, and Joe Lee. 1982. "Community Service within the Urban University." Urban Education 17 (October): 267-89.

Diesing, Paul. 1982. Science and Ideology in the Policy Sciences. New York: Aldine.

Domhoff, William. 1970. The Higher Circles. New York: Vintage.

Durkheim, Emile. 1893. The Division of Labor. Glencoe, Ill.: Free Press, 1947.

Dynes, Russell. 1984. "The Institutionalization of COSSA: An Innovation Response to Crises by American Social Sciences." Sociological Inquiry 54 (Spring): 211-29.

Engels, Frederich. 1845. The Condition of the Working Class in England. London: International Publishers, 1962.

Evans-Andris, Melissa. 1982. "Legitimacy and Rationality Through Human Services Integration." M.A. thesis. Department of Sociology, University of Louisville, Louisville, Ky.

Faegin, Joe R. 1983. The Urban Real Estate Game. Englewood Cliffs, N.J.: Prentice-Hall.

Fainstein, Susan, and Norman Fainstein. 1972. The View from Below: Urban Politics and Social Policy. Boston: Little, Brown.

_____. 1974. Urban Political Movements. Englewood Cliffs, N.J.: Prentice-Hall.

Faris, Robert E. L. 1970. Chicago Sociology: 1920-32. Chicago: University of Chicago Press.

Fischer, Claude. 1976. The Urban Experience. New York: Harcourt Brace Jovanovich.

Gist, Noel, and Sylvia Fava. 1974. Urban Society. New York: Thomas Y. Crowell.

Gouldner, Alvin. 1968. "The Sociologist as Partisan: Sociology and the Welfare State." American Sociologist 3 (May): 103-16.

Habermas, Jurgen. 1971. Toward a Rational Society. Boston: Beacon Press.

_____. 1975. Legitimation Crisis. Boston: Beacon Press.

_____. 1978. "Theory and Practice in a Scientific Civilization." In Critical Sociology, edited by Paul Connerton. New York: Penguin.

Harris, Chauncey, and Edward Ullman. 1945. "The Nature of Cities." Annals of the American Academy of Social Science 242 (November): 7-17.

Hartman, Chester. 1978. Yerba Buena: Land Grab and Community Resistance in San Francisco. San Francisco: Volcano Press.

Harvey, David. 1973. Social Justice and the City. Baltimore: Johns Hopkins University Press.

Hawley, Amos. 1971. Urban Society. New York: John Wiley.

Himmelstein, Jerry, and Mayer N. Zald. 1984. "American Conservatives and Government Funding of the Social Sciences and the Arts." Sociological Inquiry 54 (Spring): 171-87.

Horowitz, David. 1969. The Universities and the Ruling Class. San Francisco: Bay Area Radical Evaluation Project.

Horowitz, Irving. 1963. "Sociology for Sale." Studies on the Left 3 (Winter): 109–15.

Hoyt, Homer. 1939. The Structure and Growth of Residential Neighborhoods in American Cities. Washington, D.C.: Federal Housing Administration.

Jaret, Charles. 1983. "Recent Neo-Marxist Urban Analysis." In Annual Review of Sociology, Vol. 9, edited by Ralph Turner and James Short. Palo Alto, Calif.: Annual Reviews.

Kamin, Leon. 1974. "Science and Politics of I.Q." Social Research 41 (Autumn): 387–425.

Kologowski, Leszek. 1968. The Alienation of Reason. New York: Doubleday.

Ladd, Everett, and Seymour Lipset. 1976. The Divided Academy. New York: W. W. Norton.

Leggett, John C. 1984. "Getting the Data but Not Having the Bucks." Humanity and Society. Forthcoming.

Lekachman, Robert. 1982. Greed Is Not Enough: Reaganomics. New York: Pantheon.

Levitan, Sar, and Robert Taggart. 1976. The Promise of Greatness. Cambridge, Mass.: Harvard University Press.

Lipset, Seymour M. 1976. Rebellion in the University. New York: Beckman.

Lyman, Sanford. 1972. The Black American in Sociological Thought. New York: Capricorn Books.

Madge, John. 1962. The Origins of Scientific Sociology. New York: Free Press.

Maine, Henry. 1870. Ancient Law. London: John Murray.

Mannheim, Karl. 1936. Ideology and Utopia. New York: Harcourt, Brace, and World.

Marx, Karl, and Frederich Engels. 1846. The German Ideology. London: International Publishers, 1962.

McKenzie, Roderick. 1933. The Metropolitan Community. New York: McGraw-Hill.

Meadows, Edward. 1981. "Laffer's Curveball Picks up Speed." Fortune, February 23, 85–88.

Mills, C. Wright. 1959. The Sociological Imagination. New York: Oxford University Press.

Molotch, Harvey. 1984. "Tensions in the Growth Machine: Overcoming Resistance to Value-Free Development." Social Problems 3 (June): 483–99.

_____. 1976. "The City as a Growth Machine." American Journal of Sociology 82: 309–30.

Nicolaus, M. 1968. "Remarks at the American Sociological Association Convention." American Sociologist 14 (May): 154–56.

O'Connor, James L. 1972. The Fiscal Crisis of the State. New York: St. Martin's.

Palen, J. John. 1975. The Urban World. New York: McGraw-Hill.

Park, Robert. 1952. Human Communities. New York: Free Press.

Park, Robert, and E. Burgess. 1925. The City. Chicago: University of Chicago Press.

Perry, David, and Alfred Watkins. 1977. The Rise of Sunbelt Cities. Beverly Hills, Calif.: Sage.

Piven, Frances Fox, and Richard Cloward. 1977. Poor People's Movements. New York: Pantheon.

Ridgeway, James. 1968. The Closed Corporation. New York: Ballantine.

Rossi, Peter H. 1972. "Testing for Success and Failure in Social Action." In Evaluating Social Programs, edited by Peter H. Rossi and Walter Williams. New York: Seminar Press., 11–38.

Rubin, Lillian. 1976. Worlds of Pain. New York: Basic Books.

Rudnick, Andrew J. 1983. "The American University in the Urban Context: A Status Report and Call for Leadership." Washington, D.C.: National Association of State Universities and Land Grant Colleges.

Savas, E. S. 1982. Privatizing the Public Sector. Chatham, N.J.: Chatham House.

Schumpeter, Joseph. 1954. History of Economic Analysis. New York: Oxford University Press.

Schwab, William. 1982. Urban Sociology. Reading, Mass.: Addison-Wesley.

Sennett, Richard, and Jonathan Cobbs. 1972. The Hidden Injuries of Class. New York: Random House.

Shaw, Clifford. 1930. The Jackroller. Chicago: University of Chicago Press.

Shevsky, Eshref, and Wendell Bell. 1949. The Social Area of Los Angeles. Los Angeles: University of California Press.

Smith, Michael Peter. 1979. The City and Social Theory. New York: St. Martin's.

_____. 1984. Cities in Transformation. Beverly Hills, Calif.: Sage.

Stark, Irwin. 1983. "Industrializing Our Universities." Dissent (Spring): 177–82.

Suttles, Gerald. 1968. The Social Order of the Slum. Chicago: University of Chicago Press.

————. 1972. The Social Construction of Communities. Chicago: University of Chicago Press.

Szymanski, Albert. 1978. The Capitalist State and the Politics of Class. Englewood Cliffs, N.J.: Prentice-Hall.

Tabb, William. 1970. The Political Economy of the Black Ghetto. New York: W. W. Norton.

Tabb, William, and L. Sawers. 1978. Marxism and the Metropolis. New York: Oxford University Press.

Taylor, Lee. 1980. Urbanized Society. Santa Monica, Calif.: Goodyear.

Thomlinson, Ralph. 1969. Urban Structure. New York: Random House.

Thrasher, Frederick M. 1927. The Gang. Chicago: University of Chicago Press.

Toennies, Ferdinand. 1956. Community and Society. East Lansing, Mich.: Michigan State University Press.

Whitt, J. Allen. 1982. Urban Elites and Mass Transportation. Princeton, N.J.: Princeton University Press.

Wirth, Louis. 1928. The Ghetto. Chicago: University of Chicago Press.

————. 1939. "Localism, Regionalism, and Centralization." American Journal of Sociology 44 (May): 485-98.

————. 1964. Louis Wirth on Cities and Social Life: Selected Papers, edited by Albert Reiss. Chicago: University of Chicago Press.

Zorbaugh, Harvey. 1929. The Gold Coast and the Slum. Chicago: University of Chicago Press.

Zuiches, James. 1984. "The Organization and Funding of Social Sciences in 16 NSF." Sociological Inquiry 54 (Spring): 18-210.

9

Economics and Urban Policy Analysis

Jeffrey I. Chapman, Gary J. Reid, and Donald R. Winkler

The birth of economics as a discipline is usually assigned to the year 1776, the publication date of Adam Smith's The Wealth of Nations. However, only 50 years later, in 1826, Von Thunen published the first significant work in urban economics, his treatise on location theory.

Subsequent to these dates, the field of economics primarily dealt with market phenomena, while urban economics focused principally on the location of economic activity. Major contributions to economic theory and location theory were made in the late-nineteenth and early-twentieth centuries by Alfred Marshall (1890) and Alfred Weber (1909). Public economics was not ignored in this period but was not the focus of intense research and writing. One would, however, be remiss in not mentioning the contributions of Ricardo (1819) to the theory of taxation and the writings of Wicksell (1896) and Lindahl (1919) on the theory of public choice.

Modern contributions to the literature of public economics include Samuelson's (1957) and Musgrave's (1959) work on the theory of public goods and writings on externalities by Scitovsky (1957), Coase (1960), and Buchanan and Stubblebine (1962). This theoretical literature provided an important basis for application of microeconomic theory to urban-policy problems.

Active interest in applying economic analysis to urban policy largely parallels these theoretical breakthroughs in public economics. In 1959, the Resources for the Future established the Committee on Urban Economics, which helped to foster the development of modern urban economics. This effort was not hindered by the newly awakened social conscience of the 1960s, which resulted in federal-government and private-foundation funding of research on urban-policy problems.

The theoretical work and subsequent empirical investigations produced a large literature applying economic analysis to urban problems, beginning in the 1960s and peaking in the early 1970s. Among some of the more significant books that exemplify this effort are the research monographs of Muth (1969) and Netzer (1970) and the compilation of important research in urban economics, edited by Edel and Rothenberg (1972). Academic research interest in urban economics has waned from its peak in the mid-1970s, partly in response to reduced research funding. On the other hand, economics is more widely used by a large variety of urban analysts than ever before. This partly reflects the successful dissemination of economic thought to a new generation of urban planners and public administrators. As recently as ten years ago, economic theory was not an important component of the curricula of most professional schools involved in the training of urban planners, analysts, and administrators. Today economics is an integral component of the curricula of most departments or schools of planning and is gaining increasing importance in public-administration and public-policy programs as well.

The situs of economics-oriented academic research has also changed. Initially, such research was done primarily by faculty and graduate students in the nation's economics departments. Increasingly, much of the applied research in urban-economic analysis is being done in departments or schools of urban planning, public-policy analysis, and public administration. This is a natural progression, given the basic interdisciplinary nature of urban-policy analysis and the quest by academic economists to become more rigorous and mathematical in approach, and thus, less accessible to the potential consumer of urban-policy research.

One of the most important contributions of this change in situs to the analysis of the applied microtheorists is that the institutional structure is being more explicitly included in the design and verification of the theoretical constructs. Economists in these departments have emphasized that when institutional constraints and incentives are included in urban analysis, they add a robustness to the economic reasoning that is in their work. A type of symbiotic relationship among the disciplines has thus developed, with the noneconomists gaining from the internal logical consistencies of the economic analysis and the economists gaining from the increased sensitivity to the way that institutions affect, constrain, and stimulate individual behavior.

Economic theory, as applied to urban-policy problems, is at a watershed. The noneconomist often perceives the predictions of the macrotheorists as useless. Because of this, the specific recommendations and analysis of the applied microtheorist are often ignored. At the same time, the pure microtheorist often has little time for pure policy questions; and often the use of applied theory, coming from outside economics departments, seems slightly disreputable. When colleagues of economists within noneconomics departments read and critique work by the applied theorists, they tend to question as unrealistic the traditional theoretical definitions and empirical assumptions that are made in order to get the models to "work." And, finally, applied economists are sometimes criticized for their tendencies (although clearly not uniform) to submerge the problems of income distribution and political implementation to those of efficiency.

In what follows, this chapter reviews some of the more important economic concepts used in urban-policy analysis. It then briefly reviews economic contributions to urban-policy analysis with special attention paid to two substantive areas--fiscal limitations and the production of human capital. Finally, the contribution of economics to urban policy is critically examined.

ECONOMIC CONCEPTS USED IN URBAN-POLICY ANALYSIS

The discipline of economics is divided into the study of the macroeconomy and the study of the microeconomic behavior of individuals, firms, and public organizations. It is microeconomics that provides the set of tools and concepts that are used to analyze urban-policy problems. In order to understand more fully the contribution of economics to urban-policy analysis, it is first necessary to appreciate these economic tools.

Demand Theory

The theory of consumer demand explains the factors that influence consumers' demands for goods and services; empirical work on demand has estimated the magnitude of the relationships among incomes, prices, and quantities demanded of particular goods and services. This theoretical and empirical work contributes to urban-policy analysis in two principal ways. First, it has helped focus attention on the constraints and potential for policy intervention in private markets such as housing, transportation, and health care. For example, transportation economists have estimated models of demand for alternative transit modes. These models provide, among other things, implications for the most effective policies to encourage ridership on mass transit.

Demand theory has also contributed to the development of a political analogue, public-choice theory, which views the level of public-service provision as being determined in a political marketplace. The result has been theoretical and empirical work that attempts to explain voting behavior and variations in public service-tax level combinations. For example, public-choice theory has been used to explain the recent fiscal-limitation movement.

Supply Theory

Economic theory also contributes to our understanding of the determinants of the costs of producing goods and services and the relationship between these costs and the amount of goods and services provided to the market by private firms. Again, the nature of this relationship is critical if one is to assess the impacts of urban-policy alternatives accurately. For example, studies of the supply of housing to low-income families suggest how alternative public policies influence the price and quantity of such housing provided (Struyk and Bendick, 1981).

Production Theory

The nature of economic production is one of the oldest subjects in economics, having been a major contribution of Adam Smith. Production theory provides an understanding of how inputs are combined to produce outputs, the marginal productivities of inputs, and returns to scale in production. Empirical work in production functions provides estimates of the marginal productivities of inputs, an essential piece of information when combined with input prices for assessing the efficiency of resource allocation in production.

Only recently has attention focused on production functions in the public sector. Several studies have investigated production functions in education and crime deterrence (Chapman, 1976) with the aim of increasing efficiency in the public sector. Other studies have explicitly compared efficiency in production of the same service between the public and private sectors, with implications for direct provision of services of government versus contracting with private providers (Bennett and Johnson, 1980).

Efficiency

Efficiency in economics means more than the full utilization of resources (a necessary but not sufficient condition). It also means that those resources are allocated so that consumer welfare (as measured by individual consumers) is maximized, given resource constraints. Efficiency as used in public-policy analysis is usually interpreted as maximization of some policy objective given a budget or resource constraint. Efficiency can often be easily assessed when consensus exists around some specific policy objective. Efficiency is not, however, so easily assessed when no consensus exists or when policies have several objectives. However, even in this latter case, studies of efficiency can demonstrate how much of one objective needs to be foregone to attain some other objective.

Externalities

Externalities refer to the uncompensated costs or benefits one party imposes on another. Externalities exist because property rights do not exist or cannot be enforced. From society's perspective, the lack of property rights and compensation results in either insufficient or excess production of the externality. Hence, government intervention may be required to either increase production of externalities (in the case of positive externalities) or to decrease production of externalities (in the case of negative ones). Externalities are a contributing cause to many urban problems, ranging from air and water pollution to traffic congestion and crime. Understanding the nature of externalities and how they cause urban problems provides guidance for public policies to treat them.

Opportunity Costs

Opportunity costs means that in a world of fully utilized resources anytime one activity is undertaken, some other activity must be given up. This is an extremely important and useful concept in urban-policy analysis. It suggests, among other things, that specific policies should not be evaluated solely on their own merits but should also be evaluated relative to other policies they displace. An example is given by urban transportation policy. Many local decision-makers strongly prefer fixed-rail transit, arguing that local cost is low due to federal grants. This reasoning often ignores the opportunity costs of not spending the local share of capital and operating costs on other potential solutions to the problem, for example, better bus service.

Marginal Decision Making

The concept of marginal analysis or marginal decision making helps clarify which policies should be subjected to evaluation and analysis. Marginal decision making means that expansion or contraction of any program should be made on the basis of the changes in costs and benefits associated with the expansion or contraction, not on the total costs and benefits of the entire program. Fixed costs are regarded as sunk costs in economics and, since they cannot be altered, should not influence the decision-making calculus. There are, of course, many examples of projects and programs being continued or expanded on the basis of fixed costs or on the basis of total net benefits, when in fact marginal net benefits are negative and the program should be discontinued or reduced in size. Increased use of marginal analysis would enhance efficient resource allocation in urban programs and policies.

Incidence

Another important concept that economists bring to urban-policy analysis is that of incidence. Economic incidence refers to the ultimate bearer of the costs or benefits of public-policy actions. The distinction between economic and legal incidence is a critical one. For example, the legal incidence of the property tax falls upon the owner of property, but recent analysis suggests that much of the effective economic incidence falls upon all owners of capital.

While discussions of incidence have typically involved taxation, the concept has much broader application. For example, the benefits of subsidies to mass transit may be largely enjoyed by automobile drivers who experience less traffic congestion and faster travel times. And, there is some evidence that the benefits of compensatory-education programs that segregate students in order to provide the enriched service largely accrue to the students who remain in the traditional classroom, that is, the nontargeted students. The incidence of the costs and benefits of policies are widely misunderstood and are often difficult to demonstrate empirically. However, the simplistic assumption often made in project evaluations that the legal or intended beneficiaries of public policies are the actual beneficiaries is often erroneous. Economists can contribute to analysis of the effective incidence of costs and benefits of public policy. The contribution has been insufficiently exploited to date.

The economic concepts discussed above are some of those most frequently used by economists in urban-policy analysis. The listing of concepts has not been exhaustive, and the usefulness of the concepts has not been adequately demonstrated in the last few paragraphs. Indeed, to discuss thoroughly all economic concepts and demonstrate their use in urban-policy analysis would require a textbook, and several have been written on this very topic. Interested readers might consult, for example, Mills (1980).

In the paragraphs below we discuss in some more detail the urban-policy areas which have been the subject of economic analysis using the concepts delineated above. Two urban-policy areas—fiscal limitations and educational production—have been selected for more thorough discussion.

ECONOMIC LITERATURE ON URBAN-POLICY ANALYSIS

Microeconomic concepts have contributed to the analysis of a multitude of urban problems. Perusal of textbooks and edited books of readings in urban economics provides a survey of the uses and contributions of economics. The urban-problems studies by economists include local government finance, the causes and consequences of the fiscal-limitation movement, urban crime, housing, education, poverty, employment, and the environment.

Since it is not possible in a few pages to explore adequately the range of economic contributions to analysis of all the above problems, we have selected only two to discuss in some detail. The first topic is the contribution of economics in explaining why voters have passed fiscal limitations in recent years. The second is the production of human capital or learning among schoolchildren. These topics are characteristic of much applied urban microeconomic theory. Their predictions were reasonable, accurate, and the work did add insight to the phenomena. And, with respect to the educational studies, some changes in policies were ultimately implemented.

During the late 1970s and early 1980s, citizens' dissatisfaction with their governments' taxing and spending packages evidenced itself in votes on numerous tax and expenditure limitations. Proposition 13 in California, a 1978 state constitutional amendment significantly restricting local property-taxing powers, was the first major victory for tax and expenditure limitation proponents. Other major victories included the Headlee Amendment (1978) in Michigan and Proposition $2\frac{1}{2}$ (1980) in Massachusetts. The Headlee Amendment limited state revenues from own resources, prohibited new, state-mandated local expenditures unless paid for by the state, and also limited the rate of growth of local property-tax revenues by imposing automatic rate reductions if assessments grew more rapidly than overall inflation. Massachusetts's Proposition $2\frac{1}{2}$ required, among other things, that effective local property-tax rates not exceed 2.5 percent of full market value.

Two important features of these and many other recent tax and expenditure limitations are: (1) They were passed into law via the initiative process, rather than via the normal legislative process, and (2) They were imposed at the state level, but placed constraints upon local governments (the Headlee Amendment constrains both state and local governments).

Economists have contributed to our understanding of recent voter support for such tax and expenditure limitations in at least two distinct ways. First, they have developed a number of models of the public-service provisions process, which provide important suggestions as to why individual voters might believe the public sector is too large. Second, they have conducted empirical analyses of voter support for particular tax and expenditure-limitation initiatives, which have tested a number of hypotheses as to the motives of voters supporting those initiatives. One puzzle, however, is brought into focus, but left unsolved by the research done by economists on public choice and public-service provision; namely, why did local governments suffer the brunt of the tax and expenditure limitation movement's ire?

The Public-service Provision Process

Early economic research on the determinants of public-expenditure levels focused on voters' demands for public services, while largely ignoring the supply side. More accurately, the supply side was modeled as highly competitive, with politicians (incumbents and challengers) vying frequently for election. The complete dependence of politicians upon voters assured that political choices would reflect the demands of voters, not the desires of politicians (see, for example, Hotelling, 1929; Downs, 1957). Under such circumstances one would, indeed, be surprised to find voters tying their own hands by imposing constitutional constraints on the ability of such a political process to raise and spend the revenues desired by those same voters.

More recently, economists have dissected the supply side of the public-service determination process with an eye to identifying reasons why that process might not be completely demand-driven. In so doing, they have identified three types of reasons why the public sector might absorb more resources than voters would like.

Budget-maximizing public-service provision agencies may be in a position to force the level of publicly provided services to exceed that desired by voters. Several analysts have posited such models. Niskanen (1975) invests bureaucracies with monopoly power over key information about the production process, and assumes that bureaucrats try to maximize their own power and prestige by maximizing their budgets. Other analysts obtain similar conclusions about excessive service levels by focusing on the ability of certain high-demand voting blocs or politicians to control the way in which proposals are presented and voted on (Romer and Rosenthal, 1979). These agenda-setter models predict higher service levels and expenditures than would be obtained if all options were voted upon directly by voters and the median voter were decisive.

Courant, Gramlich, and Rubinfeld (1979) have carefully analyzed the limits to the ability of public employees to obtain wage rates in excess of those paid to their private-sector counterparts. While public-employee wage rates are limited by, among other things, the self-interest of those employees in protecting their jobs, there is reason to believe that when those employees can exercise bargaining power, their wages will exceed competitive wage rates. This will drive up the cost to voters of any given level of public services.

Public-service provision agencies may operate inefficiently, by employing less than optimal combinations of factors of production (for example, too much labor and too little capital). Fiorina and Noll (1978) have analyzed why and how this might occur.

The economic research on the public-service provision process provides the above insights, which suggest reasons why voters might have believed that government was absorbing too much of society's scarce resources when they voted on initiatives such as Proposition 13, the Headlee Amendment, and Proposition 2½. Other economists have employed these insights, plus the observation that any particular tax limitation can be expected to redistribute the tax burden, to guide their research on the factors behind the tax and expenditure-limitation movement. This research suggests that all of these factors, with perhaps the exception of excessive public employee wages, help to explain tax cap support. Analyses of the vote on Proposition 13 in California found evidence that voters were seeking to shift the tax burden from themselves as local property taxpayers to state taxpayers (Citrin, 1979). Other researchers also found evidence that California voters wanted lower services (Shapiro, 1980). Analyses of the votes on Michigan's Headlee Amendment (Courant, Gramlich, and Rubinfeld, 1980) and Massachusetts's Proposition 2½ (Ladd and Wilson, 1983) found, in contrast, strong evidence that voters were more interested in reducing ineffi-

ciency and waste in government than in shifting tax burdens, reducing services, or cutting public-employee wage
rates.

In sum, the theoretical analyses by economists of
the public-service provision process identified three potential reasons why voters might want to limit the ability of
their governments to raise and spend taxes: excessive
services, excessive public-employee wages, and inefficient
service provision. Economic and public-choice theory also
identify a fourth potential voter motivation for supporting
a particular tax cap: namely, to shift the tax burden
from oneself to other voters. Empirical research guided by
these insights has found their importance to vary, depending on the particular tax and expenditure-limitation being
examined. Only the excessive public-employee wage rate
motivation has failed to gain substantial empirical support.

Production of Human Capital

Another urban-policy problem to which economists
have contributed analysis and understanding is the production of human capital. This is a topic which social
scientists of various persuasions have studied; indeed,
economists long ignored this subject area, leaving it to
sociologists and educational psychologists. The breakthrough in terms of stimulating interest by economists in
human-capital issues was provided by the theoretical work
of Gary Becker (1964). Becker demonstrated that economic
theory provided powerful explanations for observed variations in human-capital investments by individuals and
firms; indeed, compared with sociological and psychological
explanations of such phenomena, economics often gave simp-
ler and more elegant answers.

Becker's theoretical work stimulated a number of
studies of the rates of return to investments in education
and the contribution of education to both productivity and
economic growth. However, economists largely ignored the
production of human capital until two developments occurred.
One was the growing concern in the 1960s with economic
inequality and the role of education in generating those
differences; of particular concern was educational and economic inequalities between ethnic groups. The second was
a study of educational opportunity in the United States,
commissioned by Congress. That study, by sociologist

James Coleman (1966), evidenced some of the methodological differences between economics and sociology and, also, generated a significant research response by economists.

The Coleman study concluded that variations in school resources explained very little of the variation in learning among schoolchildren in the United States. The economists' response was provided by Bowles and Levin (1968) who argued first that for policy purposes Coleman should have attempted to determine the marginal productivity of school resources and, second, that Coleman's methodology was erroneous.

Subsequently, Hanushek (1972) reanalyzed the Coleman data and concluded that, using the appropriate methodology, school resources were in fact significantly related to learning. Other economic studies that followed used different data sets to estimate production functions for learning among elementary and secondary schoolchildren. Winkler (1975), for example, studied learning differences between black and white schoolchildren and concluded that differences in school resources, including peer-group composition, explained an important part of those learning differences.

Other studies that followed explored facets of educational production. Ritzen and Winkler (1977a), for example, argued that estimates of educational production functions assumed that the sole objective of schools was to maximize learning; they showed that acknowledging schools have multiple objectives resulted in different estimates of the productivity of school resources. They also argued (1977b) that what was important for policy considerations was the level of learning at the end of the elementary-secondary schooling period, and that public policy should attempt to distribute school resources over the school life of the child so as to maximize the final learning level.

Economic analysis has contributed theory to understand the production of human capital, has focused attention on those parameters and variables most important for cost-effective policy considerations, and has contributed to the determination of public policy. In terms of theoretical understanding, economics highlighted the importance of the returns to education in explaining some of the learning differences among children. In particular, theory demonstrates how perceived differences in the monetary rewards associated with schooling can explain the time and resource investments made by children and parents. In addition, theory indicates that differences in the discount rate (rate of time preference) individuals apply to the stream of future benefits can, also, explain variations in personal effort and motivation to learn. Economic theory also demonstrates the importance of opportunity costs as a component of total costs in the individual cost-benefit calculation regarding how much schooling to undertake. Finally, economic theory demonstrates the importance of estimating marginal productivity in order to maximize learning with a given set of resources.

A CRITICAL EXAMINATION OF ECONOMICS' CONTRIBUTIONS TO URBAN-POLICY ANALYSIS

Economics has clearly contributed to our understanding of urban problems and the evaluation of possible policies to treat those problems. The impact of economic research on urban policies, however, is difficult to measure. To some extent, economists have succeeded in educating current and future policy analysts and informing the decision-maker with respect to desirable policy alternatives. However, in spite of this education, the economists' policy prescriptions are frequently ignored in the short run. One example is given by the recent adoption by several cities of fixed-rail transit systems, which transportation economists typically rate among the least cost-effective transit alternatives. Another example is the focus in educational policy on improving educational quality for poor children by reducing class size rather than by providing higher-quality teachers, in spite of economic research that shows a very weak relationship between learning and class size and a very strong relationship between learning and teacher quality.

The limited immediate policy impact of economic research on urban problems is in part attributable to the largely insular nature of that research; interdisciplinary research has been the exception, not the rule, among academics. Formal research grants are rare for applied, policy-relevant work. Indeed, the great gulf between knowledge and policy adoption demonstrates the need for interdisciplinary efforts that pay explicit attention to implementation as well as analysis.

Economists have traditionally viewed their role as one of providing objective policy advice and information to decision-makers. However, if economics is to have greater policy impact, attention needs to be paid to the institutional and political constraints on the adoption of new policies. This is an area which lends itself to inter-disciplinary cooperation. One example of this relates to organizational theory. Recently, significant books by Breton and Wintrobe (1982) and Hoenack (1983) have applied economics to the analysis of organizations. As economists increasingly interact with other disciplines in multi-disciplinary schools of planning, policy, and public administration, one can expect increasing use of economics to study public organizations and better understand how government actually works. The result of this research endeavor may be the successful integration of implementation feasibility in the policy-analytic process.

REFERENCES

Attiyeh, Richard, and Robert F. Engle. 1979. "Testing Some Propositions about Proposition 13." National Tax Journal: Supplement 32(2): 131–46.

Becker, Gary. 1964. Human Capital. New York: Columbia University Press.

Bennett, James T., and Manuel H. Johnson. 1980. "Tax Reduction without Sacrifice: Private Sector Production of Public Services." Public Finance Quarterly 8(4): 363–96.

Bowles, Sam, and H. Levin. 1968. "Some Determinants of Scholastic Achievement--An Appraisal of Some Recent Evidence." Journal of Human Resources 3(2): 3–24.

Breton, André, and R. Wintrobe. 1982. The Logic of Bureaucratic Conduct. New York: Cambridge University Press.

Buchanan, James, and W. C. Stubblebine. 1962. "Externality." Economica 29: 347–75.

Chapman, Jeffrey I. 1976. "An Economic Model of Crime and Police: Some Empirical Results." Journal of Research in Crime and Delinquency, 48–63.

Citrin, Jack. 1979. "Do People Want Something for Nothing: Public Opinion on Taxes and Government Spending." National Tax Journal: Supplement 32(2): 113-30.

Coase, Ronald. 1960. "The Problem of Social Cost." Journal of Law and Economics.

Coleman, James, et al. 1966. Equality of Educational Opportunity. Office of Education, U.S. Government Printing Office.

Courant, P. N., E. M. Gramlich, and D. L. Rubinfeld. 1979. "Public Employee Market Power and the Level of Government Spending." American Economic Review 69(5): 806-17.

Downs, Anthony. 1957. An Economic Theory of Democracy. New York: Harper and Row.

Edel, M., and J. Rothenberg, eds. 1972. Readings in Urban Economics. Macmillan.

Fiorina, Morris P., and Roger G. Noll. 1978. "Voters, Bureaucrats and Legislators: A Rational Choice Perspective on the Growth of Bureaucracy." Journal of Public Economics 9: 232-54.

Hanushek, Eric. 1972. Education and Race. Lexington Press.

Hoenack, Stephen. 1983. Economic Behavior within Organizations. Cambridge University Press.

Hotelling, Harold. 1929. "Stability in Competition." Economic Journal 39: 41-57.

Ladd, Helen F., and Julie B. Wilson. 1983. "Who Supports Tax Limitations: Evidence from Massachusetts' Proposition 2 1/2." Journal of Policy Analysis and Management 2(2): 256-79.

Lindahl, E. 1919. "Positive Losung." Die Gerechtigkeit der Besteurung. Lund, Sweden.

Marshall, Alfred. 1890. Principles of Economics. London: Macmillan.

Mills, Edwin S. 1980. Urban Economics. Glenview, Ill.: Scott, Foresman.

Musgrave, Richard. 1959. The Theory of Public Finance. New York: McGraw-Hill.

Muth, Richard. 1969. Cities and Housing. Chicago: University of Chicago Press.

Netzer, Dick. 1970. Economics and Urban Problems. New York: Basic Books.

Niskanen, William A. 1975. "Bureaucrats and Politicians." Journal of Law and Economics 18(3): 617-43.

Ricardo, David. 1819. The Principles of Political Economy and Taxation. London: Dent.

Ritzen, J., and D. Winkler. 1977a. "The Revealed Preferences of a Local Government Bureaucracy." Journal of Urban Economics 4(3): 310-23.

_____. 1977b. "The Production of Human Capital Over Time." Review of Economics and Statistics 59(4): 427-37.

Romer, T., and H. Rosenthal. 1979. "Bureaucrats versus Voters: On the Political Economy of Resource Allocation by Direct Democracy." Quarterly Journal of Economics 93: 563-87.

Samuelson, Paul. 1957. "The Pure Theory of Public Expenditure." Review of Economics and Statistics.

Scitovsky, T. 1957. "Two Concepts of External Economies." Journal of Political Economy 62: 70-82.

Shapiro, Perry. 1980. "Population Response to Public Spending Disequilibrium: An Analysis of the 1978 California Property Tax Limitation Initiative." In Tax and Expenditure Limitations, edited by Helen F. Ladd and T. Nicolaus Tideman. Washington, D.C.: Urban Institute Press.

Shapiro, Perry, David Puryear, and John Ross. 1979. "Tax and Expenditure Limitation in Retrospect and in Prospect." National Tax Journal 32(2): 1-10.

Smith, Adam. 1937. An Inquiry into the Nature and Causes of the Wealth of Nations. New York: Random House.

Struyk, Raymond J., and Marc Bendick, Jr. 1981. Housing Vouchers for the Poor. Washington, D.C.: Urban Institute Press.

Tiebout, Charles. 1956. "A Pure Theory of Local Expenditures." Journal of Political Economy 64: 416-24.

Von Thunen, J. 1826. Der Isolierte Staat in Beziehung Auf Landwirtschaft und Nationalokonomie. Hamburg und Rostock.

Weber, Alfred. 1909. Uben den Standort der Industrien. Tübingen.

Wicksell, K. 1896. "Ein Neues Prinzip der Gerechten Besteurung." Finanztheoretische Untersuchungen. Jena.

Winkler, D. 1975. "Educational Achievement and School Peer Group Composition." Journal of Human Resources 10(2): 189-204.

10

Equity and Efficiency in Urban-Service Delivery: A Consumption and Participation Costs Approach

Robert Warren

INTRODUCTION

The issues of equity and efficiency in the delivery of urban services have been long-standing matters of policy concern in the United States. However, each has been the center of attention at different times. After World War II, for example, considerable emphasis was placed on increasing the "economy and efficiency" of urban services by creating metropolitan-wide governments in large urban areas. Equity and social justice at the local level were important goals of public programs in the 1960s. Currently, production efficiency has again become the primary criterion in decisions about the provision of services at the local level. Academic research in political science and public administration has followed a similar pattern of swings between concern over efficiency and equity.

A number of elements have contributed to the dominance of efficiency as a goal in local government in the 1980s. The shift away from equity began more than a decade ago as cities faced weakened public economies and revenue shortfalls. The seriousness of this urban fiscal crisis was symbolized by New York City's near-bankruptcy in the mid-1970s (Newfield and DuBrul, 1981; Bailey, 1984). Since then, other factors have emerged which have reinforced the demand for greater efficiency in urban services. In some cases, voters have enacted revenue limitations and limitations and spending caps on local government (Kirlin and Kirlin, 1982; Rosentraub and Harlow, 1983; Porter and

Peiser, 1984). The Reagan administration has substantially cut back or ended federal programs that related to local delivery of urban services, especially those with redistributive effects (Palmer and Sawhill, 1982; Nathan and Doolittle, 1983; Clarke, 1984). Finally, the increased strength of politically conservative attitudes in the country has resulted in a good deal of support for the idea that much of what local government has traditionally provided in services can be produced by the private or voluntary sectors for less cost and should be either contracted out to them by cities or the provision left entirely to the private or nonprofit sectors (Poole, 1980; Savas, 1982).

Although many communities have been innovative in responding to economic and political hard times, there has been a general pattern of reduction in "nonessential" services, with only basic, public-safety functions more or less protected from cuts. Further, the reduction in federal funds and local revenue sources have encouraged a good deal of experimentation and, frequently, significant shifts in cities to more reliance on user charges, contracting with private firms, and the involvement of volunteer associations and individuals in the coproduction of services which were previously produced exclusively by public personnel. Positive aspects of coproduction and privatization have been found in the form of such things as more positive citizen attitudes toward government and increased production efficiency (Ostrom and Whitaker, 1974; Sharp, 1980; Parks et al., 1981). However, these judgments have tended to be made without considering the effects of these strategies on service distribution and social equity.

In fact, the dominant perspective from the view of city decision-makers has been to treat equity and efficiency in a trade-off situation. If there are fewer public services or lower levels of what can be provided as a result of these adjustments to gain greater efficiency, it is assumed that the effects will be the same for everyone. However, this assumption of equity of deprivation is seldom correct. Some citizens are more able than others to supplement reduced public services or replace those that are eliminated by turning to the private market. This is known, but treated as a contextual fact rather than a moral dilemma. The possibility that the services which the city continues to provide may now be in a form that is more costly to consume or are simply not accessible for some citizens is not even recognized as a fact in most cases. If these effects are unavoidably apparent, they tend to be accepted as the necessary consequence of making do with fewer resources. Levy et al. (1974:240) point out that efficiency and distributive equity must be treated as separate criteria if politics is to be approached "as we know it: people bargaining over their expected gains and losses."

This fiction that efficiency is being achieved and requires the subordination of equity has been reinforced by the tendency of urban scholars to use only production inputs in measuring the performance of public services. Indeed, a paradigm of sorts has emerged for political scientists and students of public administration, where only production costs are considered when efficiency and equity are studied. The purpose of this chapter is to consider the implications of an alternative framework and paradigm for the study of efficiency and equity. It will be argued here that there are substantial costs to the consumption of publicly provided services that, for the most part, are ignored by students of public policy. Yet, an inclusion of these costs would dramatically change the conclusions of studies of efficiency and equity.

To develop this paradigm, this chapter is divided into four sections. Following this introduction, Section II considers the costs of citizenship and the consumption of public services, and Section III formally presents the alternative paradigm for the study of efficiency and equity. The fourth and final section discusses the implications of an alternative paradigm for the analysis of the distribution of public services.

EQUITY, EFFICIENCY, AND THE COSTS OF CITIZENSHIP

Efficiency in the abstract has no meaning in a public-policy context. Generally it is understood as a measure of whether specified values are being achieved for the least cost. Put another way, Levy et al. (1974:238) state that "an agency is inefficient if it can (but does not) produce more outputs for its existing budget." The efficient performance of the agency cannot be measured by the amount of resources utilized without reference to the organization's goals. If this were not the case, efficiency would be synonymous with zero costs. Thus, efficiency, for a public agency, necessarily means the provision of a specified set of services for the least cost.

There is another point to be raised as well. It concerns what costs and whose costs are accounted for in measuring efficiency. The usual assumption that efficiency is achieved through a reduction in a governmental agency's production costs overlooks the fact that there are other costs involved in the successful provision of public services which are borne by citizens and are not reflected in the agency's budget. For example, to have a service provided normally requires <u>participation costs</u>--time, effort, and money--expended in the policy-decision process, to have it authorized. Yet, to achieve this does not guarantee that all citizens will have access to it or find it usable without further expenditures--<u>consumption costs</u>. If these participation and consumption costs exist and are not equally distributed among citizens they must be accounted for in assessing both the efficiency and equity of the distribution of a service.

Concept of Costs

At one time steps were being taken to incorporate the concept of consumption costs in the provision of services. Many of the efforts of the Great Society programs of President Johnson, such as Community Action and Community Service Centers, were aimed at reducing the net administrative cost of production of various kinds of social services. These programs, however, went one step further. They tried to make services more accessible and usable to low income and minority inner-city populations (Weschler et al., 1968; Altshuler, 1970). The physical facilities were located in the neighborhoods where the users lived, multiple services were available and coordinated at one place and workers were employed from the local area to enhance communication both linguistically and psychologically. Thus measures of efficiency began to account for a wider range of costs. They included those paid by citizens to make use of the services as well as those represented in the formal agency budget.

With the shift in the political and economic conditions of the nation in the 1970s and 1980s, little remains of this orientation in the public sector. However, the experience helps make it clear that viewing equity and efficiency as opposing values and assuming that all costs related to urban services are equally distributed misstates the policy problems that arise in dealing with public goods and services under conditions of resource scarcity. An emphasis on production costs and the neglect of other costs borne by citizens results in efficiency coming to be narrowly defined as a reduction in production costs to the exclusion of other resource-use and cost issues.

Attention to a wider range of costs, including those which citizens face in attempting to acquire and use services, can radically alter the calculation necessary to measure both efficiency and equity. Regardless of how low the unit cost of an urban service, this is not an adequate measure of efficiency if the service is not accessible, except at additional cost, or is unusable by citizens for whom it is intended. The recognition of citizen transaction costs pulls equity and efficiency together so that they are complementary rather than opposed values. The concept of operational citizenship provides a framework within which the logic of including citizens, as well as agencies, among those expending resources in the provision of public services can be further discussed (Warren and Weschler, 1975).

A useful distinction can be drawn between formal citizenship and operational citizenship. The former deals with legal status and the rights and privileges derived from it. In the political sphere, voting, holding office, interest-group participation, and attitudes toward government have often been used as measures of viable citizenship at the local level. Even if persons do not involve themselves in political activity, this is assumed to be evidence of satisfaction with the system.

Operational Citizenship

The concept of operational citizenship assumes that, in addition to legal rights and privileges, persons must have the capacity to participate in all relevant policy processes involving the use of public authority and resources which do or can affect their interest. It also assumes a capacity on the part of individual citizens to consume or have effective use of the public goods and services mandated by public decisions to which he or she is legally entitled.

Thus, from a citizen's perspective, there are several interrelated types of costs which exist for individuals and can affect their ability to function as operational citizens. These include costs associated with:

—participation in making public-policy choices;
—the production and delivery of goods and services
  mandated by these choices;
—acquiring and consuming the goods and services.

Participation costs have been a topic of importance
to social scientists reflecting a variety of ideological positions (Dahl, 1961; Buchanan and Tullock, 1962; Bachrach,
1967; Parenti, 1978). Indeed, federal legislation and programs during the late 1960s and early 1970s were based
upon the assumption that many of the problems of the poor
and minorities in obtaining and using public goods and
services were the result, in part, of barriers to their participation in local, public decision making, which prevented
their interests from being reflected in policy outputs.

The enforcement of the right of black persons to
register to vote, cast a ballot, and hold public office was
intended to reduce their participation costs in community
decision making from high or prohibitive to a level similar
to that for whites. Similarly, provisions for "maximum
feasible participation" of low-income and minority groups
in making policy concerning the use of federal funds at
the local level in community-action, economic-development,
and educational programs were designed to lower the costs
of participation for them by literally creating decision-
making mechanisms which did not exist before and dictat-
ing their involvement (Warren, 1969; Gittell, 1980). While
many of the costs associated with low-income and ethnic
minority involvement in community policymaking remain,
most federally mandated provisions intended to reduce cost
barriers no longer exist or are not enforced under the
Reagan administration.

There has been a historical interest among political
scientists and public-administration scholars in the theoretical and empirical examination of the production and
delivery costs of urban services, going back to the origins
of these disciplines in the United States (Goodnow, 1909;
Stewart, 1950). While it waned during the 1960s, work on
measuring efficiency and reducing production costs has regained its ascendancy. At the same time, there has also
been a stream of research that has continued to deal with
the question of equity in the distribution of services. It
was largely stimulated by the federal-court decision in
Hawkins v. Shaw (437 F. 2d 1286), which found that municipal services were not equally available to blacks or of
equal quality.

A number of studies generated by the Shaw case have addressed the question of whether there is an urban underclass which experiences systematic bias in the distribution of urban services. The main body of this research has a number of common features. With few exceptions, they use input equality as the standard by which the distribution is judged. They compare spatial areas, neighborhoods, in terms of the amount and type of services that are provided to each one. The neighborhoods compared are controlled for race and socioeconomic class.

The majority of the studies have found that there are service inequities among neighborhoods but that they are not predictable in terms of race or class. The explanation most frequently offered is that this "unpatterned inequality" is a function of bureaucratic rules which are race and class neutral (Antunes and Mladenka, 1976; Antunes and Plumlee, 1977; Lineberry, 1977; Mladenka and Hill, 1978; Jones, 1980; Boyle and Jacobs, 1982).

Several problems with this research can be noted. There are a number of services not analyzed in these studies which might be expected to show class or race discrimination in their distribution. These include health and welfare services, transportation, job training, and air quality. The distributional bias for some of these, as well as other services, cannot be measured by the spatial comparisons. Further, race and class, while obviously important, far from exhaust the array of citizen characteristics with which distributional inequalities could be associated. Gender and sexual preference, age, and ideology, as well as intra-class or race distinctions, might also be significant.

Finally, and most important for this discussion, there is a general failure in this research to deal with the question of end use and a virtual absence of any consideration of consumption costs other than the proximity of a service facility to a neighborhood. As will be seen, there are a variety of other forms that acquisition costs can take and even the presumed advantage of proximity to a point of service delivery is no guarantee that it is consumable.

Consumption costs can be defined as those costs that a potential user must pay to acquire and use urban services. Thus a person may have to add an increment to consume the outputs of public agencies, in addition to any participation costs to have the service mandated or con-

tributions to production through tax payment or user
charges. Traveling considerable distances or being required to fill out innumerable forms to obtain public
health services are obvious examples. At the extreme,
some services may be delivered in a form that makes them
unusable by some citizens or may not be equally available to everyone. The costs of consumption to the citizen
here are not simply the increment necessary to obtain outputs otherwise available. To remedy such conditions,
citizens would have to go beyond consumption costs and
incur participation costs as well, in the form of political
pressure upon the city bureaucracy and elected officials
or legal action to force the government to make services
available which are already mandated.

From the perspective of operational citizenship,
then, the structure of consumption costs becomes an important policy issue. On the one hand, a reduction or increase in consumption costs can make the service more or
less accessible to some people. On the other hand, such
variations in cost to the citizen consumer can increase or
decrease the efficiency by adding to or reducing the total
costs involved in the end use of the service. Thus, efficient provision of services may not be different from equitable provision of services. In fact, efficiency may require equity. A reduction in consumption costs makes a
service more equitable by being more accessible and usable.
The service is also more efficient because less cost is required for local consumption.

AN ALTERNATIVE ANALYTICAL FRAMEWORK

If the questions of equity and efficiency in urban
services are to be dealt with adequately in policy analysis,
more than production costs and the spatial distribution of
services must be considered. Neither equity nor efficiency
can be determined without considering the type, amount,
and distribution of consumption costs and participation
costs which it may be necessary for citizens to incur before having the effective use of a service. These costs
constitute a necessary step in approaching a study of
equity. Even if outcomes were equal, consumption and
participation costs may still be unequal for some citizens.

By designing an analytical framework which includes
the perspective of citizens as consumers, it becomes obvi-

ous that several conditions can exist which affect the capacity of the residents of certain areas, as well as groups of people who are not spatially identifiable, to acquire and consume the products of governmental agencies. These include cases in which mandated public services are:

- not produced;
- provided in smaller quantities or are of lower quality than available in other areas or to other groups;
- not consumable; and
- not accessible without additional costs that may not be equally distributed among areas or groups and may be prohibitively high for some.

Under any of these conditions, subsets of a community's population, such as blacks, women, or the poor, or citizens generally, who are legally entitled to consume public services, must forgo them or invest additional resources in consumption or participation costs to try to acquire and use them. Even these expenditures, however, do not ensure that the service will become accessible or consumable.

Thus, such inequalities which deny operational citizenship can involve a range of services, take a variety of forms, and affect a diverse array of individuals and groups. By considering the four categories set out above in more detail, the importance for policy analysis of attention to the acquisition and end use of services can be elaborated.

Failure to Provide Services and Discrimination in Delivery

The court case filed against Shaw, Mississippi has become the classic model of public goods and services being produced by a municipality but not delivered or delivered in lesser quality to some community residents. Nearly 98 percent of all houses fronting on unpaved streets in Shaw were black-occupied and 97 percent of the houses not served by sanitary sewers were located in black neighborhoods. There also were significant disparities in the provision of stoplights and fire hydrants (Anderson, 1972). Similar patterns of service inequalities have occurred in other communities and been recognized judicially. In the 1978 case of Johnson v. City of Arcadia (450 F.Supp 1363)

the court agreed with the black plaintiffs that the Florida
city had shown a long-run pattern of unequal service distribution (Nutter, 1980).

Such findings have not been limited to rural communities. A federal district court found that Montgomery
County, Ala., had a recreation program that staged separate activities in the black community and, in some cases,
did not provide similar services to those available for
whites (Poverty Law . . ., 1979). Neither are local governments the only public agencies charged with service
discrimination. In 1982, the federal government filed a
civil-rights suit against the Chicago Park District for
having fewer field houses, craft houses, senior centers,
ice-skating rinks, tennis courts, and day camps in black
and Hispanic areas than in white sections (New York Times,
1982).

It must also be noted that the courts have been far
from consistent sources of support for citizens claiming
that they are receiving unequal treatment in services. As
Rossum (1980:2) puts it:

> The "other side of the tracks" phenomenon
> has not been seriously assaulted by efforts
> at service equalization nor has the discre-
> tion municipal authorities have traditionally
> enjoyed in the delivery of urban services
> been noticeably trenched upon by the courts.

In the 1972 Beale v. Lindsay case (468 F.2d 287)
the U.S. Appeals Court for the Second Circuit ruled in
favor of the City of New York against citizens of a Puerto
Rican area. The case involved the unequal condition of
one of four parks in the Bronx. A park in the Puerto
Rican neighborhood was in significant disrepair in comparison with those in white areas. The city argued that it
had actually put more resources into the park in question
than the others and that its poor condition was due to
vandalism. The court concluded that the city was consti-
tutionally responsible only for equal input among neighborhoods and not equal output (Rossum, 1980:7, 8).

The fact that the park was less accessible and
usable than others in the vicinity was not questioned by
either the city or the court. In reaching its decision,
however, the court failed to consider the extent to which
vandalism was, in part, the result of the city's cumulative

failure to provide adequate levels of other services, such as law enforcement or building- and housing-code regulation in the neighborhood. The logic of the court ruling would seem to be that, in the absence of a level of law enforcement by the city to prevent vandalism, the residents of the neighborhood must absorb the costs of eliminating this presumably illegal behavior if the park is to become more usable.

Education

Education is another service about which there has been a long history of contention about inequities, usually based on race and class. Numerous studies have found that schools in minority and poor neighborhoods are less likely to have science laboratories, libraries, experienced teachers, and advanced courses than those in white, middle-, and upper-income areas within the same school district. While a massive infusion of federal funds in the late 1960s and 1970s helped redress some of these imbalances, the gaps were seldom completely closed in terms of outcome. Under current economic and political conditions, even equality of input may be in jeopardy. In 1984, for example, it was reported that a teacher shortage in New York City was disproportionately affecting students in the poorest neighborhoods (Purnick, 1984). The superintendent of District 5 in Harlem characterized the situation as one in which:

> These kids are being ripped off twice--
> once because they're perceived as being in
> a school district incapable of properly
> educating them, and secondly because
> they're incapable of being served by
> qualified teachers (Purnick, 1984:B5).

Gender

Gender also has been the basis of service discrimination in education. Until quite recently it was standard policy in most school districts to exclude females from courses in mechanical and craft skills. This is still the practice in some districts, although it is clearly illegal (Ross and Barcher, 1983:107). Some districts have sought also to maintain a policy of excluding pregnant girls and unwed mothers from regular school, though not the fathers.

While Title IX of the Educational Amendments of 1972 Act forbids such exclusions, the courts have not been consistent in upholding the provision (Ross and Barcher, 1983: 109). A failure to provide the same or comparable sports programs for girls in public schools also is illegal under Title IX. However, large discrepancies remain. Of the 29 sports activities that are offered on the interscholastic level, 22 are more available to male than female high-school students. For example, in 1978-79, 9,437 schools provided golf for boys and 2,907 for girls (U.S. Commission . . ., 1980:12).

This pattern of gender inequity in education continues even in rehabilitation training for incarcerated juveniles. One report, based on a national survey, found that boys had twice as many options for such training with 36 different types of programs available, as compared with 17 for girls (Flaste, 1977). The same inequities also exist for adults. In a 1979 court case, a Michigan judge found that the rehabilitation opportunities offered women in prison were substantially inferior in both variety and quality to those provided for males (Ross and Barcher, 1983).

At times the withholding of service is freely admitted and justified as being in the best interest of those who are being deprived. This is common in the failure to enforce building and housing codes. In Wilmington, Del., the head of the city agency responsible for housing-code enforcement stated in 1984 that the code was not strictly enforced and claimed that if it had been, "many low income families who at least have a roof over them now [in building cited as violating the housing code] would instead be out on the street (Jackson, 1984a:A1)."

However, there are costs beyond rent, in terms of safety risks, which are assumed by the tenants whom the city allows to remain in houses that it has condemned as unfit. The city fully recognizes them and takes steps to ensure that it does not share these costs. When a building is declared unfit in violation of the housing code, the city informs the tenants that they remain there at their own risk in order to take "the city off the legal hook if there were any injuries to the tenants (Jackson, 1984a:A8)."

Police

Much of the research on equity in police services has compared input measures and response time to citizen calls by geographical area. If, however, a wider range of variables in the criminal-justice system and considering specific types of requests for aid the common conclusion that there is equity in protection of person may not hold. By looking at gender rather than race or class as the variable, the performance of the police in cases where a wife is physically abused by her spouse can be considered. The research literature indicates that the police frequently fail to give adequate protection to a battered wife. In addition to concern for the safety of officers involved, the reasons cited for this behavior include a "low priority status given domestic disturbances," attitudes by police that family disputes are "essentially verbal in nature, not serious, and causing no one injury," and "police training that often reinforces a nonarrest policy (U.S. Commission . . ., 1982:24)."

Whether police will assume that the arrest of the abuser is an appropriate response to such violence has been raised as a key issue in a growing body of writing on this topic. One researcher has concluded that the fact that such violence constitutes a crime and someone has been harmed may not be the basis of a decision to arrest when wife abuse is occurring and states that

> . . . in domestic violence cases, more arrests occur when the peace of the neighborhood has been disrupted, a deadly weapon has been used, or when the assault is so serious that the police have no alternative. Even then the charges filed may not reflect the severity of the crime committed (U.S. Commission . . ., 1982:25).

The question of the quality of police service has been raised in a different way in the case of gay males. Historically, when the behavior of gays has made it possible to identify their sexual preference--such as patronizing homosexual bars--they have found police services to constitute harassment rather than protection. In San Francisco, police behavior was changed only after sustained political organizational efforts in the gay community and the election of a gay to the city's legislative body (Castells 1983:141-44).

There are further variations in the circumstances under which services can be withheld. Though mandated, they may not be provided to anyone or modified in such a way that, contrary to policy intent, special interests rather than the general public are benefited. In New York City, for example, the Consumer Affairs Department had a trade waste division which was responsible for regulating the private-cartage industry, which handled waste collection from private firms. One of its responsibilities was to prevent price gouging. However, three independent studies of pricing in the cartage industry found overcharges of up to 400 percent in the vast majority of cases. In 1974, after seven years of operation by the division, a Brooklyn grand jury found it to be ineffective as a regulatory body and largely controlled by organized crime. Efforts by business firms to have the division act on their behalf and prevent overpricing were normally unsuccessful (Village Voice, 1974). A report issued by the mayor's office in Seattle, Wash., concluded that a police unit established to protect the public from bunco and other fraudulent activities was basically acting to help businesses collect debt from individuals (Suffia, 1970).

At times, technological change can produce short-run service inequities which may become longer-term. A class- and race-based pattern of inequality has emerged, for example, in schools' provision of courses in computer literacy, and in students' access to computers. In the current squeeze on educational budgets, schools with the largest number of minority students are faring the worst in developing computer-oriented curricula. One recent survey found that 80 percent of the country's largest and richest public high schools now have at least one microcomputer, while 60 percent of the 2,000 poorest schools have none (Johnson, 1982:22, 23).

Cable Television

Cable television, another link to the emerging information society, may be delayed, if not denied, to low-income and minority areas of cities. In most states, municipal governments have the authority to franchise and regulate cable-television systems. This includes determining areas of the city that will be provided with cable service and a time schedule. However, telecommunication analysts have questioned whether cable-system operators have adequate incentives to meet deadlines for serving poorer, black, and Hispanic neighborhoods (Dawson, 1982; Moss

and Warren, 1984:250).   The general problem has been described as one in which

> . . . construction sequences calling for
> poor neighborhoods to be wired last are
> used by cable companies to buy time.   A
> lot of things can happen in three or four
> years before the company gets to build
> these neighborhoods.   Inflation, interest
> rates, new services, the changing cost of
> equipment, programming, and a change in
> the local government all promise some po-
> tential for the cable company to get out
> from some of the onerous provisions that
> were in the original franchise (Rothbart
> and Stoller, 1983:32).

There is also evidence to suggest that city governments
are reluctant to enforce franchise conditions and, particularly, unlikely to attempt to cancel the franchise for non-
performance (Stoller, 1982:34, 35).

In such cases, the inability or unwillingness of a
city to act has the effect of validating the withholding of
a service by a private firm from some citizens who, under
the franchise agreement, have a legal right to it.   Inaction,
or lack of facilitative behavior, by a government can also
affect the ability of citizens to acquire services that the
public agency itself is responsible for providing.   Indeed,
what has been termed governmental passivity can be a determinant in whether or not public services are accessible
and usable, especially those which are available on demand only.

Ringeling has commented on the importance of recognizing that there is a difference between production and
supply of services by government.   On the basis of research in Europe, he has concluded that people "do not
always get what they should get according to the rules."
He goes on to characterize those responsible for allocating
public services as passive, explaining that by "passivity
of the administration" he means that

> . . . the government effectuates the rights
> allocated to citizens only when this effec-
> tuation is asked for. . . .   If sections of
> the population do not know what is their

due, if they do not ask for anything, if
they do not succeed in taking other barriers [sic] for the effectuation of their
rights, then provision fails to take place,
even though they have every right to in
the view of their condition of life
(Ringeling, 1981:300).

Providng services which are available on demand
only, without facilitative action by the producing agency,
has been reported in a variety of circumstances in the
United States. Piven and Cloward (1971:294) found that,
in the midst of the Great Society era, the official policy
of the New York Department of Welfare was to allow additional grants to clients for winter clothing but "they were
rarely made unless requested and even then the investiga-
tors often allocated less than the prescribed amount."

MacDonald, in another context, concluded that perhaps the most obvious reason persons eligible for sizable
food-stamp benefits do not enroll is ignorance of the existence of the program or the amount of benefits to which
they are entitled. He goes on to note that in a class-
action suit, a federal district court found that the State
of Minnesota and the U.S. Department of Agriculture had
never conducted outreach activities to inform eligible persons about the program benefits in a manner prescribed by
federal law (MacDonald, 1977:98).

In cases of domestic violence, such as discussed
above, when the police do not arrest the husband engaging
in physical abuse, a woman has the option of making a
citizen's arrest. However,

police often fail to inform women of their
right to make such an arrest and thus effectively deny it to the woman who is not
aware of this alternative. If she is aware
of it, the police may still discourage her
from using it and may refuse the help
necessary to take the man into custody and
complete the arrest (U.S. Commission . . .,
1982:25).

According to Hartman (1984:239), a recently adopted
rent-control ordinance in San Francisco has proven to be
of little aid to the renters for whom it was ostensibly

designed. Based on a comparison of the neighborhoods from which petitions and complaints have been filed with the rent-stabilization board, Hartman (1984:239) concludes that:

> Relying on tenant complaints to trigger effective implementation of the law was of course a major weakness in the ordinance: the reality is that tenants—particularly lower income, minority and recent immigrant tenants—are often not aware of their legal rights and not likely to use a bureaucratic mechanism they perceive as inaccessible or unresponsive. This is particularly true in San Francisco, where tens of thousands of residents do not have legal immigration status or facility with the English language.

Hartman goes on to note that the problems faced by citizens attempting to use the ordinance to keep their rent increases within the legal limits do not end, even if they are able to file a complaint and have it supported by the rent-stabilization board. When the board has referred cases to the city attorney's office for prosecution, action has seldom been taken. As a result in 1984,

> tenants brought suit . . . to compel [the city attorney] to seek injunctions against landlords in such cases, to establish written procedures for handling these referrals, and to require written explanations when no notice is given (Hartman, 1984:240).

Citizens do not always find it necessary to move outside the consumption process and incur participation costs to gain the use of services which agencies are generally withholding through passivity or inaction. But the citizens who do succeed tend to have special characteristics and are not representative of the universe of potential consumers. For example, a 1975 study of AFDC clients in New York City was designed to measure the "bureaucratic competence" of applicants. It looked at clients in terms of such variables as literacy, education, experience in filling out forms, and understanding bureaucratic language.

The study found that the higher the score on these measures, the more likely a caseworker's decision would be in
the client's favor. Further, more errors by caseworkers
would favor those with greater rather than lesser bureaucratic competence (Urban Institute, 1980). The observation
of similar patterns in England has led Hall to comment
that it may be (as quoted in Ringeling, 1981:298)

> the government does not supply its commodi-
> ties and services to those who are most in
> need of them. Instead of that the govern-
> ment provides for those who are most elo-
> quent, most persistent, most able to under-
> stand the rules and workings of bureau-
> cracy, the cleverest or the best informed.

It is obvious that passivity and inaction can be an
effective and intended way to raise the consumption costs
of citizens for services. So, too, can the manipulation of
rules concerning access to services. Here administrative
behavior is far from passive and is able to regulate demand without direct involvement in the production process
by reducing requests for a service and eliminating existing users. In 1973, for example, the California Supreme
Court invalidated the state's Department of Welfare rules
that had cut benefits to children. In its decision the
court stated:

> The department's desire to cut welfare ex-
> penses at any cost has led it to disregard
> the clear guidelines of its legislative man-
> date and to construct a contrived and tor-
> tured concept of "income" in an attempt to
> camouflage an impermissible administrative
> reevaluation of recipient needs.
> An analysis of the complexities of
> the department's novel determination of
> "income" is reminiscent of a journey into
> the fictional realms visited by Alice through
> the looking glass (Lembke, 1973).

A significant controversy developed in 1983 and 1984
over federal policy in reviewing the eligibility of people
receiving social-security disability benefits. While the example is on a national scale, the behavior of the govern-

ment and its effects on citizens makes quite clear the power
of administrative agencies at any level to adopt policies
that both deny a service to legally eligible persons and
force them to incur the costs of litigation if they wish to
regain their benefits.

When President Reagan took office, a review was
initiated of 1.2 million cases of citizens receiving disability benefits. As a result, more than 490,000 were declared
no longer eligible (Rangel, 1984). In turn, there was a
tremendous increase in the number of social-security cases
pending in the courts, growing from 19,000 in 1981 to
48,000 in 1984 (Pear, 1984).

A decision by Judge Jack B. Weinstein of the U.S.
District Court in Brooklyn in 1983 ordered the Social Security Administration to restore benefits denied to 50,000 mentally ill persons in New York. In his ruling, Weinstein
found the Social Security Administration to have engaged
"in a covert policy" from 1978 to 1983 to deny citizens the
right to have their eligibility properly assessed. This decision was upheld by a court of appeals in 1984 (Rangel,
1984).

The rate at which the Social Security Administration's actions were being overturned in the courts led
Judge H. Lee Sarokin to take judicial notice. In his
court, over a six-month period, 56 percent of the cases
dealing with appeals on ineligibility rulings were either
reversed or remanded. The reversal rate for the country
as a whole was 49 percent. Judge Sarokin described the
reversal rate as

> staggering and paints an undeniable pic-
> ture of a heartless and indifferent bureau-
> cratic monster destroying the lives of dis-
> abled citizens and creating years of agony
> and anxiety by ignoring both facts and
> legal precedent (Narvaez, 1984).

Judge Sarokin was particularly concerned by the fact that
the government "usually had nothing to lose" by being
taken to court over denials of eligibility. Consequently,
in a case before him, he ordered the government to pay
the legal fees incurred by a citizen who had successfully
regained his disability benefits through litigation (Narvaez,
1984).

In the examples which have been discussed, the services, if they can be acquired, have been assumed to be consumable. While this may be generally true, it is far from universally so. Even when a service is accessible it may not be effectively usable by some subset of citizens.

Nonconsumable Services

The idea that a public decision can be made, services produced and made available but not be consumable by some citizens has seldom been articulated as a policy problem. It is far from rare, however.

A conceptual question can be raised in discussing the conditions that preclude individuals or groups from consuming services to which they are legally entitled. It concerns the issue of whether a distinction is possible between services which can be classified as "nonconsumable" and those which are too costly. For purposes of this discussion, it is assumed that such a distinction is possible and useful. In a very broad sense, the former can be thought of as involving cases in which the relevant variables are outside the control of the consumer or which would require modifications of a systemic character by the citizen to make the service usable as packaged, such as changes in cognitive structure, cultural patterns, or language. Instances of the latter type can be said to include situations in which citizens can and do make some rough calculation and determine that the costs associated with consuming the product are greater than the benefits to be derived.

Although only recently recognized and responded to, public transportation, for years, was largely unusable for handicapped citizens (Hull, 1979). In the 1970s, for the first time, substantial efforts were made to provide access to fixed-route transit systems and identify alternative, publicly supported means of mobility for the handicapped under federal leadership and funding. However, the problem of making public transportation consumable for handicapped, as well as elderly persons, has been far from resolved. As one analyst has concluded:

> U.S. policy aimed at increasing the mobility of the elderly and handicapped is fraught with inconsistencies and complica-

tions. Most national program efforts have
begun in some confusion; many have generated into open conflict (Rosenbloom, 1982).

Education, which is probably the most critical public service provided in a community in terms of the long-
run consequences of its successful consumption, ironically,
offers a range of examples of problems with consumability.
Perhaps the best-known case of identifying learning difficulties from this perspective is the Head Start program. A
major assumption in initiating Head Start was that the
standard package of education designed to reflect middle-
class values and experience was not consumable by children from poor and minority families entering the first
grade.
     The solution, however, was more to change the cog-
nition of children through preschool training, rather than
redesigning the content of education to deal with consumability problems beyond the lower grades. Educational
difficulties can stem from the attributes of school administrators and teachers as well as students (Ryan, 1976:61).
Thus, those who design and deliver education can systematically behave in ways that undermine the intellectual
and psychological development of students. Reference has
been made to this phenomenon in a variety of studies
(Clark, 1965; Kozol, 1967; Kohl, 1968).
     A recent example and attempted remedy for the prob-
lem of educational consumability concerns the sexual preferences of students. In 1985, the New York City Board of
Education approved the establishing of Harvey Milk School
for homosexual high-school students. The initial 20 male
and female students had had difficulty in fitting into conventional high schools because of their sexual identity and
had dropped out. Harassment by other students and teachers was frequently cited as a reason for leaving. The
chancellor of schools, in explaining the decision to author-
ize the school, is quoted as saying that, in most instances,
these youngsters would never have been able to complete
their education in their previous schools and "the alternative was to abandon the students (Rother, 1985)."
     Language can affect the consumability of education
delivered in English for students who can communicate only
in another language. The nature of the problem has been
judicially recognized. In Lau v. Nichols, the Supreme
Court found that the rights of Chinese-speaking children

in San Francisco to an education could not be met without having classes conducted in Chinese. The court held that:

> There is no equality of treatment merely
> by providing students with the same facili-
> ties, textbooks, teachers, and curriculum;
> for students who do not understand English
> are effectively foreclosed from any meaning-
> ful education (Hull, 1979:261).

How schools deal with "black English" has also been a matter of controversy in terms of its effect on the education of children (Newell, 1981). A federal judge in Michigan ruled that the teaching of standard English in a public school must "recognize the existence of a child's 'home language' if it is different from standard English . . . and that knowledge be used in teaching those children how to read standard English." The decision was based upon the view that the unconscious, but evident, negative "attitude of teachers toward home language causes a psychological barrier to learning by students (Stuart, 1979)."

Differences in the language which a service is delivered in and the language of the end user can result in other barriers to consumption. For example, many city hospitals that have large Hispanic populations do not have bilingual personnel. A lawsuit by the California Rural Legal Assistance Agency forced San Francisco General Hospital, 40 percent of whose patients are Mexican-American, to hire 30 translators. An anecdotal but, perhaps, not unique report, states that "a call in Spanish to the Houston Fire Department met with the response, 'get somebody who speaks English to call us back' (Crewdson, 1979)."

Consumption Costs

The actual costs incurred by citizens in the process of consuming public services can assume a variety of forms—time, effort, money, physical, and psychological. They can be recurring or nonrecurring, and of shorter or longer duration. The investment of time in travel to or in queueing at a facility and the effort required to complete extensive and complex paperwork have become an expected part of obtaining welfare-related services. This point is

so well recognized that there is no need to discuss it in
detail, apart from noting that the costs can be and are
manipulated by service providers to reduce or eliminate
users legally entitled to them.

Direct user charges for services can be structured
in ways that discriminate against some consumers as a
matter of policy. In a study of water and sewerage services in Australian cities, Rees (1981:103) concluded that:

> The evidence is clear that families at the
> bottom of the housing market, living in
> high densities in units and flats, are ef-
> fectively charged more for each unit of
> waste discharged than are households in
> other residential properties. The per unit
> disparity is increased still further by the
> fact that the costs of provision are lower
> in areas of high population density.

While these effects in utility services are also well known,
pricing is seldom adjusted in favor of either equity, ability to pay, or economic efficiency, or actual production
costs (Rees, 1981:102).

There are other types of consumption costs for citizens which can be more complex, less direct, and more
difficult to identify, let alone measure. At times they may
price a citizen out of the market for a public service. At
other times they are absorbed because the person has no
choice. Cox (1973) has noted that, after the initial experience in the United States with urban-redevelopment
programs, adjustments were made with the intent of allow-
ing at least some lower-income residents who had been living in the area to remain after massive public investment
to upgrade it. Renamed "urban renewal," rehabilitation
rather than demolition of existing houses was done when-
ever possible. This goal was often defeated, however, because many homeowners in renewal areas were not able to
improve their property to the level required by the rehabilitation program and had to sell. This process occurred in a number of lower-class areas containing older
buildings of some architectural merit and appeal to higher-
income buyers. As the physical quality of the neighborhoods improved, the original residents were priced out.
They were unable to consume the benefits of the publicly
subsidized upgrading, although the intent of the program
was that they should (Cox, 1973:83, 84).

A less direct set of costs arose in a relocation program described by Gans in a Boston redevelopment project.
In designing a plan to relocate large numbers of people
who would be forced to move because of extensive demolition of existing buildings, housing-authority staff projected that 60 percent of this group would be eligible for
public housing and all would make use of it. Yet only 10
percent did. The citizens, primarily Italian-American and
part of closely knit family and social networks, rejected
the public housing for several reasons: they did not want
to be stigmatized by living in public housing; they knew
that they would not be able to stay close to relatives,
friends, and neighbors; and they did not wish to be subjected to administrative restrictions, especially the family-
income limitation (Gans, 1962:321-24). The consumption
costs were simply too high.

Efforts have been made to reduce the consumption
costs of public housing. Yet for some they have increased
or taken new forms. Residents of housing projects maintained by the Wilmington (Del.) Housing Authority have
sought for three years to have paint removed from their
homes, which exceeds the lead content allowed under federal law by 100 times. A number of negative physical effects can result from exposure to excessive levels of lead,
including blood clots, nerve and kidney damage, and im-
pairment of learning ability in children. A chemical analysis of 152 housing-authority units indicated that 131 exceeded a safe level. Residents are seeking a court order
to have the paint removed. The housing authority has
maintained that it does not have the funds to do so (Jackson, 1984b).

At times, the cost of consuming services--especially
public housing--can be psychological, in terms of stress
and not simply stigma, as well as physical. In 1983, a
San Francisco grand jury visited both the San Bruno jail
and the Yerba Buena Plaza West public-housing project.
It concluded that "it is far more dehumanizing" to be a
resident of the housing project than the jail (Hartman,
1984:256).

In New York City, a shortage of inexpensive rental
housing has caused the city to place homeless families in
hotels in the notorious Times Square area. It is characterized as a "neighborhood of drifters and derelicts, where
sex and drugs are bought and sold on every grimy corner
and violence and pornography and exploitation are the

traditional values (Dowd, 1984)." Yet by mid-1984 there were 570 families with 1,271 children placed in the area by the city. Some of the families had lived in hotels there for more than a year (Dowd, 1984).

The psychological costs of the stigma associated with welfare services are generally less dramatic than these examples; but they are enduring and real to citizens who are subjected to them. Weisbrod (1970) has commented that there are "stigma costs associated with the loss of self-respect, dignity and acceptance by the rest of society that occurs when persons make their poverty known to others in order to receive benefits from a transfer program."

Ringeling states that all the prejudices attached by society to unemployment, sickness, or supplementary benefits may make people reluctant to resort to them. He reports:

> The Dutch government has tried several times to do something to counteract this stigma. The introduction of the Supplementary Aid Act was accompanied by extensive publicity campaigns. Central in these campaigns was the idea that social aid was not a favor from the government but a right of the citizen. It did not help much; there remained considerable inhibitions to make use of that right (Ringeling, 1981:297).

Page, drawing upon extensive data from England, reports a wide range of research corroborating that the stigma attached to welfare services both deters some from using them and causes psychological disturbance for those who do (Page, 1984). In discussing the food stamp program in the United States, MacDonald (1977:99) observes that the procedures required to obtain and use the stamps creates ample opportunity for recipients to suffer these stigma costs.

One of the most basic functions that government offers is its judicial system. If a crime is committed, victims are presumably able to have charges brought against the perpetrator. Similarly, individuals charged with crimes are expected to have a right to trial. However, the cost structure of the use of the criminal courts makes it too costly for some persons to consume.

Beginning in the 1970s, a series of issues were raised concerning the crime of rape. Evidence was publicly discussed which made it clear that many women did not report rapes and few of those who did, sought to bring the rapist to trial. This reluctance to use the criminal-justice system grew out of the psychological costs incurred by the victim in dealing with male police and trial procedures. In case of trial, her entire sexual history was open to question and she was required to prove that she did not consent and used every possible means of physical resistance (victims of no other crime have such a test imposed upon them) against the attack (Grimstad, 1973; DeCrow, 1974). In San Francisco in 1970, a study estimated that 6,000 rapes were committed, 621 were reported and, of these, only 59 went to trial. The chief of police of Los Angeles was quoted, in reference to these statistics, as saying that most rapists were never brought to trial because ". . . of the reluctance of women to subject themselves to something that is really worse than the rape itself and that's the rape they suffer in the court room (Los Angeles Times, 1974)."

By the mid-1980s, many police departments have modified the way they receive and handle reports of rape and treat the victim; and the federal government and half of the states have revised rules of evidence in rape trials. However, where departmental procedures and attitudes have not been reformed and in the states without changed evidentiary rules, the "humiliation from the salacious inquiries the police sometimes indulge in" and "the outrageous cross-examination the woman is often subject to when she testifies" continue (Ross and Barcher, 1983:165).

Persons charged with crimes face a different set of costs associated with using their right to a trial. Considerable evidence exists that, other things equal, a suspect who demands a trial, and is found guilty, will receive a longer sentence than a person who pleads guilty to a similar offense (Dawson, 1969). Consequently, it is not unlikely that an innocent person, without resources or connections in the community or with a past conviction, will plead guilty on the assumption that acquittal is unlikely and a shorter sentence is preferable to a longer one (Landes, 1971). The right to seek a new trial after a conviction can also be constrained by the threat that the state will retaliate by substituting a more serious charge in a new trial. Even though this practice has been ruled against by the United States Supreme Court, it is still attempted (Greer, 1977).

CONCLUSIONS

There is little that is new in the knowledge that some people may receive public services while others do not and that the costs of acquiring them may differ among subsets of the population and neighborhoods. What is done with this knowledge, however, is an issue of importance in both analytical and policy terms. Is it adequate and is it being used in ways that allow an accurate measurement of efficiency and a full understanding of the equity implications of current policies in the distribution of urban services? The conclusion reached here in both cases is no.

This discussion has made a number of assumptions. One is that equity and efficiency are complementary rather than conflicting criteria in the provision of public services. This is necessarily tied to a second assumption, that costs--monetary, psychological, and physical--absorbed by citizens in the acquisition and consumption of public services must be accounted for in measuring the efficiency of their provision. A critical point is that consumption, as well as acquisition, costs exist and may be high or prohibitive for some citizens. End-use costs are just as real as production or input costs. Normatively, the logic developed here is based on the belief that people should be operational citizens. To achieve this they must be able to participate freely and effectively in public decision making and be able to consume public services that have been mandated and to which they are entitled.

Expanding the framework for the study of service provision to include the concepts of end use and operational citizenship leads to a further enlargement of the boundaries of analysis. It has been shown that citizens may not receive a service at all, receive it in smaller amounts or lower quality than they should, or in a form that is not consumable. It also has been made clear that, at times, citizens will engage in political and legal action in an attempt to obtain services they are entitled to. From an analytical perspective, agency production costs and citizen acquisition, consumption, and participation costs must be jointly considered in any assessment of equity and efficiency, and their interrelationship recognized.

Numerous examples have been given of instances in which citizens have lobbied with public officials, sought to change state and local laws, and brought suit to obtain a fair distribution of services. To the extent that they fail, they are being denied operational citizenship. Even if they succeed, they will still have been forced to expend resources to obtain a service well beyond the amount normally required and expected.

It has also been shown that, by looking at the end use of services, it becomes possible to fit bureaucratic behavior that raises or lowers acquisition and consumption costs into a conceptual framework, which allows an understanding of how such actions affect equity and efficiency in service provision, rather than diverting attention from the issue.

The main body of research on urban-service equity has tended to move in the direction of narrowing rather than expanding the phenomena. As the data presented above indicate, the adequate study of service distribution cannot only include a comparison of service inputs to neighborhoods or use race and class as the only independent variables. Some services cannot be compared spatially. Others are primarily consumed by one subset of the population. Services such as law enforcement and education are a bundle of discrete services. Which of these are selected for study can significantly affect the findings in relation to equity. Further, the separate analysis of the distributional effects of each of several services has failed to consider the possibility that, in the aggregate, they may have a collective effect which is different and significant. Finally, the primary focus on input equality as the measure of distributional equity has meant that acquisition, consumption, and participation costs and the complementary nature of equity and efficiency have not been considered.

A normative position which assumes that operational citizenship is a desirable goal for society and an analytical approach which accounts for the costs to citizens, as well as agencies, in the provision of services allows a far broader range of questions to be asked and potentially answered. How acquisition and consumption costs can be reduced or redistributed to gain greater efficiency as well as equity become salient issues. If such cost modifications are achieved, participation costs would also be lowered to the extent that political or legal action were no longer required to gain effective use of a service.

In a time of resource scarcity and political conservatism in the public sector, it is not surprising that the strategies adopted by public officials to reduce provision and production costs are likely to increase service acquisition and consumption costs, particularly for politically and economically marginal groups. It is surprising, however, that the political-science and policy-analysis literature accepts and fails to go beyond a conceptual framework that reinforces, intended or otherwise, a fiction that efficiency and equity are being satisfied by current public policies.

REFERENCES

Altshuler, A. 1970. Community Control: The Black Demand for Participation in Large American Cities. Indianapolis: Pegasus.

Anderson, D. R. 1972. "Toward the Equalization of Municipal Services: Variations on a Theme by Hawkins." Journal of Urban Law 50(2): 177-97.

Antunes, G. E., and K. Mladenka. 1976. "The Politics of Local Services and Service Distribution." In Toward a New Urban Politics, edited by L. Masotti and R. Lineberry. Cambridge, Mass. Ballinger.

Antunes, G. E., and J. P. Plumlee. 1977. "The Distribution of an Urban Public Service: Ethnicity, Socioeconomic Status and Bureaucracy as Determinants of the Quality of Neighborhoods." Urban Affairs Quarterly 13 (March): 313-32.

Bachrach, P. 1967. The Theory of Democratic Elitism. Boston: Little, Brown.

Bailey, R. W. 1984. The Crisis Regime. Albany, N.Y.: State University of New York Press.

Boyle, J., and D. Jacobs. 1982. "The Intra-city Distribution of Services: A Multivariate Analysis." American Political Science Review 76 (June): 371-79.

Buchanan, J. M., and G. Tullock. 1962. The Calculus of
    Consent. Ann Arbor, Mich.: University of Michigan
    Press.

Castells, M. 1983. Grassroots and the City. Berkeley,
    Calif.: University of California Press.

Clark, K. B. 1965. Dark Ghetto. New York: Harper and
    Row.

Clarke, S. E. 1984. "Neighborhood Policy Options."
    Journal of the American Planning Association 50
    (Autumn): 493-501.

Cox, K. R. 1973. Conflict, Power, and Politics in the
    City. New York: McGraw-Hill.

Crewdson, J. M. 1979. "Hispanic Influx Moving U.S.
    Closer to Bilingualism." New York Times, August 8, 1.

Dahl, R. A. 1961. Who Governs? New Haven, Conn.:
    Yale University Press.

Dawson, F. 1982. "The Hottest Story in Town." Cable-
    Vision 8 (November 22): 219-29.

Dawson, R. O. 1969. "Sentencing, the Decision as to
    Type, Length and Condition of Sentences." Report of
    the American Bar Foundation's Survey of Administra-
    tion of Justice in the United States." Boston: Little,
    Brown.

DeCrow, K. 1974. Sexist Justice. New York: Vintage.

Dowd, M. 1984. "Childhood in 'Hell': Growing up in
    Times Sq." New York Times, June 25, B1.

Flaste, R. 1977. "Law Inequality for Girls Cited."
    Morning News, Wilmington, Del., September 9, 42.

Gans, H. J. 1962. The Urban Villager. New York: Free
    Press.

Gittell, M. 1980. Limits to Citizen Participation. Beverly
    Hills, Calif.: Sage.

Goodnow, F. 1909. Municipal Government. New York: Century.

Greer, T. 1977. "Court Calls for Justifying 'Upping the Ante' in Retrials." Morning News, Wilmington, Del., December 8, 6.

Grimstad, K., ed. 1973. New Women's Survival Catalog. New York: Coward-McCann and Geoghagen.

Hartman, C. 1984. The Transformation of San Francisco. Totowa, N.J.: Rowman & Allenhead.

Hull, K. 1979. The Rights of Physically Handicapped People. New York: Avon Books.

Jackson, M. 1984a. "Housing Code Often Ignored." Sunday News Journal, Wilmington, Del., December 2, A1, A8.

_____. 1984b. "WHA Nears Lead Paint Settlement." Morning News, Wilmington, Del., February 3, B1.

Johnson, J. P. 1982. "Can Computers Close the Educational Equity Gap?" Perspective 14 (Fall): 20-25.

Jones, B. D. 1980. Service Delivery in the City. New York: Longman.

Kirlin, J. J., and A. Kirlin. 1982. Public Choices--Private Resources. Sacramento, Calif.: California Taxpayer's Association.

Kohl, H. 1968. 36 Children. New York: Signet Books.

Kozol, J. 1967. Death at an Early Age. Boston: Houghton Mifflin.

Landes, W. M. 1971. "An Economic Analysis of the Courts." Journal of Law and Economics 14 (April): 61-107.

Lembke, D. 1973. "High Court Kills Two Rules Cutting Welfare." Los Angeles Times, July 3, 3.

Levy, F. S., A. J. Meltsner, and A. Wildavsky. 1974. Urban Outcomes. Berkeley, Calif.: University of California Press.

Lineberry, R. L. 1977. Equality and Urban Policy: The Distribution of Municipal Public Services. Beverly Hills, Calif.: Sage.

Lineberry, R. L., and R. W. Welch, Jr. 1974. "Who Gets What: Measuring the Distribution of Urban Services." Social Science Quarterly 54 (March): 700-12.

Los Angeles Times. 1974. April 7, part 1, 27.

MacDonald, M. 1977. Food Stamps and Income Maintenance. New York: Academic Press.

Mladenka, K., and K. Hill. 1978. "The Distribution of Urban Police Services." Journal of Politics 40 (February): 112-33.

Moss, M. L., and R. Warren. 1984. "Public Policy and Community-oriented Uses of Cable Television." Urban Affairs Quarterly 20 (December): 233-54.

Narvaez, A. A. 1984. "Judge Criticizes U.S. Agency on Denial of Benefits." New York Times, June 8, B5.

Nathan, R. P., and F. C. Doolittle. 1983. The Consequences of Cuts: The Effects of the Reagan Domestic Program on State and Local Governments. Princeton, N.J.: Princeton Urban and Regional Research Center.

Newell, R. C. 1981. "Giving Good Weight to Black English." Perspective 13 (Spring): 25-29.

Newfield, J., and P. DuBrul. 1981. The Permanent Government. New York: Pilgrim Press.

New York Times. 1982. "U.S. Sues Chicago Park District over Rights Policy." December 1, A17.

Nutter, E. 1980. "Equal Services at Issue." 46 (June): 11.

Ostrom, L., and G. P. Whitaker. 1974. "Community Control and Governmental Responsiveness: The Case of Police in Black Communities." In Improving the Quality of Urban Management, edited by D. Rodgers and W. Hawley, 303-34. Urban Affairs Annual Reviews, Vol. 8. Beverly Hills, Calif.: Sage.

Page, R. 1984. Stigma. London: Routledge and Kegan Paul.

Palmer, J. L., and I. V. Sawhill, eds. 1982. The Reagan Experiment. Washington, D.C.: The Urban Institute.

Parenti, M. 1978. Power and the Powerless. New York: St. Martin's.

Parks, R. B., P. C. Baker, L. L. Kiser, R. Oakerson, E. Ostrom, V. Ostrom, S. L. Percy, M. A. Vandivort, G. P. Whitaker, and R. Wilson. 1981. "Consumers as Coproducers of Public Services: Some Economic and Institutional Considerations." Policy Studies Review 9 (Summer): 1001-11.

Pear, R. 1984. "Administration Would Curtail Payments Granted in Court." New York Times, November 5, 1.

Piven, F. F., and R. A. Cloward. 1971. Regulating the Poor. New York: Vintage.

Poole, R. W. 1980. Cutting Back City Hall. New York: Universe Books.

Porter, D. R., and R. B. Peiser. 1984. Financing Infrastructure to Support Community Growth. Washington, D.C.: Urban Land Institute.

Poverty Law Review. 1979. "Montgomery County 'At-Large' Plan Voided." Vol. 7 (January/February): 1.

Purnick, J. 1984. "City's Poor Districts Are Hard Hit by a Severe Shortage of Teachers." New York Times, February 29, 1.

Rangel, J. 1984. "Court Assails U.S. on Benefit Cuts for Mentally Ill." New York Times, August 8, 1.

Rees, J. 1981. "Urban Water and Sewerage Services." In Equity in the City, edited by P. N. Troy, 85-103. Sidney, Australia: George Allen and Unwin.

Ringeling, A. 1981. "Passivity of the Administration." Policy and Politics 9 (July): 295-308.

Rosenbloom, S. 1982. "Federal Policies to Increase the Mobility of the Elderly and the Handicapped." Journal of the American Planning Association 48 (Summer): 335-50.

Rosentraub, M. S., and K. Harlow. 1983. "Local Budgets and Tax Revolts: A Review of Four Scenarios." Policy Studies Review 3 (August): 79-84.

Ross, S. D., and A. Barcher. 1983. The Rights of Women. Toronto: Bantam Books.

Rossum, R. A. 1980. "The Rise and Fall of Equalization Litigation." Urban Interest 2 (Spring): 2-10.

Rothbart, G., and D. Stoller. 1983. "Cable at the Crossroads." Channels 3 (July/August): 32-37.

Rother, L. 1985. "Chancellor Supports City School Serving Homosexual Youths." New York Times, June 7, 1, B4.

Ryan, W. 1976. Blaming the Victim. New York: Vintage.

Savas, E. S. 1982. Privatizing the Public Sector. Chatham, N.J.: Chatham House.

Sharp, E. B. 1980. "Toward a New Understanding of Urban Services and Citizen Participation: The Coproduction Concept." Midwest Review of Public Administration 14 (June): 105-18.

Stewart, F. J. 1950. A Half-Century of Municipal Reform: The History of the National Municipal League. Berkeley, Calif.: University of California Press.

Stoller, D. 1982. "The War Between Cable and the Cities." Channels 2 (April): 34-37.

Stuart, R. 1979. "Help Ordered for Pupils Talking 'Black English.'" New York Times, July 13, A8.

Suffia, D. 1970. "'Tolerance' on Consumer Fraud Here?" Seattle Times, September 9, 1.

Urban Institute. 1980. "Reading, Writing and Welfare." The Urban Institute Policy and Research Report 10 (Spring): 17–18.

U.S. Commission on Civil Rights. 1980. More Hurdles to Clear. Washington, D.C.: Government Printing Office.

_____. 1982. The Federal Response to Domestic Violence. Washington, D.C.: Government Printing Office.

Village Voice. 1974. New York, June 20, 3.

Warren, R. 1969. "Federal-local Planning: Scale Effects in Representation and Policy Making." Public Administration Review 30 (November/December): 584–95.

Warren, R., and L. F. Weschler. 1975. "The Costs of Citizenship." In Governing Urban Space, edited by R. Warren and L. F. Weschler, 10–23. Los Angeles: University of Southern California.

Weisbrod, B. 1970. "On the Stigma Effect and Demand for Welfare Programs: A Theoretical Note." Discussion Paper 82–70. Madison, Wis.: Institute for Research on Poverty.

Weschler, L. F., P. D. Marr, and B. M. Hackett. 1968. California Service Center Programs: Neighborhood Anti-poverty Centers. Davis, Calif.: Institute for Governmental Affairs.

INDEX

ABOUT THE EDITOR AND CONTRIBUTORS

MARK S. ROSENTRAUB is associate professor of urban affairs at the Institute of Urban Studies, the University of Texas at Arlington. He is currently involved in studies of the effects of the DRG payment system on health costs and hospitalization.

JEFFREY I. CHAPMAN is professor of public administration at the University of Southern California, Sacramento campus.

SCOTT CUMMINGS is professor and chairperson of sociology at the University of Louisville.

ROBERT E. ENGLAND is assistant professor of political science at Oklahoma State University.

PATRICIA A. HUCKLE is associate professor of political science and women's studies at San Diego State University.

DAVID R. MORGAN is director of the Bureau of Governmental Research and professor of political science at the University of Oklahoma.

MITCHELL L. MOSS is associate professor of public administration at New York University.

JAMES C. MUSSELWHITE, JR., is a project director for the Urban Institute's study of nonprofit agencies.

MYRNA R. PICKARD is dean of the school of nursing, the University of Texas at Arlington.

GARY J. REID is assistant professor of public administration at the University of Southern California.

ROBERT C. RODGERS is associate professor of management at the school of business, the University of Texas at Austin.

LESTER M. SALAMON, a former deputy associate director of the Office of Management and Budgeting, is director of the Center for Governance and Management Research, the Urban Institute, Washington, D.C.

JEFFREY D. STRAUSSMAN is associate professor of public administration at the Maxwell School, Syracuse University.

LYKE THOMPSON is assistant professor of public administration at the Center for Public Administration Programs, Western Michigan University.

ROBERT WARREN is professor of urban affairs and public policy at the University of Delaware.

DONALD R. WINKLER is associate professor of public administration at the University of Southern California.